Reconciling International Trade and Labor Protection

Reconciling International Trade and Labor Protection

Why We Need to Bridge the Gap between ILO Standards and WTO Rules

Wolfgang Plasa

LEXINGTON BOOKS
Lanham • Boulder • New York • London

Published by Lexington Books
An imprint of The Rowman & Littlefield Publishing Group, Inc.
4501 Forbes Boulevard, Suite 200, Lanham, Maryland 20706
www.rowman.com

Unit A, Whitacre Mews, 26-34 Stannary Street, London SE11 4AB

British Library Cataloguing in Publication Information Available

Library of Congress Cataloging-in-Publication Data Available

ISBN 978-1-4985-2138-3 (cloth : alk. paper)
ISBN 978-1-4985-2139-0 (electronic)

∞™ The paper used in this publication meets the minimum requirements of American National Standard for Information Sciences Permanence of Paper for Printed Library Materials, ANSI/NISO Z39.48-1992.

Printed in the United States of America

Contents

Acknowledgment

I wish to thank most warmly my good friend John Wilson. Without his valuable, tireless, and humorous advice, this study would never have been completed.

Preface

This book arrives at the right time, as Europe is beginning, once more, to look for ways of combating the deplorable working conditions in many developing countries that we are implicitly condoning and encouraging when buying vast quantities of imported goods produced in conditions that would not be unfamiliar to Dickens. It is, however, not yet another incendiary pamphlet denouncing the violation of principles or rights close to the author's heart. Above all, it is a practical, realistic call for action. It is therefore the opposite of a dogmatic treatise, far away from the one-track-mind approach that has led so many otherwise worthy causes to defeat. It provides a sober, realistic, practical analysis of the situation. Above all, it provides a number of concrete, feasible options for action. It should be read by anyone concerned about the impact of our actions or inactions, as consumers or decision makers, about our relations with the rest of the world, and especially by those who can influence public or private policy and decision making.

The author largely takes it for granted that his readers know what the problems are that he wants to address. His book is therefore not a catalogue of the violations of basic labor rights and standards that are the daily fare of tens of millions of workers in China and many other developing countries. Public opinion does wake up once in a while, when a textile factory collapses in Bangladesh burying more than a thousand workers under its debris, or when the number of suicides in the gigantic Foxconn factory in China reaches proportions that even you and I, as fervent buyers of the latest smartphones produced there, begin wondering whether we are really putting our money where our (moralistic) mouth is. It is, however, also a constant that public opinion and the media have a very brief attention span. Once the dead have been buried and the companies concerned have done their *mea culpa* and promised to enforce strict standards, we, the consumers, rarely hesitate before resuming our purchases of goods that we know, in our heart of hearts, are still likely to be produced in morally repellent conditions. To avoid any misunderstanding, by this is meant the *conditions* of work, not the *level of remuneration.*

Attitudes toward these problems do not, at least in Europe, depend on where you find yourself on the political spectrum, left or right. Nor does the relative indifference toward the "moral hazard" caused by indirectly encouraging such violations of basic conditions of decent working conditions follow party lines. So if it is not a question of political controversy, why are we doing nothing, and why have the problems become greater than ever before?

A quiet (r)evolution has taken place over the past thirty years in the developed countries: trade barriers (tariffs) have been sharply reduced, often eliminated; there has been a drastic fall in the cost of transport and a quasi-elimination of customs controls; the rules of the WTO have been strengthened through the introduction of a powerful dispute settlement system, with the result that WTO (free) trade obligations are (most) often being enforced. Add to this the concomitant decline of government authority, accompanied, perhaps even hastened by the spread of neo-liberal theses, easy to comprehend and, like the medieval purchase of indulgencies, dispensing us of any sense of responsibility ("the market does it all") and a general distrust in the public of anything smacking of ideology. The result? A world in which imports into the developed countries are largely subject to no controls other than sanitary spot checks or those aiming at the drug traffic.

The practical economic and social consequences of this in the developed countries have been enormous over this relatively short period of time. Imports of manufactured products are now virtually free of any but the lowest tariffs, with a few exceptions irrelevant for the purpose of the issue under discussion in this book. Before the 1990s, tariff protection, transport costs, quantitative restrictions (textiles, apparel, footwear) provided a cushion or buffer against imports. This has gone. The consequence is that differences in other aspects of social organization or public policy, like conditions of work and environmental protection, now have a much higher potential impact than before in terms of determining the location of production and trade flows.

This would be of little consequence if conditions of work and environmental protection were reasonably comparable between countries. There is, however, as much of a difference between the quasi-prison mega-factories spewing out millions of smartphones or other electronic products in China and their US or European counterparts as there is between the London of Dickens and today's metropolis.

So why is nothing being done? One of the main reasons is that huge vested interests have emerged. These vested interests include those of *consumers*, able to buy cheap apparel or high-tech electronic goods at a price-quality relationship never seen in modern times. They include the *producers* in China and elsewhere, benefiting from very cheap, disciplined labor, the *shipping companies* transporting the goods, and *retailers* in the developed countries. The political weight of these combined self-interests is enormous. I have experienced this when I was Director-General for Trade in the European Commission but, if anything, the lobbies have become more powerful, in the case of imports from China with the help of a very activist government. I believe that this is the basic explanation of why the issue of trade and labor, from being actively discussed in Europe and the United States only fifteen years ago, seemed to have disappeared from the political agenda until the Rana Plaza disaster. To this you can add the fact that those whose jobs have disappeared and who often find themselves among the long-term unemployed, at least in Europe, are not organized nor defended by organized labour, which largely defends the interests of those who remain employed, that is, around 90 percent of the work force. The rest of society, you and I, after wringing our hands, also accept this situation because of the existence of generous unemployment benefits. The end result: if not a "conspiracy of silence" at least a tacit "conspiracy of indifference."

This has emerged concomitantly with the ever-increasing impact of the neo-liberal schools of thought, at least in Europe. Neo-liberals will argue that substandard working conditions encourage economic growth in the exporting countries, improve the terms of trade of the importing countries, and that loss of industrial employment in the "old" industrialized countries will be compensated by growth in other sectors. This, incidentally, perpetuates the confusion between low wages, justified up to a point by differences in levels of productivity, and working conditions. This can also be described as the school of flipping hamburgers rather than assembling goods. Others have, excessively, referred to this development as "slaves working for the unemployed."

Such extreme theses represent an unhelpful simplification of the real world. In the case of the neo-liberals, the essence of the argument is virtually Panglossian: all is for the best in the best of all possible worlds as long as one gives free rein to the operation of the market which will solve all problems over time. They also suggest that extremely poor pay and working conditions are necessary to continue economic development through capital accumulation. Such over-simplifications, which, en passant, treat human beings as simple expendable pawns, completely ignore the experience of other countries where economic development has taken place without sacrificing whole generations on the altar of "growth" and "the market."

This preface is, however, not the place for discussing the calamitous impact of neo-liberal thought on public policy (or the absence thereof). The basic questions are much more straightforward than some economists would have us believe; to quote Wolfgang Plasa: ". . . *what is fundamentally immoral can hardly be described as normal. We have to realise that we are responsible for promoting immoral and inhumane working conditions in other countries if we import and consume more and more goods produced under such conditions."*

What, then, should and could be done? Once more, the author shuns easy, sweeping answers.

Do we have the right to *impose* our "standards," with or without quotation marks, on other countries? The simple answer is no (although, to be honest, one would often wish to do so . . .). But nor do such other countries have the right to *impose* their goods on us. We have a basic right to buy or not to buy. Do we have the right to "*encourage*" other countries to adopt and implement minimum standards? The author's answer is yes.

One of the problems is, however, that this does not fit well, or at all, with classical (international) trade policy and rules. WTO rules basically prohibit the use of criteria such as working conditions in establishing government-imposed barriers on imports. The use of classical trade policy tools, for example, special tariffs applied against imports of products considered to have been produced in inhumane conditions, is therefore very circumscribed, indeed virtually impossible, with one exception: an importing country may offer an easier access to its market, for example by reducing or eliminating whatever remains of its tariff barriers, if the exporting country can demonstrate that it has undertaken, or is in the process of undertaking, reforms of its domestic policies in areas such as social conditions, protection of the environment, etc. This could also be described as using the approach of the carrot rather than the stick, and is, within certain limits, compatible with the WTO.

The problem is that this somewhat starry-eyed approach hardly works in practice. I am well placed to know and so is Wolfgang Plasa: we were both participants in the development of this policy several years ago. I do not regret having tried, but nor should one regret abandoning policies that do not work. The reasons for failure are quite simple: in the European context, the grant of "GSP Plus" status (i.e., the abolition of all tariffs in favor of certain developing countries) is predicated on those countries demonstrating that they have ratified and implemented an impressive number (twenty-seven!) of international conventions relating to social conditions, the protection of the environment, etc. This policy therefore rewards those who have, *apparently*, already acted. It only constitutes an encouragement to do better to the extent that it is seen as a goal to be obtained by "good behavior." So far, so good. The problem that has emerged is that some (several? many?) of the beneficiary countries either rest on their laurels once they have achieved GSP Plus status, or succeed in obtaining it against promises of good behavior in the future. From the practical, political viewpoint, this quickly becomes very difficult to manage. New, vested interests emerge as trade flows develop, frustrating any attempt to withdraw preferential treatment, even in the light of continued violations by the beneficiary country. Other, political considerations of a classical type come into play: country X is in the throes of an insurgency or threatened by one or the other fundamentalist movement. Once obtained, this makes its GSP Plus status virtually untouchable.

In any event, the attractiveness of the carrot has diminished considerably. Customs duties have gone sharply down and quantitative restrictions on textiles and clothing have disappeared. Furthermore, the EU decided ten years ago to abolish all of the above in respect of imports from the fifty-odd least developed countries, in one fell stroke depriving it of any carrot-like approach in respect of these countries, including, for example, the Bangladesh of the Rana Plaza disaster.

Decision makers are therefore faced with a difficult situation: classical trade policy tools of the coercive type, for example, "labour tariffs," are politically unacceptable and also illegal in terms of the WTO. Carrot-type approaches are difficult to manage and of doubtful value. What then to do?

Wolfgang Plasa suggests a number of possible approaches. Since you will read his book, I will not try to summarize them but rather provide a complementary set of arguments and suggestions.

Who are the potential actors? Who can do something? The usual collection of suspects . . . consumers, governments, private companies, NGOs. In my view, shared, I believe, by the author, all of the above need to contribute, but how? So far, we have focused on what governments cannot, should not or will not do, acting or rather NOT acting, in isolation.

Governments cannot legislate directly against imports, except in certain very limited circumstances identified by the WTO and subject to its rules. *They can, however, provide a legal or regulatory framework for action by private companies or individuals*. This is done here, at home, by adopting relevant legislation, enforced by courts of law. No one would imagine leaving this role to private companies or NGOs. Why should one do so with respect to working conditions in third-world countries? The main message of this preface is to insist on the indispensable role of governments in setting the standards and to make them comprehensible and practically applicable, not to abandon this basic role by shifting the burden to someone else. Let us return to that below.

Private persons, consumers, you and I, can act, but on the basis of what information? Refusing to buy all apparel produced in Bangladesh would make no sense and in any event contribute to the continued misery of that country, and how do I know that one electronic gadget is better or worse than another in terms of the conditions in which it was produced? Reliable information is not generally available and few consumers are, in any event, going to spend the time and energy necessary to inform themselves about the working conditions around the world. This is one area where governments have a clear role to play.

Private companies can act, but, once more, on the basis of what information? They are not law enforcement agencies, nor should they be expected, with some common sense exceptions, to inform themselves about the conduct of the numerous actors in the supply chain that leads from a factory in Outer Mongolia to an assembly plant in Düsseldorf or Chicago. Private companies, as much as private consumers, need clear guidelines and information, expressed in terms of common sense and proportionality of effort. (A "common sense exception" would, for example, occur if a company was the owner and responsible for the operation of another company somewhere in what used to be called the "third world.")

Therefore, although the operational responsibility for buying and distributing goods manufactured in unacceptable conditions lies, by definition, with the "Western" companies engaged in such business, one should not draw from this the conclusion that they should be legally compelled to act as labor rights vigilantes or enforcers.

However, in a political climate favoring "privatization" of even core government functions (see for example the failed attempt to privatize procurement decisions for military equipment in the UK), "privatizing" the enforcement of core labor standards in foreign countries seems like an easy way of getting rid of the problem, especially to governments that are exposed to the contradictory pressure of public opinion, fear of losing a case in the WTO, and an even greater fear of upsetting the emerging Chinese giant.

Shifting the burden to industry is, for example, the sense of a draft law currently being discussed in the French Parliament and which would render companies with more than 5,000 employees in France responsible for ensuring that their subcontractors in foreign countries comply with very general, sweeping definitions of the activities and rights covered by its provisions. This is not the place to engage in a critique of this draft, other than to regret its practical inapplicability and the fact that it gives a misleading impression that something effective is being done. In order to be effective, obligations imposed on private operators have to be reasonably precise, proportionate, and manageable, and this is where the problems associated with this kind of approach begin. For example, the imposition of an obligation on a company to ascertain that his supplier in country X is complying with ILO decision no. 14 sounds very nice on paper. In reality, this would make it necessary for each importer to conduct verifications on the spot that go far beyond their competence: they are not law enforcement agencies and they would quickly be tempted or obliged to employ armies of outside consultants (armies, because there are hundreds of companies and thousands of subcontractors potentially concerned; see also the very illustrative example of national implementation of the OECD agreement on combating the purchase of conflict minerals, much to the advantage of the private consultants supposed to carry out on-the-spot verification).

Voluntary approaches/codes of conduct: Wolfgang Plasa rightly, in my view, derides voluntary codes of conduct. These suffer from the same drawbacks as above. What should be the relevant criteria? How should they be interpreted on the spot? By whom? In case of non-compliance, what are the sanctions? What I am trying to say is stated, convincingly in my view, by the author: "Codes of conduct are based on the erroneous belief that law enforcement can be privatized. In the final analysis, codes are not a panacea for achieving social justice. In other words, they cannot replace regulations." Indeed.

The problems inherent in both types of approaches are similar: how to define the subject matter, that is, what conduct is unacceptable, or how to translate the generalities of international treaties into concrete obligations. Once this has been done, how to define the action that can reasonably be expected from the Western companies concerned in a manner that is proportionate and practical: to repeat, they are not law enforcement agencies and the role of the latter should, in my view, not be assumed by consultants or NGOs but by the public authorities.

This brings us back to the role of government. Governments are supposed to promote the public good, writ large, and to set the standards of conduct that correspond to the aspirations of their populations. In the case of (foreign) working conditions, this would then imply that our governments, individually or in the OECD, decide what should be the minimum standards acceptable to an informed citizen, applied in factories abroad that produce goods sold on our markets. The problem is that this also brings us back to the impossibility of crossing a certain line vis-à-vis the WTO that prohibits "discrimination."

Is there a way to circumvent this problem? The key WTO-related question is the issue of constraint: prohibitions or restrictions are WTO incompatible. There is, however, nothing in the WTO to prevent a government from defining what are decent standards of work and/or which are not (child labor), nor is there anything to prevent them from *offering* companies, groups of companies, or associations *the possibility* of obtaining a verification report from a publicly authorized agency to the effect that the goods imported originate in factories compliant with such standards. This would then allow them to label the goods originating in such factories as being "socially responsible."

The advantage of such a government-sponsored approach would be its reliability for consumers, otherwise exposed to the certainty of being bombarded with the same type of PR statements regarding "sustainability" and "saving the planet" which now seem to adorn virtually all products and the reliability of which is highly questionable (it would, indeed, today be far easier to count the number of companies that do *not* pretend to be saving the planet). Furthermore, it would create a level playing field between importers and a marketing advantage for those able and willing to obtain the "label."

To simplify and to be practical, it could be applied to the most important consumer goods such as textiles, clothing, toys, and electronics: the definition of the product is clear and visible, but it hardly makes sense to appose labels on sacks of cement or bars of steel or semi-conductors. . . . In other words, it seems of little relevance, and conducive to a vast paper chase of the conflict mineral type, to apply such an approach to intermediate products that go through successive stages of processing. But then one should not refrain from acting simply because of the difficulty of applying a certain approach to all products. The purpose would be to put pressure on foreign governments and encourage their companies to do better.

This kind of approach has been applied, more or less effectively, in other areas. For example, the EU "eco-labeling" scheme, also voluntary, is based on criteria defined by the public authority (in this case the Commission, after working closely with the producers of the product concerned) and allows companies to affix an "eco-label" to their products, subject to verification by independent bodies. Those that are prepared to make the effort gain a competitive advantage. Another example, less convincing perhaps in terms of its effectiveness, may be found in the field of the application of sanitary standards. Minimum standards for the hygiene, etc., of slaughterhouses are set by the EU. Non-EU slaughterhouses may be certified, *by their national authorities*, as being in conformity with EU rules, opening therefore the possibility of exporting the products concerned to the EU. EU inspectors may, in certain circumstances, decide to verify compliance on the spot. None of this has been challenged in the WTO, nor would any challenge be likely to succeed. These are just a couple of examples of how to translate such approaches into practice.

There will, of course, be a Pavlovian reaction among governments to try to shift the burden elsewhere, to the OECD or the WTO, just as they have tried to shift the burden to industry in the case of conflict minerals. The OECD has in principle the capability of working out an approach, and it has demonstrated its capacity to do so in other areas with extraterritorial implications, such as its agreement to combat corruption. The problem is, however, that this would require a consensus among its thirty-four members, and that any consensus on an issue like this would most likely be at the level of the lowest common denominator. I would be more confident if one major member were to establish a convincing approach at the national level that could then become the basis for an OECD agreement. This would, of course, from the political perspective vis-à-vis the non-OECD world, have the advantage of "safety in numbers." As to the WTO, the chances are extremely remote of its members agreeing to something which has been rejected as a matter of principle by most developing countries for years, unless this were to happen as a reaction to the adoption by some (developed) countries of measures. Other members might then come to realize that carefully circumscribed

WTO agreement would be better than suffering the imposition of de facto extraterritorial measures by industrialized countries.

Let me conclude on a very different note. Public opinion in Europe was made aware, partly by personal observation, partly by the works of authors like Dickens or Zola or their modern equivalents, of the existence of sweat-shops and their incompatibility with certain basic principles. Action was taken, and capitalism, as the saying goes, acquired a human face. This awareness only rarely exists with respect to what is happening thousands of kilometers away from our shores. In certain (many?) cases, access to factories by the media is denied. In any event, we, as individual consumers, even if we may occasionally be informed about what is going on behind closed factory gates, have no means at our disposal other than a purely symbolic, ineffective boycott of the products concerned. This is where the media, NGOs, and especially public authorities need to play their role. If properly informed, public opinion can become a very powerful force, which it is not today. There is no shortage of public opinion campaigns to save the earth, the polar bears, the climate, etc., etc. Why not launch a public information campaign to help our fellow human beings escape from inhuman working conditions? This will put pressure on the governments to play their role. This is, indeed, the main operational message of this preface, *to insist on the indispensable role of governments to set the standards and to make them comprehensible and applicable in practice, not to abandon this basic role by shifting the burden to someone else.*

Mogens Peter Carl
Former Director-General of Trade in the European Commission

Foreword

This study deals with certain problems arising at the interface between international trade in goods and the labor conditions under which such goods are produced. I had the opportunity of gaining some insight into these problems during the years that I managed the Generalized System of Trade Preferences (GSP) of the EU. In 1999, the European Commission decided to update the scheme, including the special incentive arrangement concerning labor rights. I consulted foreign exporters and European importers to find out how to make GSP preferences more attractive for traders and more effective in improving labor conditions. From time to time, entrepreneurs came to see me to find out about preferential treatment for imports from countries where they envisaged investing or to complain about the loss of such treatment as a result of "graduation." In these conversations, I learned how much it costs—and pays—to establish a garment factory in Bangladesh or Nepal. When visiting these and other developing countries in Asia and Latin America, I also saw the reality of sweatshops.

As a member of the European Commission's Permanent Delegation in Geneva, I participated in GATT, WTO, and ILO activities as well as in the negotiations of the Uruguay Round. Those were the years when decisions were taken to trigger the dynamics now commonly referred to as globalization. In retrospect, I am not so sure whether today's world really looks like that expected and hoped for twenty-five years ago.

A good deal of what is discussed in this study concerns poverty reduction, an area of which I had extensive experience in the field. I served as Head of Delegation of the European Commission in several developing countries where I was responsible, *inter alia*, for the implementation of EU development assistance. I undertook some studies into the living conditions of underprivileged groups of society and into the policies of their governments to improve these conditions. In order to know more about this, I met and discussed with people living on less than $2 a day, people who, if you ask them in the morning what they will have for lunch, may reply that they are not sure whether they will actually have lunch.

In essence, it was my personal experience of the issues discussed in this study that motivated me to undertake it. I wish to emphasize that this book is not conceived as a contribution to academic research into these problems, but as an attempt to contribute to their solution. It is meant to breathe life back into a debate that has been obfuscated by political polemics and partisan publications. It is intended to help reconcile international trade and labor protection.

Introduction

What This Book Is About

THE THEME OF THIS STUDY

Over the last two decades or so, several developing countries have become important suppliers of manufactured goods. In these countries, a significant number of new jobs were created, with wages often higher than in agriculture or the informal sector. At the same time, consumers in importing countries were pleased to be offered electronics, apparel, footwear, and other products at amazingly low prices.

However, this goes hand in hand with some less pleasant developments. A good deal of these goods are produced under atrocious working conditions by people who are denied fundamental rights and who are paid miserable wages. But this situation does not only affect the workers concerned. It also adversely affects trade and development, in both exporting and importing countries.

There are numerous initiatives which attempt to address these problems. Fair trade organizations endeavor to convince consumers to buy goods produced and sold under "fair" conditions. Multinationals (MNEs) claim that they respect codes of conduct that ensure proper working conditions. There is also an international organization, the ILO, whose mission is to establish minimum labor standards which all countries in the world should meet. Yet, ILO reports show that there are serious violations of these standards in many countries.

So why do governments not do more about it? Why do they not restrict the import of goods produced under conditions that do not meet certain minimum labor standards? Actually, they cannot. They are members of the

ILO, but they are also members of the WTO. WTO rules do not allow restrictions on imports on the grounds that the goods concerned were produced in violation of ILO labor standards. Indeed, there is a gap between ILO standards and GATT rules. The question that this study attempts to answer is whether there is a need to bridge that gap by linking international labor standards to the rules of the multilateral trading system.[1]

This issue is not new. In the 1990s, there were passionate discussions of the merits of a link between trade and labor standards. Several WTO members requested a debate of the issue at the WTO Ministerial Meeting in Seattle in December 1999. On that occasion, President Clinton told the press that the WTO should at some point use trade sanctions to enforce core labor rights around the world. This proposal was commented on by the Egyptian trade minister Boutros-Ghali, observing that "if you start using trade as a lever to implement non trade-related issues, that will be the end of the multilateral trading system, maybe not this year, but in 10 to 15 years."[2] Shortly thereafter, in 2001, WTO Director-General Michael Moore expressed the view that "WTO members will never agree to trade sanctions to enforce labor standards. It is a line in the sand that developing countries will not cross. They fear that such provisions could be abused for protectionist purposes."[3] Developing countries have indeed been unwilling to cross this line. Some of them blocked any real debate of the matter in the WTO.

Meanwhile, a number of developments have changed the context of the discussion. First, China joined the WTO at the end of 2001. Second, the Multi Fiber Agreement (MFA) expired at the end of 2004. Third, both the United States and the EU have begun to include references to labor standards in all of their respective bilateral and regional trade agreements. Fourth, in 2008, the ILO adopted a "Declaration on Social Justice for a Fair Globalization" which states that "the violation of fundamental principles and rights at work cannot be invoked or otherwise used as a legitimate comparative advantage." Fifth, the number of ratifications of the eight ILO conventions on so-called "core labor standards" (CLS) has increased considerably since 1998, when the ILO agreed on the list of these standards by adopting the "Declaration on Fundamental Principles and Rights at Work."

On the other hand, one development did not materialize, at least not to the extent that economists had predicted: in spite of high and sustained economic growth in certain countries, labor conditions did not improve as much as one would have expected. Again and again, we learn of dramatic events that throw the spotlight on appalling working conditions in some of these countries. Thus, it is about time to revisit the issue of linking compliance with international labor standards to the rules of the multilateral trading system.

THE FOCUS OF THIS STUDY

When I told my friends and colleagues about my plans to write this book, most of them had reservations. They pointed to the fact that this would add just another opus to the already more than abundant literature on the subject. Others argued that it would not make sense to enforce labor standards through trade sanctions. Some were of the view that the idea of enforcing minimum labor standards should be dismissed altogether as this would come at a high cost in terms of unemployment, loss of productivity, etc.

From the beginning, the debate on trade and labor has been dominated by two arguments: the ethical and the economic. A century ago, when the ILO was founded, there were proposals to ban imports of goods produced by children. More recently, the ethical arguments in favor of a link have resurfaced, this time invoking the need to respect human rights. However, there is not only disagreement about the scope of human rights, but also about their binding force and ultimately their value.

Initially, economic arguments were brought up by importing countries afraid that competition from countries with lower standards might harm their domestic industries and put pressure on the level of labor protection achieved at home. Until fifteen years ago or so, there was support in major importing countries for the idea of linking trade to labor standards, for the sake of labor protection and of market protection. Meanwhile, other economic interests, namely those of exporting countries and foreign investors in these countries, came to the fore. These favor trade over labor protection. They are supported by economists who claim that free trade and poor labor conditions promote economic growth. It is quite questionable, though, whether the empirical evidence available supports these theories. The sheer number of publications shows that they remain rather controversial.[4]

Yet, even if it was certain that poor labor conditions favor economic growth, this would not necessarily rule out linking trade to labor standards, as many authors seem to claim. These authors consider economic growth as an overarching political priority. I do not share this view. I do not believe that economic growth should be used as the main criterion, let alone the only one, for evaluating the merits of a policy linking trade and labor standards.

I wrote this book because so much has been said about the macro-economic implications of linking (or not linking) trade to labor standards and the importance of the latter as human rights—but so little about other economic, legal, political, and moral considerations that may suggest a link between trade and labor. They are examined in this book.

When discussing with my colleagues the ideas in this book, I realized that all of them had a clear idea of what a link between trade and labor would look like—but most of them had a different one in mind. Not surprisingly, their personal opinions on the merits of linking trade and labor differed as much as the links that they imagined. Besides, most of my interlocutors focused on the *effects* of trade restrictions on imports from countries not respecting minimum labor standards. Interestingly, none of them saw a need to clarify the *purpose* that a link should serve.

A link between trade and labor is not an end in itself, but a means to solve a specific problem. Accordingly, the starting point of the discussion has to be the particular problem that such link may solve. Non-compliance with labor standards is not only an issue of economics and ethics. It also creates problems for sustainable development and for international trade. This study examines, one by one, the major problems which result from non-compliance with international labor standards in order to answer the question of whether any of these problems needs to be addressed by linking trade to these standards.

This book focuses on results, not on causes. It asks the question of whether certain developments are acceptable and not so much whether they are the work of corrupt governments, greedy CEOs, capitalism or globalization, trade, or consumer preferences.

The issues examined in this study are of a political nature. They cannot be assessed solely on the grounds of scientific or technical considerations or by weighing benefits against costs. Ultimately, the answers to the questions discussed here depend on personal opinions and political preferences, and as far as this study is concerned on mine.

THE STRUCTURE OF THIS STUDY

This study starts with an attempt to clarify the nature and extent of certain problems stemming from insufficient labor protection. It tries to answer the question of whether trade restrictions would be a necessary and appropriate means to solve them. It concludes that for two of these problems, this is actually the case. Subsequently, it examines the question of whether these problems could be solved without restricting trade. Thereafter, the study analyzes links between trade and labor that exist in the trade regimes of some major trading partners. Finally, it discusses how the two links proposed in this study should be shaped.

The book is structured in the following manner. Chapter 1 will look at the ILO and the WTO. It will examine the nature of the gap between the rules of the multilateral trading system and international labor standards and recall earlier attempts to bridge it. Chapter 2 will clarify the framework of the debate starting with a definition of what a link would mean. Chapter 3 will attempt to answer the question whether there are non-trade-related reasons that may justify such link. Chapter 4 will examine whether there are trade-related reasons that would do so. Chapter 5 will discuss alternative approaches, such as fair trade initiatives and codes of conduct, which could make a link between trade and labor standards redundant. Chapter 6 will present the experience made with links that the EU and the United States established in the framework of their unilateral and bilateral trade regimes. Chapter 7 will examine the question of how best to shape the proposed links. Chapter 8 will discuss the objections that are commonly presented against proposals to adopt a link. Chapter 9 will consider further benefits that a link would produce. Chapter 10 will assess the chances of getting agreement on the proposed links between trade and labor standards. Finally, chapter 11 will sketch out new ways and means that might contribute to solving the problems discussed in this study.

I like to emphasize that this is not a book on who said what. It is not research on research. The way in which arguments and objections are examined here follows a theoretical framework. I do not say that they have ever been presented in the same way as they are here. None of the arguments reflect the official position of any government or international organization.

NOTES

1. Issues similar to the ones examined in this study may arise in the framework of trade in services. This study only considers trade in goods.
2. S. Greenhouse and J. Kahn, U.S. Effort to Add Labor Standards to Agenda Fail, *The New York Times*, December 3, 1999.
3. M. Moore, The WTO: what is at stake? 6th John Payne Memorial Lecture, European Business School London, March 12, 2001.
4. D. K. Brown, International Trade and Core Labour Standards, A survey of the recent literature, OECD Labour Market and Social Policy Occasional Papers No. 43, Paris, 2000.

Chapter One

The Institutional Framework

Trade and labor conditions influence each other in the real world.[1] Labor conditions have a bearing on production costs which, in turn, affect competitiveness in international trade. Conversely, export opportunities are an important determinant of investments, which, in turn, have an impact on labor conditions. Yet, there is no formal link between the WTO rules which govern international trade and ILO obligations which govern labor conditions. This chapter begins with a brief description of the institutional arrangements of the ILO and WTO. It will then examine the origin and scope of the gap between trade rules and labor standards in more detail and recall earlier attempts to bridge it. It will also provide a definition of a link between the two.

THE ILO

The chaos created by World War I provided an opportunity to found a new world order. Part I of the Versailles Peace Treaty of 1919 established the League of Nations as its centerpiece. Part XIII of the same Treaty (Articles 387 to 427) created the International Labor Organization as one of the League's agencies. Although this new world order was largely inspired by American proposals, the United States did not ratify the Treaty of Versailles. They joined the ILO only in 1934, without ever joining the League of Nations.

The ILO is the only international organization which survived the demise of the League of Nations. It became the first UN specialized agency. The ILO's mandate was confirmed in the Declaration of Philadelphia, adopted in 1944, which became an annex to the 1946 ILO Constitution.

ILO's Mandate

The mandate of the ILO is to ensure that labor conditions in all countries of the world abide by certain minimum standards.

The Rationale of International Labor Standards

The ILO came into being as a compromise between intentions to establish socialism and recognition of the need to improve social conditions that otherwise would fuel those intentions. While the international labor movement claimed that workers deserved better social protection and more social justice, not least as a compensation for the hardship they had suffered during the war, many governments and employers agreed on limited social reforms in order to improve political stability and to rebut more radical requests made by revolutionary movements. Both goals—*social justice* and *political stability*—are referred to in the preamble of the ILO Constitution:

- ". . . universal . . . peace can be established only if it is based upon social justice;
- . . . conditions of labor exist involving such injustice, hardship, and privation to large numbers of people as to produce unrest so great that the peace and harmony of the world are imperiled . . ."

According to these provisions, social justice is a condition for political stability and both are conditions for peace in the world. In line with the overarching mandate of the League of Nations, the ILO is meant to promote permanent and universal peace. The preamble mentions yet another reason for which the agency was established:

- ". . . the failure of any nation to adopt humane conditions of labour is an obstacle in the way of other nations which desire to improve the conditions in their own countries."

The fourth objective of the ILO is to reconcile international competition with social justice. The fact that this objective cannot be achieved without international cooperation provides the *raison d'être* of the ILO.

The "Methods and Principles for Regulating Labor Conditions"

Article 427 of the Treaty of Versailles enumerates the "methods and principles for regulating labor conditions which all industrial communities should endeavor to apply." They are:

- labor should not be regarded merely as a commodity or article of commerce;

- the right of association by the employed as well as by the employers;
- a wage adequate to maintain a reasonable standard of life;
- an eight-hour day or a forty-eight-hour week;
- a weekly rest of at least twenty-four hours;
- the abolition of child labor and the imposition of such limitations on the labor of young persons as shall permit the continuation of their education and assure their proper physical development;
- equal remuneration of men and women for work of equal value;
- equitable economic treatment of all workers lawfully resident in a foreign country;
- a system of inspection . . . in order to ensure the enforcement of the laws and regulations for the protection of the employed.

International cooperation in order to promote the above objectives may use different methods. One is to set benchmarks and targets, which may be more or less binding. Another one is to impose procedures like collective bargaining which promise to achieve the said objectives. The ILO combines both approaches. Its fundamental credo, however, is the belief that freedom of association and the right to collective bargaining will enable workers to obtain adequate labor protection. So these rights may be portrayed as the "mothers of all labor standards."

The Institutional Framework of the ILO

At present, the ILO has 185 member states (out of 193 states that are members of the UN). This means virtually universal membership.

The Tripartite Structure

The main organs of the ILO have a unique tripartite structure. The International Labor Conference, which meets annually, has four delegates from each member country, two of which represent the government and one each representing employees and employers. Between annual sessions of the Conference, the work of the ILO is guided by the Governing Body composed of twenty-eight government, fourteen worker, and fourteen employer members.

All delegates have equal and individual voting rights. Thus, they may coordinate their votes either with delegates from the same country or from the same group. In practice, workers' delegates of different countries often coordinate their voting, and so do employers' delegates. Progress in the framework of the ILO requires compromise not so much between divergent interests of different countries, but rather between those of different groups. Coordination between delegates from the same country will depend on internal relations between them and on their respective political power. In some countries governments control trade unions. In other countries governments are controlled by employers. In both cases, the conditions for an efficient functioning of the tripartite structure of the ILO are not in place.

The Instruments

The ILO prepares and adopts conventions and recommendations establishing international labor standards. New standards may be proposed by employers, workers, governments, the ILO industrial committee, or the UN. A proposal for new standards is followed up by a comparative study of the relevant laws and national practices of member states and submitted to the latter for comments. After examination by a tripartite committee, the draft is discussed at the annual ILO Labor Conference. New standards are usually discussed and voted by two successive annual labor conferences. Each clause is voted separately.

Over the last ninety years, international labor standards have been established in virtually all work-related matters. By 2014, the ILO had adopted 189 conventions and 203 recommendations. Conventions that have not been ratified by a member country have the same legal status in that country as recommendations. The ILO Constitution requires member states to submit all conventions adopted by the ILO to the authorities competent for ratifying them.

The ILO uses various means to promote the effective implementation of labor standards in all member states. It monitors compliance and publicizes violations to persuade countries to stop them. It may also decide to sanction countries that are found to persistently fail to comply with ILO labor standards. And it provides technical assistance to countries facing difficulties to meet their obligations under the ILO conventions.

Monitoring Compliance

The ILO monitors compliance with ILO conventions in the framework of its "regular" system of supervision. Under this system, the government of each member state is required to periodically present reports on the measures taken to apply each Convention it has ratified. It must also send these reports to employers' and workers' organizations, which have a right to comment and supplement the information provided by the government. The reports are examined by the Committee of Experts on the Application of Conventions and Recommendations (CEARC) composed of twenty independent experts. This Committee submits an annual report to the International Labor Conference's Tripartite Committee on the Application of Conventions and Recommendations, which may invite governments to respond to allegations of serious problems in public session. The Conference Committee in turn prepares a report to the International Labor Conference. Some of this information is published, with the intention to spur compliance.

Member states are also required to report on the follow-up of recommendations as well as on matters falling within the scope of conventions that they did not ratify, and explain the difficulties which prevent them from doing so. Moreover, the "Declaration on Fundamental Principles and Rights at Work" of 1998 establishes, as its follow-up, a special mechanism to monitor compliance with the conventions on CLS. This mechanism requires all ILO members that have not ratified these conventions to report annually their efforts to remove obstacles to ratification. These reports are reviewed by the ILO's Governing Body. On this basis, the Director-General prepares an annual global report on one of the four CLS. This mechanism is of a "strictly promotional nature" as its aim is to identify areas where ILO technical cooperation and advice may be required. Although not all reports are submitted in time to be examined by the CEARC, it is fair to say that the regular system of supervision provides a comprehensive review of compliance with ILO conventions.

Complaints Procedures and Enforcement Mechanisms

The ILO investigates complaints alleging non-compliance with ILO conventions in the framework of its "special" system of supervision. This system includes different procedures set in motion by individual complaints. These procedures are laid down in Articles 24 and 26 of the ILO Constitution. In addition, there is a special procedure to investigate infringements of freedom of association.

Under Article 24, any employers or workers organization may make "representations of non-observance" against a member state that, in their view, does not comply with a convention that it has ratified. If such complaint is not resolved through informal consultation, the Governing Body may refer it to the Committee on Freedom of Association or a tripartite *ad hoc* committee composed of some of its members.

Under Article 26, a complaint may be filed against a member state by another member state, a delegate to the International Labor Conference, or the Governing Body itself. However, only those member states may file such complaints that have ratified the conventions whose standards are allegedly violated by the other member state. Upon receipt of a complaint, the Governing Body may appoint a Commission of Inquiry, consisting of three independent members, which will investigate the case, prepare a report, and, if necessary, make recommendations on measures to be taken to address the problems raised by the complaint. A Commission of Inquiry is the ILO's highest-level investigative procedure. It is set up when a member state is accused of committing persistent and serious violations and has repeatedly refused to address them.

There is a special procedure to investigate infringements of Convention 87 on Freedom of Association and Protection of the Right to Organize and Convention 98 on the Right to Organize and Collective Bargaining. In the framework of this procedure, governments, workers or employers organizations, international organizations of workers and employers when one of their members is directly concerned, or such international organizations that have consultative status at the ILO may file complaints against member states even if the latter have not ratified the relevant conventions. This special procedure involves two different bodies. One is the Fact-Finding and Conciliation Commission, which can carry out investigations, but only with the consent of the government concerned. It works in a way similar to a Commission of Inquiry. The other body is the Committee on Freedom of Association, appointed by the Governing Body and composed of members of the latter.

Governments may not accept the recommendations of a Commission of Inquiry and refer the matter to the International Court of Justice. If a country found to commit persistent and serious violations of its obligations as a member of the ILO does not accept the recommendations of a Commission of Inquiry, action can be taken under Article 33 of the ILO Constitution. This provision states that:

> In the event of any Member failing to carry out within the time specified the recommendations, if any, contained in the report of the Commission of Inquiry, or in the decision of the International Court of Justice, as the case may be, the Governing Body may recommend to the Conference such action as it may deem wise and expedient to secure compliance therewith.[2]

The ILO Objectives in the Present Context

It is quite remarkable that almost a century ago the international community was able to agree on the objectives listed above. The ILO Declaration on Social Justice for a Fair Globalization adopted in 2008 highlights the relevance of the agency's mandate and objectives in the present context.

Social Justice and Social Protection

Some of the founding members of the ILO had adopted domestic legislation in the area of workers' rights and labor protection half a century before. When the ILO came into being, such laws had become part of the concept of a "modern" society. Subsequently, this concept has been developed far beyond the minimum standards of social protection that the ILO founders had in mind. The Declaration of Philadelphia reflects the growing importance of material welfare on the agency's agenda. It states that "poverty anywhere constitutes a danger to prosperity everywhere," and refers to the "war against want," echoing President Roosevelt's call for "freedom from want."

Meanwhile, industrialization in a number of developing countries—among them very important ones—advanced considerably, giving rise to issues concerning the protection of workers employed in the newly created industries. At the same time, many states recognized the right of the individual to a decent life under conditions preserving human dignity. The situation in some of these countries bears striking similarities with Europe at the time of early industrialization. The gap between that situation and internationally recognized minimum standards is, in some cases, serious. More recently, these shortcomings have been branded as violations of human rights. Many states signed and ratified international conventions and declarations enshrining fundamental economic and social rights. Indeed, the ILO has actively participated in the efforts of other UN agencies to promote human rights in the world. In essence, the first objective of the ILO—better social protection for workers—remains as important as is was a century ago.

Social Peace and Political Stability

Just before the ILO was founded, the Soviet Union was established as the first communist state in history. In several other European countries, attempts were made to follow that example. The mood of politicians who in 1919 decided to commit themselves to international cooperation in the field of social protection was certainly influenced by these events. They realized that granting a minimum protection satisfying the most urgent claims would dampen more radical requests for social reforms.

Most industrialized countries have overcome the "class struggle" which was a reality at the time when the ILO was founded. The concept of the social market economy has become the model of a society which widely satisfies the aspirations both of employers and of employees. While support for communist ideas has become considerably weaker, the risk of political unrest is real in many countries, in particular where working conditions are extremely poor and wages extremely low. Nevertheless, the governments of many countries seem to be very reluctant to undertake the necessary social reforms. Unfortunately, recent events show that still today in some countries "conditions of labor exist involving such injustice, hardship, and privation to large numbers of people as to produce unrest." Moreover, it has become clear that political stability is a major condition of sustainable development. Insofar, it is as important as it was when the ILO was founded.

World Peace

According to the ILO preamble, social justice is a condition for political stability and both are conditions for peace in the world. While it would be difficult to assess the causal links between working conditions in a given country, its degree of political stability, and its role in international conflicts, there is little doubt that better social protection improves political stability and reduces the risk of conflicts.

The present debate on global threats focuses on climate change, poverty, the increase of world population, the use of natural resources and energy, HIV, nuclear arms, and other weapons of mass destruction. In my view, the threats stemming from social injustice are equally dangerous. Growing inequalities bear the risk of new conflicts and possibly even new forms of conflict.[3] To that extent, the third reason for which the ILO was founded—ensuring peace in the world—remains as relevant as it was in 1919 and in 1944.

Fair Competition

The founding members of the ILO were well aware that no country could have afforded to improve working conditions in the absence of similar and simultaneous action by its competitors. They knew of the impact of trade on social protection and vice versa. Nowadays, as a result of progressive trade liberalization, more international trade, and growing competition, the risk that low labor conditions in one country might impede improvements of labor conditions in other countries is at least as high as a century ago. Besides, free trade will not yield the gains it promises unless competition is fair. Particularly low labor conditions may result in unfair competition. This risk is as real now as it was almost a century ago when the ILO was founded.

Cooperation versus Coercion

Over the last ninety years, the ILO has adopted a significant amount of international legislation in the field of its responsibilities. In addition, the agency has at its disposal a comprehensive and sophisticated set of instruments to monitor compliance with labor standards. They provide the ILO with a detailed and pertinent knowledge of the situation in each member state. In contrast, the agency's means to enforce standards are limited and the number of cases where they were actually used even more scarce. This, however, has been a deliberate choice. The ILO would not work if governments were not willing to cooperate. And governments may not be willing to cooperate if they face sanctions as a result of non-compliance with labor standards.

THE MULTILATERAL TRADING SYSTEM

The chaos left behind by World War II provided the opportunity to establish a new world order, more efficient and better equipped to handle the problems which the previous one had failed to address. The new order, whose centerpiece is the United Nations Organization, was also largely inspired by American proposals.

The major elements of this new economic and financial order are the International Bank for Reconstruction and Development (the World Bank), the International Monetary Fund (IMF), and the International Trade Organization (ITO). The latter was prepared by the United Nations Conference on Trade and Employment, held in Havana, Cuba, in 1947–48. However, when it became clear that the United States would not ratify the Havana Charter, it was agreed to provisionally apply its essential rules and principles, enshrined in the General Agreement on Tariffs and Trade (GATT).

GATT became de facto an international organization and provided the institutional framework of the multilateral trading system for almost half a century. As a result of successive rounds of trade negotiations, new rules were adopted in various areas such as investment, technical barriers to trade, sanitary and phytosanitary measures. Moreover, the Marrakech agreements which codify the results of the Uruguay Round establish similar rules for trade in services. They also include an agreement on trade-related aspects of intellectual property rights (TRIPS) and replace the provisional GATT by a genuine international organization, the WTO, on the basis of previously existing institutions and rules.

WTO's Mandate

The GATT agreement describes its own objectives as follows:

> Their relations [of the contracting parties] in the field of trade and economic endeavor should be conducted with a view of raising standards of living, ensuring full employment and a large and steadily growing volume of real income and effective demand, developing the full use of the resources of the world and expanding the production and exchange of goods.

These objectives should be promoted by

> . . . entering into reciprocal and mutually advantageous arrangements directed to the substantial reduction of tariffs and other barriers to trade and to the elimination of discriminatory treatment in international commerce.

The overarching objective of the multilateral trading system established by GATT and WTO is to facilitate trade between countries in order to promote economic growth and development. The GATT agreement is not meant to achieve total liberalization of trade, but rather to provide a rule-based framework facilitating international trade in order to promote economic development. The signatories' intention was to avoid the dilemma experienced between the two World Wars, when countries resorted to trade restrictions in order to fight economic recession, yet achieved exactly the opposite.

The Rationale of Free Trade

Free trade enables countries to buy products from the cheapest supplier and to sell products to countries where it is more expensive to produce them. Countries able to produce a certain good at lower costs than others have an "absolute" advantage. The benefits of trade are quite obvious where countries having such advantages produce more of the goods concerned than needed for the domestic market and exchange them with goods from other countries able to produce the latter at lower costs. This seems more difficult for countries not having an absolute advantage in any sector. However, according to the theory of comparative advantage, all countries gain from participating in international trade (and from letting others participate) if they export goods of sectors where their advantages are *comparatively* high (or their disadvantages are *comparatively* low) and import goods of sectors where their advantages are *comparatively* low (or their disadvantages *comparatively* high).[4]

In order to reap the benefits of international trade, two conditions have to be met: first, trade has to be (relatively) free. This means that countries do not only seek access to the markets of other countries, but have to open their own markets. Second, countries with competitive advantages in many sectors should abandon sectors where opportunity costs are high, in order to allow other countries to use their comparative advantages in these sectors. Both conditions require some kind of cooperation. The WTO provides the framework for achieving the first one.

GATT Rules and Principles

GATT and WTO agreements establish a legal framework based on a number of basic rules and disciplines.

Bound Tariffs and No Quantitative Restrictions. Among the most important ones are Article II which requires members to bind their individual tariffs at certain levels and Article XI which prohibits submitting imports to quantitative restrictions.

Non-Discrimination. Free trade means competition between domestic and foreign suppliers. Competition must be free and fair, meaning that all suppliers must receive equal treatment. Equal access *to* the market of importing countries for products originating in different exporting countries is ensured by the principle of "most-favored nation treatment" (MFN). Article I (1) of the GATT agreement states that "any advantage, favor, privilege or immunity granted by any contracting party to any product originating in or destined for any other country shall be accorded immediately and unconditionally to the like product originating in or destined for the territories of all other contracting parties." This provision prohibits discrimination between a country's trading partners.

Equal treatment between trading partners and domestic suppliers on the market of importing countries is required by the principle of "national treatment," which is defined in Article III. Paragraph 2 of this provision requests that "the products of the territory of any contracting party imported into the territory of any other contracting party shall not be subject . . . to internal taxes . . . in excess of those applied . . . to like domestic products." The provisions of this article prohibit discrimination of imports that would "afford protection to domestic production."

In practice, products from different suppliers compete where consumers consider them as basically the same. In the language of GATT, such products are called "like products." GATT and WTO agreements do not provide a legal definition of like products. GATT panels define like products as those whose essential physical characteristics are the same.[5] Panels found that discrimination is not allowed on the basis of production and processing methods (PPM) where these methods have no impact on the consumption of the products concerned. The labor conditions under which goods are produced do not determine the physical characteristics nor do they have an impact on consumption of the products concerned. Hence, importing countries may not apply import restrictions on the grounds that the goods concerned were produced under conditions violating labor standards.

Other GATT Principles. Arguably the most important principle underlying the philosophy of the multilateral trading system is fairness. The system seeks to establish a global balance of benefits (in terms of market access, not in terms of actual trade flows). The GATT agreements provide for compensation, under the circumstances defined in Article XXIII, where benefits of one country are nullified or impaired by others—even in the absence of violations of any specific rule. Also in order to ensure fairness, other GATT rules aim at making international trade transparent and predictable.

Moreover, the multilateral trading system incorporates a dynamic of progressive trade liberalization. Although there is no legal commitment, there is a kind of basic understanding between WTO members to gradually liberalize trade. Members are also expected to accept new rules and disciplines, where such rules turn out to be necessary in order to ensure that trade remains free and that competition remains fair.

The Institutional Framework of the WTO

Ever since its inception, the multilateral trading system has expanded. Present membership of the WTO includes 160 states and independent territories. They account for approximately 97 percent of world trade. Some twenty-three countries are currently in the process of negotiating their accession to the organization. Countries that are neither members of the WTO nor in the process of becoming members are either marginal as far as their participation in international trade is concerned or pursue isolationist policies which marginalize them in the framework of the international community.

WTO activities belong to one of two categories. On the one hand, there are the regular activities of the main bodies which include all members. Decisions in these bodies are generally taken by consensus. If there is no consensus, a vote may be called. Each country has one vote. Important decisions require qualified majorities.

On the other hand, since the creation of GATT, the agency has organized eight rounds of trade negotiations, aimed at amending and supplementing trade rules and at further liberalizing world trade. The latest round started in November 2001 in Doha, Qatar. Trade negotiations in the framework of such rounds continue until everything on the agenda is agreed by everybody.

Three Classes of Members

Roughly half the number of the original GATT Contracting Parties were developing countries. At present, 124 WTO members—that is, three-quarters of the organization's membership—are developing countries or independent territories. Thirty-four of them are "least developed countries" (LDCs). Over the last few decades, many developing countries succeeded in actively participating in international trade. Some have become manufacturers of high-tech industrial goods. And others, including countries belonging to the group of least developed countries, now play an important role as suppliers of less sophisticated, labor-intensive products.

In contrast, the GATT has not been very successful in addressing the needs of developing countries. For some years, the GATT simply ignored the fact that these countries find it difficult to compete with industrialized and richer nations. In 1971, GATT members finally agreed to provide special and more favorable treatment to developing countries, also known as "special and differential treatment" (SDT). This treatment includes more rights (better access to the markets of developed countries) and fewer obligations. As far as obligations of developing countries are concerned, SDT generally burns down to delaying the date at which new disciplines become binding. For LDCs, SDT means that they are exempted from virtually all rules and disciplines. As a result, the WTO has become a three-class society where developed countries are obliged to respect all obligations, where developing countries are granted some longer transitional periods, and where LDCs have rights but virtually no obligations.

In spite of this, many developing countries have been unable to fully comply with WTO disciplines at the end of the additional period that they were granted. Only a third of the thirty-four LDCs which are WTO members have a permanent mission in Geneva. A claim that these countries are actually integrated into the multilateral trading system belongs to the realm of fiction. On the whole, the GATT had only mitigated success in integrating developing countries into the multilateral trading system.

Three Pillars

The Marrakech agreements finalizing the Uruguay Round of Trade Negotiations added new organs in parallel to the ones in charge of trade in goods. The present institutional framework of the WTO includes three (similar) pillars, one for trade in goods, another for trade in services, and a third for intellectual property rights. A number of subsidiary bodies manage and monitor the application of the various WTO agreements at the level of day-to-day business. They report to the Goods Council, the Service Council, or the Intellectual Property Council. These three councils, in turn, report to common bodies, the Ministerial Conference which meets approximately every two years, and the General Council which conducts the organization's business during the intervals.

Monitoring Compliance

WTO members have to inform the organization (which subsequently informs all other members) of all measures, policies, and laws affecting international trade. Moreover, the WTO conducts regular monitoring of each country's trade policy, in the framework of the "Trade Policy Review Mechanism" (TPRM) established during the Uruguay Round. These peer reviews provide information—and occasionally early warning—on how closely members follow WTO rules and disciplines.

Complaints Procedures and Enforcement Mechanism

The most important feature of the WTO institutional framework is undoubtedly the dispute settlement mechanism (DSM) established by the Marrakech agreements in 1994.

The Dispute Settlement Mechanism

Settling disputes is the responsibility of the Dispute Settlement Body (DSB; the General Council in another guise). In line with the quasi-jurisdictional nature of the dispute settlement procedure, fact finding (and presenting evidence) is basically left to the party requiring the establishment of a panel.

The DSB has the authority to establish panels, adopt reports of panels and the Appellate Body, monitor the implementation of rulings and recommendations, and authorize retaliatory measures if rulings are not implemented. The DSM provides for a structured process with clearly defined stages of procedure. The DSB may establish a panel of three independent experts if consultations between the interested parties have failed. The first instance ends with the ruling of a panel. An appeal may be filed against any legal points of a panel's findings. Appeals are heard by three members of a permanent seven-member Appellate Body. A country losing a case cannot block the adoption of a ruling.

Sanctions

If the losing defendant does not comply with the ruling or recommendations of a panel or the Appellate Body, the complaining side may ask for compensation pending full implementation. If there is no agreement on compensation, the DSB may authorize retaliation. In principle, trade sanctions should be applied in the sector where the dispute arose. If this would not be effective, sanctions may be imposed in other sectors covered by the same agreement or even by other agreements. This is commonly referred to as "cross-retaliation." The DSB monitors the implementation of panels' and Appellate Body's rulings and recommendations until the issue is solved.

The WTO Objectives in the Present Context

Trade liberalization has made tremendous progress since World War II. Consequently, competition has become fiercer. At the same time, an increasing number of issues and policies have become relevant for trade. GATT and WTO dealt with a number of these issues by adopting rules applying the same principles as those enshrined in the original agreements, in particular non-discrimination and fairness. The 1994 agreements finalizing the Uruguay Round confirmed the principles agreed in 1947 and extended their application to trade in services and TRIPS. These principles are as important as they were when the foundations of the multilateral trading system were laid.

Trade versus Other Policies

GATT and WTO are widely acclaimed as a success story. One of the reasons of this success are the rather strict provisions imposing non-discrimination, as well as a fairly narrow interpretation of these rules. These rules make a clear distinction between trade and production. In addition, trade policy has generally been understood as a strictly commercial function, in isolation from social and environmental concerns.

As a result of this approach, certain problems arising at the interface between trade and other policies are ignored by the multilateral trading system. On the one hand, this leaves governments free to choose policies in such areas as the environment and labor standards that enhance their competitiveness on foreign markets. On the other hand, governments are not allowed to adopt policies in these areas which would conflict with their obligations under the WTO agreements, meaning those that would restrict trade. For these reasons, the multilateral trading system has come under heavy attack.

THE GAP BETWEEN TRADE AND LABOR STANDARDS

Due to the ILO principle of "no sanctions" and the GATT principle of "non-discrimination," there is a gap between the rules of multilateral trading system and the international labor standards adopted by the ILO. Nonetheless, certain WTO rules and other provisions of international law may be applied or construed in order to narrow that gap.

The UN Charter

Under Chapter VII of the UN Charter, the Security Council can take sanctions as an enforcement tool to maintain or restore international peace and security when peace has been threatened and diplomatic efforts have failed. The use of sanctions is intended to apply pressure on a state to comply with decisions taken by the Security Council. Sanctions may include comprehensive economic and trade embargoes. Sanctions adopted by the Security Council are mandatory for all member states of the UN. Article 103 of the UN Charter (Chapter XVI) states that "in the event of a conflict between the obligations of the members of the United Nations under the present Charter and their obligations under any other international agreement, their obligations under the present Charter shall prevail." A trade ban decided by the Security Council would therefore also prevail over WTO obligations.

In theory, under Chapter VII of the Charter, the Security Council could adopt a mandatory trade ban against a country violating labor standards in a way that puts peace and security in jeopardy. In practice, though, it is unlikely that violations of labor standards have such effects. The possibility of linking trade and labor offered by Chapter VII are, for all practical purposes, rather limited.

ILO Rules

As stated above, under Article 33 of its Constitution, the ILO can take action against a member state found to violate its standards. Such action may include the authorization of trade sanctions. However, the ILO has traditionally refrained from using Article 33, for the reasons mentioned above.

So far, this provision has been invoked only once. In 1998, an ILO Commission of Inquiry issued a set of recommendations to stop widespread forced labor practices in Myanmar. After a series of unfruitful attempts to convince Myanmar to comply with these recommendations, the International Labor Conference voted a resolution under Article 33 in 2000. Yet, this resolution does not explicitly recommend the use of trade sanctions, but calls on ILO members and UN organizations to take appropriate actions, which only a few did. The empirical experience confirms that, indeed, Article 33 does not bridge the gap between trade and labor standards.

Moreover, if the ILO was to authorize its members to apply trade measures under Article 33, such measures might be incompatible with the rules of the multilateral trading system. Contrary to the UN Security Council, the ILO lacks the power to override the obligations of its members as members of the WTO.

WTO Rules

As stated above, WTO rules prohibit restrictions on imports of goods and impose non-discrimination between foreign suppliers and between the latter and domestic producers. But these rules do not give free trade unconditional preference over all other policies and concerns. They provide for exceptions from these principles both for trade-related and for non-trade-related reasons. Some of these exceptions may be interpreted in a way that would allow trade restrictions for reasons related to substandard labor conditions.

GATT Article VI: Anti-Dumping

Article VI and the Anti-Dumping Agreement authorize WTO member states to apply anti-dumping duties on products which are sold on the market of the importing country for a price that is less than their "normal value." Exports of goods produced under substandard labor conditions are often described as "social dumping." Could Article VI and the Anti-Dumping Agreement be applied to such exports?

Article VI determines the normal value by reference either to the domestic price or the price for the like product for export to other countries or to the costs of production. To the extent that savings from substandard working conditions reduce the price of the product concerned on any market, including the domestic one, the normal value of the goods concerned would include these savings. If the dumping margin of social dumping is calculated in reference to that value, it would be zero. Thus, under the terms of this provision, social dumping would not appear as dumping. Accordingly, anti-dumping rules cannot bridge the gap between trade and labor.

GATT Article XVI: Subsidies

Article XVI and the Agreement on Subsidies limit the use of subsidies by WTO member states. Arguably, in terms of economics, substandard labor conditions amount to subsidies to companies which offer these conditions. But they do not meet the legal definition of subsidies of this provision. Article XVI defines a subsidy as a financial contribution or any income or price support *by the government* of the exporting country. Although some governments seem to be engaged in wage-suppressing policies, this can hardly be regarded as a subsidy as defined in Article XVI.[6] Therefore, this provision cannot be applied to bridge the gap between trade and labor.

GATT Article XIX: Safeguard Measures

Under certain conditions, GATT Article XIX authorizes safeguard measures which may take the form of customs duties and quantitative restrictions of imports. Such measures may be imposed if there is a sharp increase in imports which results from unforeseen developments and causes (or threatens to cause) serious injury to domestic industry. Such an increase in imports may be triggered—wholly or in part—by substandard working conditions in the exporting country. In that case, Article XIX would authorize the importing country to impose trade restrictions for reasons linked to labor conditions.

Unlike anti-dumping and anti-subsidy measures, safeguards do not respond to a situation where trade is considered to be unfair. This is why they can only be applied under exceptional circumstances. Besides, developing countries are given some protection from safeguard measures. Finally, safeguard measures can only be applied *erga omnes*, meaning to all countries supplying the same goods. Hence, safeguard measures as authorized under GATT Article XIX do not provide an adequate tool to bridge the gap between trade and labor standard.

GATT Article XX: General Exceptions

Article XX (a) and (b) allow for exceptions from GATT rules and disciplines where such exceptions are necessary to protect public morals, human, animal, or plant life or health. Arguably, these exceptions could be construed in a way allowing the application of trade measures against countries where labor conditions are incompatible with public morals or present a threat to health. This may be the case as far as child labor and forced labor are concerned. However, it is a basic rule of treaty interpretation that exceptions should be interpreted in a narrow sense. It would be difficult to argue that the exceptions of Article XX (a) and (b) also cover labor conditions. As one provision—Article XX (e)—refers to prison labor, there is no reason to assume that other labor conditions are covered by any of the other exceptions listed in Article XX without being explicitly mentioned.

The possibility of applying Article XX (d) on "measures necessary to secure compliance with laws or regulations not inconsistent with the GATT" to labor standards was discussed during the preparation of the Havana Charter, but was rejected.[7]

Article XX (e) authorizes WTO members to restrict imports of "products of prison labor." This provision seems to establish a link with the international labor standard prohibiting forced or compulsory labor. However, the relevant ILO conventions do not ban prison labor in general, but only under certain specific circumstances. Thus, the area in which GATT Article XX (e) overlaps with ILO labor standards is very limited.

Article XX (h) allows for exceptions necessary to honor *obligations* under commodity agreements. Some of these agreements contain provisions on "fair labor standards." Yet, these provisions do not *oblige* signatories to apply trade restrictions against countries where labor standards are not fair.

GATT Article XXI: Security Exceptions

Article XXI (c) enables WTO member states to act "in pursuance of its obligations under the United Nations Charter for the maintenance of international peace and security." The International Confederation of Free Trade Unions (ICFTU) has suggested that this provision be construed as to permitting trade actions authorized by the ILO.[8]

It is true that the ILO Constitution states that labor conditions should be improved in order to ensure peace in the world. But I do not believe that any generally accepted method of legal interpretation could support the above reading of Article XXI (c). Moreover, as in the case of a trade ban decided by the Security Council, it is difficult to imagine a situation where violations of labor standards are so serious as to jeopardize world peace.

GATT Article XXIII: Nonviolation, Nullification, or Impairment

Article XXIII states that if any benefit accruing to a WTO member directly or indirectly under the WTO agreement is being "nullified or impaired . . . as the result of . . . the application by another contracting party of any measure, whether or not it conflicts with the provisions of the Agreement," the matter may be referred to the Contracting Parties. Arguably, violations of labor standards in exporting countries may nullify or impair the benefits to which importing countries are entitled.[9] However, this provision does not provide an immediate remedy. Besides, the way in which panels have interpreted Article XXIII limits the possibility to use it as a tool to fill the space between trade and labor standards.[10]

GATT Article XXXV: Non-Application of the Agreement between Particular Contracting Parties

Article XXXV authorizes WTO member states, upon their own accession to WTO or upon the accession of a new member state, to declare that they will not apply the GATT Agreement in their trade relations with another member state. Although this provision may be used for reasons related to the respect of labor rights in specific countries, its scope is much to limited to solve the problems stemming from the absence of a link between trade and labor standards.

WTO Rules and Sustainable Development

Arguably, substandard labor conditions are an impediment to sustainable development. In order to make development sustainable, it may be required to apply trade measures on imports from countries not complying with CLS. While the preamble of the agreement establishing the WTO contains an explicit reference to sustainable development, none of the WTO provisions refer to this concept. Although there are general exceptions from WTO rules for environmental concerns, there is no exception that would allow restrictions on trade for the sake of making development sustainable. Thus, even a general consensus that sustainable development requires compliance with CLS would not help to bridge the gap between ILO standards and WTO rules.

Commodity Agreements

Several commodity agreements concluded under the auspices of the UN during the 1970s include references to labor standards. Article 42 of the International Tin Agreement of 1975 states that participating countries "will seek to ensure fair labor standards." Article 63 of the 1977 International Sugar Agreement stipulates that "members shall ensure that fair labor standards are maintained in their respective sugar industries and, as far as possible, shall endeavor to improve the standard of living of agricultural and industrial workers in the various branches of sugar production, and of growers of sugar cane and sugar beet." Likewise, Article 54 of the 1979 International Natural Rubber Agreement states that "members declare that they will endeavor to maintain labor standards designed to improve the levels of living of labor in their respective natural rubber sectors." None of these agreements goes as far as to establish a link between compliance with certain labor standards and trade in the relevant sectors.

Conclusion

Both the WTO and the ILO lack provisions linking one to the other. Even the most flexible interpretation of WTO rules cannot fill this gap. And there is no other provision of international law that could bridge it.

ATTEMPTS TO BRIDGE THE GAP BETWEEN TRADE AND LABOR STANDARDS

Over the last decades, numerous attempts have been made to bridge or at least narrow the gap between the rules governing international trade and labor standards.[11]

Attempts Made before World War II

Already during the preparatory stage of the ILO, proposals were made to combine labor standards with trade restrictions. In fact, the report prepared by the Advisory Commission on International Labor Legislation commissioned by the Versailles Peace Conference proposed a ban not just on child labor, but on international shipment of goods made by children.[12] Likewise, the American delegates proposed a prohibition on trading goods in the production of which convict labor was employed or permitted.[13] The British delegation proposed that "one of the principal objectives of international labour Conventions is to eliminate unfair competition based on oppressive working conditions . . . the appropriate penalty should be that . . . the signatory states should place an embargo on goods produced in those conditions of unfair competition . . ."[14] However, none of these proposals were adopted.

In 1927, the League of Nations convened a World Economic Conference which considered, *inter alia*, the problem of exports of goods that are particularly cheap because of poor labor standards. One of the recommendations of the conference was to encourage producers to apply methods of remuneration giving the worker "a fair share in the increase of output."[15] In 1937, an ILO conference suggested that "in framing their commercial policies, governments should take account of social conditions prevailing in countries with which they have trade relations."[16]

The Havana Charter

The need to accommodate labor protection with trade policy was explicitly acknowledged by the United Nations Conference on Trade and Employment of 1947–48. Article VII of the Havana Charter prepared by this conference reads:

> The Members recognize that measures relating to employment must take fully into account the rights of workers under inter-governmental declarations, conventions and agreements. They recognize that all countries have a common interest in the achievement and maintenance of fair labor standards related to productivity, and thus in the improvement of wages and working conditions as productivity may permit. The Members recognize that unfair labor conditions, particularly in production of export, create difficulties in international trade, and, accordingly, each Member shall take whatever action may be appropriate and feasible to eliminate such conditions on its territory.

This provision refers to labor standards *related to productivity*, which suggests that the labor conditions the authors were concerned about were those affecting production costs. The emphasis on the *production of export* suggests that the rationale of this provision was the impact of different production costs, resulting from different labor standards, on trade. Although this provision would not have established a formal link between trade and labor, it would have narrowed the gap between the two.[17]

Proposals Made in the Framework of GATT, WTO, and the OECD

Soon after the creation of the multilateral trading system, attempts were made to introduce a link with international labor standards. Most of these initiatives were taken by the US government.

1953: A US proposal

In 1953, the United States proposed a GATT rule stating that unfair labor conditions "create difficulties in international trade which nullify or impair benefits under this Agreement." This language borrows from Article VII of the Havana Charter and GATT Article XXIII (Nonviolation, Nullification, or Impairment). As the Contracting Parties could not agree on a definition of unfair labor standards, it was eventually abandoned.[18]

1975: The Tokyo Round

The Trade Act of 1974 which authorized the United States to participate in the Tokyo Round of multilateral trade negotiations states as one of the goals of these negotiations "the adoption of international fair standards and of public petition and confrontation procedures in the GATT." Apparently, this objective also included labor standards.[19] Sweden, drawing on ideas of the International Metalworkers Federation, proposed adding a social clause to the GATT that would establish a framework for GATT Contracting Parties to protect their workers against imports from countries with substandard labor conditions. The criteria proposed for judging the fairness of labor conditions were those of the UN and the ILO. These proposals were not taken up during the Tokyo Round negotiations.

1986: The Uruguay Round

In 1986, during the preparation of the Uruguay Round, the United States attempted to put workers' rights on the round's agenda. The US delegation made it clear that it "did not intend to impose its wage standards on the rest of the world, or to deny the legitimate comparative advantage of developing countries. Rather, the United States sought to ensure that trade expansion was not an end in itself, and that it benefited all workers in all countries and contributed to the basic objectives of GATT."[20] Nonetheless, developing countries refused to discuss the issue of labor in the framework of the Uruguay Round.

In 1987, the United States proposed to set up a GATT working party (not linked to the Uruguay Round negotiations) on the "possible relationship between international trade and respect of international labor standards," but failed to garner sufficient support.[21] Subsequently, the United States reduced its demand to examine only three standards—freedom of association, the right to collective bargaining, and freedom from forced or compulsory labor. But again, there was no agreement between GATT contracting parties.

1994: The Marrakech Conference

In April 1994, trade ministers gathered in Marrakech to sign the agreements finalizing the results of the Uruguay Round. At that time, it was envisaged to replace successive rounds of multilateral trade negotiations by regular ministerial meetings. There was intense debate on the subjects to be included in the agenda for these meetings, and many ministers pleaded for adding work on a "social clause" to the list. But there was no consensus to begin work on trade and labor standards. The only mention of the subject was a brief reference in the Chairman's lengthy list of issues that may be included in the future WTO work program.

1996: The Singapore Ministerial Meeting

The first Ministerial Meeting of Trade Ministers after the Marrakech Conference took place in Singapore in 1996. A request by the United States, Canada, Japan, and the EU to put the issue of trade and labor standards on the agenda of future ministerial meetings met with a flat refusal by developing countries to engage in any discussion, resulting finally in the withdrawal of an invitation to the ILO Director-General to address the ministerial meeting.

Nonetheless, this was the first occasion on which the issue of trade and labor standards made its way into an official statement of the WTO. Point 4 of the Declaration of the Ministerial Conference in Singapore in 1996 reads:

> We renew our commitment to the observance of internationally recognized core labor standards. The ILO is the competent body to set and deal with these standards, and we affirm our support for its work in promoting them. We believe that economic growth and development fostered by increased trade and further trade liberalization contribute to the promotion of these standards. We reject the use of labor standards for protectionist purposes, and agree that the comparative advantage of countries, particularly low-wage developing countries, must in no way be put into question. In this regard, we note that the WTO and ILO Secretariats will continue their existing collaboration.[22]

1998: The Geneva Ministerial Meeting

At the second Ministerial Meeting in Geneva in 1998, the EU and the United States proposed the establishment of a forum where "business, labor, environmental and consumer groups can speak out and guide the further evolution of the WTO." The proposal did not find consensus.

1998: The Multilateral Agreement on Investment

After the conclusion of the Uruguay Round, OECD governments decided to address the issue of protecting foreign investments. In 1995, the OECD started to prepare a draft for a Multilateral Agreement on Investment (MAI) which listed a number of principles including international labor standards, but it only confirmed the parties' commitment to respecting these standards without establishing new obligations. A proposal by the UK government for a clause requiring governments not to derogate from existing labor standards in order to attract investment did not garner the support of all other developed countries.

The MAI negotiations sparked an intense international debate about the impact of trade and investment on labor rights, environmental protection, and sustainable development. In the end, the idea of a MAI had to be abandoned because of resistance by developing countries. While the issue of labor standards may not have been crucial for the collapse of the MAI negotiations, it was certainly among the factors that hindered its success.

1999: The Seattle Ministerial Meeting

International labor standards were perhaps the most divisive issue on the agenda of the Ministerial Meeting in Seattle in December 1999. The United States and Canada made proposals to create a working group on trade and labor, while the EU proposed a joint ILO/WTO Standing Working Forum on the issue. Developing countries fiercely opposed these proposals, although the United States and the EU made it clear that they did not envisage the use of trade sanctions. This was somehow contradicted by declarations made by President Clinton in a press interview. As a result, developing countries hardened their stance and blocked any work in the WTO concerning labor standards.

2001: The Doha Development Agenda

Subsequently, during a conference convened in November 2001 in Doha, Qatar, trade ministers agreed on a new round of multilateral trade negotiations. Again, the efforts of the EU and US to put trade and labor standards on the "Doha Development Agenda" did not succeed. The Ministerial Declaration adopted in Doha includes no more than a scant reference to the issue:

> We reaffirm the declaration that we made at the Ministerial Conference in Singapore regarding internationally recognized core labor standards. We take note of the work being conducted at the International Labor Organization on the social dimension of globalization.

So far, all attempts to establish a link between trade and labor in the framework of the multilateral trading system have failed. In essence, the present situation is not much different from the one that emerged after World War I: the only organization responsible for labor standards and their interrelation with international trade remains the ILO.

The Report of the Brandt Commission

In 1980, the Independent Commission on International Development (the Brandt Commission) found that

> . . . exports that result from working conditions that do not respect minimum social standards relevant to a given society are unfair to the workers directly involved, to workers of competing Third World exporting countries, and to workers of importing countries whose welfare is undermined. They are also unfair to business concerns and countries which encourage social progress.

Accordingly, the Commission made a recommendation that "fair labor standards should be internationally agreed in order to prevent unfair competition and to facilitate trade liberalization."[23]

Attempts Made in the Framework of the ILO

The World Conference on Employment of 1976

In 1976, the ILO convened a World Conference on Employment which acknowledged that "the competitiveness of new products imported from developing countries should not be achieved to the detriment of the living conditions for their labour forces."

The ILO Working Party on the Social Dimensions of the Liberalization of International Trade

In his 1994 report to the International Labor Conference, ILO Director-General Michel Hansenne favored the idea of linking labor standards to the rules of the multilateral trading system.[24] The same year, the ILO set up a "Working Party on the Social Dimensions of the Liberalization of International Trade" (since 2000 the "ILO Working Party on the Social Dimension of Globalization"), mandated to examine the issue of linking trade and labor standards. The ILO secretariat proposed a scheme under which the ILO and WTO would share responsibilities, the ILO being in charge of monitoring compliance with labor standards and the WTO responsible for deciding trade sanctions. However, the Working Party could not agree on this approach. Eventually, the Workers' Group of the Governing Body withdrew its demand for authorization of trade sanctions for violations of labor standards. Nonetheless, the Working Party acknowledged that there is growing recognition of the significance of fundamental labor standards in the framework of globalization and international trade. Subsequently, the ILO succeeded in adopting two declarations meant to counterbalance the social consequences of globalization and trade liberalization.

The ILO Declaration on Fundamental Principles and Rights at Work of 1998

Acting in response to the 1996 WTO Ministerial Declaration and drawing on the conclusions of the Copenhagen UN World Summit on Social Development of 1995, the ILO adopted, in 1998, a "Declaration on Fundamental Principles and Rights at Work and its Follow-Up." They include:

- freedom of association and protection of the right to collective bargaining,
- the elimination of all forms of forced or compulsory labor,
- the effective abolition of child labor,
- the elimination of discrimination in respect of employment and occupation.

Since then, the term "core labor standards" has been coined for these fundamental principles and rights at work. As far as trade is concerned, the 1998 Declaration stresses

> . . . that labor standards should not be used for protectionist purposes, and that nothing in this Declaration and its follow-up shall be invoked or otherwise used for such purpose; in addition, the comparative advantage of any country should in no way be called into question by this Declaration and its follow-up.[25]

The ILO Declaration on Social Justice for a Fair Globalization of 2008

Following the 2005 Report of the World Commission on the Social Dimension of Globalization, the ILO, in 2008, adopted another declaration, the "Declaration on Social Justice for a Fair Globalization." One of the four strategic objectives mentioned in this declaration is to respect, promote, and realize fundamental principles and rights at work. It notes

> . . . that the violation of fundamental principles and rights at work cannot be invoked or otherwise used as a legitimate comparative advantage and that labor standards should not be used for protectionist purposes.

These terms signify an important departure from the position expressed in the 1998 Declaration. While that declaration states that the comparative advantage of any country should not be called into question, the 2008 Declaration recognizes that a comparative advantage obtained through substandard labor conditions is not legitimate.

Conclusion

There were numerous attempts, made over almost a century, to bridge the gap between international trade and labor standards, but none of them succeeded. While some of them were meant to improve labor protection and in particular to stop child labor, most of them were motivated by the desire to protect domestic industries against unfair competition from countries with low standards. Since the establishment of the multilateral trading system by the 1947 GATT agreements, countries where labor is cheap constantly blocked all attempts to bridge the gap in the framework of that organization.

Until the adoption of the 1998 ILO Declaration on Fundamental Principles and Rights at Work, these attempts suffered from the absence of an international consensus on the priority list of labor standards to which trade should be linked. While there is such consensus now, more recent proposals to link trade and labor meet with resistance even in the countries which tabled them. Governments of these countries are more and more often lobbied by importers to keep their markets open for cheap imports, including those which are cheap because labor standards are not complied with in exporting countries.

Realizing that there was little chance to bridge the gap in the framework of the WTO and the ILO, various members of WTO started, some twenty years ago, to adopt rules requiring compliance with labor standards in their own trade legislation and have included similar provisions in their bilateral or regional trade agreements. However, these provisions do not amend the rules of the multilateral trading system. The gap between these rules and ILO standards is as wide as half a century ago.

The sheer number of proposals made to bridge this gap suggests that it creates problems that are serious and real. On the other hand, the lack of response to those proposals suggests that there is no need to fix them. This gives rise to two questions: How serious are these problems today? Is there a need to resolve them now?

NOTES

1. The term "labor standards" as used in this study refers to norms concerning working conditions; the term "labor conditions" refers to the circumstances under which work is carried out.

2. Until it was amended in 1946, Article 33 provided that members could take "measures of an economic character." While the revised version leaves the Governing Body more discretion to adopt its action to the particular case, it does not exclude the possibility of economic or trade sanctions.

3. R. Howse, The World Trade Organization and the Protection of Workers' Rights, *The Journal of Small and Emerging Business Law*, Summer 1999, p. 13.

4. While GATT and WTO agreements do not acknowledge any economic theory as their official credo, certain declarations of the WTO and the ILO refer to "comparative advantages."

5. See R. E. Hudec, Like Product: The Differences in Meaning in GATT Articles I and III, in T. Cottier and P. Mavroidis, eds., *Regulatory Barriers and the Principle of Non-Discrimination in World Trade*, Ann Arbor, 2000.

6. E. Alben, GATT and the Fair Wage: A Historical Perspective on the Labor-Trade Link, *Colombia Law Review*, Vol. 101, p. 1418.

7. D. K. Brown, D. K., International Labor Standards in the World Trade Organization and the International Labor Organization, *Review*, Federal Reserve Bank of St. Louis, issue July 2000, p. 108.

8. K. A. Elliott and R. B. Freeman, Can Labor Stands Improve under Globalization? Institution for International Economics. Washington, DC, 2003, p. 137, footnote 11.

9. The US Commission on Foreign Economic Policy established in 1953 found that trade problems stemming from unfair labor conditions were actionable under GATT Article XXIII, US Commission on Foreign Economic Policy: Staff papers, Feb. 1954, p. 437, quoted by S. Charnovitz, The Influence of International Labor Standards on the World Trading Regime, *International Labour Review*, Vol. 126, No. 5, Sept.–Oct. 1987, p. 574. A background paper submitted in 1995 to the ILO Working Party on the Social Dimension of the Liberalization of International Trade suggested using this provision for creating a link between trade and labor standards, H. Lim, The Social Clause: Issues and Challenges, International Labor Organization, Bureau for Workers Activities, Geneva, 2001, p. 46.

10. E. Alben, GATT and the Fair Wage: A Historical Perspective on the Labor-Trade Link, p. 1419.

11. As the present study focuses on the relation between international norms, attempts to narrow the gap by national trade laws are not mentioned in this section.

12. P. S. Foner, *History of the Labor Movement in the United States*, Vol. 7, *Labor and World War I, 1914–1918*, New York, 1987, p. 358.

13. J. T. Shotwell, *The Origins of the International Labor Organization in Two Volumes*, New York, 1934, Vol. II, Documents 37 and 47.

14. Quoted by G. Caire, Labour Standards and International Trade, in W. Sengenberger and D. Campbell (eds), *International Labour Standards and Economic Interdependence*, International Institute for Labour Studies, Geneva, 1994, p. 297.

15. League of Nations, Report and Proceedings of the World Economic Conference, Geneva, 1927, p. 49, quoted by S. Charnovitz, The Influence of International Labor Standards on the World Trading Regime, p. 566.

16. ILO: Report of Proceedings, Tripartite Conference on the Textile Industry, Washington, DC, 1937, First Part, p. 42, quoted by S. Charnovitz, The Influence of International Labor Standards on the World Trading Regime, *International Labour Review*, Vol. 126, No. 5, Sept.–Oct. 1987, p. 567.

17. During the negotiations of the Havana Charter, it was also suggested that the general exceptions provision on prison labor be used in connection with labor standards. The subcommittee responsible for the general exceptions provision expressed the view that this objective was covered for short-term purposes by the provision on safeguards and for long-term purposes by Article VII of the Charter—which never took effect; see E. Alben, GATT and the Fair Wage: A Historical Perspective on the Labor-Trade Link, *Colombia Law Review*, Vol. 101, p. 1432.

18. US Commission on Foreign Economic Policy: Staff papers, Feb. 1954, p. 437, quoted by S. Charnovitz, The Influence of International Labor Standards on the World Trading Regime, *International Labour Review*, Vol. 126, No. 5, Sept.–Oct. 1987, p. 574.

19. K. A. Elliott, and R. B. Freeman, Can Labor Stands Improve under Globalization? p. 5.

20. Preparatory Committee (GATT), Prep. comm. (86) SR 14 (May 23, 1986) 81.

21. GATT doc L/6243, (October, 28, 1987).

22. I suppose that the meaning of the term "comparative advantage" as used in this declaration is not that of the theoretical concept referred to on page 10, but rather that of "competitive advantage."

23. Independent Commission on International Development Issues, North-South: A Program for Survival, Cambridge, 1980, pp. 186 and 288.

24. International Labour Organization, Defending Values, Promoting Change, Report of the Director-General to the International Labor Conference, Geneva, 1994.

25. This language repeats part of the declaration adopted by the WTO in 1996.

Chapter Two

The Framework of the Discussion

The starting point for discussing the merits of linking trade to labor standards must be a specific problem that a link may solve. This could be any problem concerning or stemming from poor labor conditions, that could be addressed through trade measures, and that is serious enough to warrant their use.

Thus, the first step is the identification of a particular problem and the assessment of its importance. This chapter will explain how the chapters that follow will assess the existence and significance of problems that arise in connection with poor labor conditions and the need of addressing them by linking trade to labor standards.

Yet, we cannot give a final answer to the question of whether a specific problem requires the establishment of a link without a clear understanding of what such a link would look like. This, however, depends on its particular objective—which we do not know as long as we do not know the answer to the question of whether a specific problem actually requires the establishment of a link. Nonetheless, any kind of link, whatever its reason or objective, would have to incorporate certain essential elements. This chapter will clarify what these elements are. It will provide a provisional definition of a link used for the following discussion. It will also explain some other terms used in the following discussion.

THE ESSENTIAL FEATURES OF A LINK

Basically, a link between international trade and labor standards means a rule allowing trade measures on imports from countries with poor labor conditions.

A link would fill the gap between two sets of norms of international law, that is, those governing the multilateral trading system and international labor standards. It must be a provision of international law itself.

A link would have to state the conditions under which it applies. One of the conditions would be non-compliance with certain labor standards. A link would have to specify the relevant standards.

It would also have to define the legal consequences of non-compliance. These would be the application of certain trade measures. A link would have to determine the type of these measures.

A Provision of International Law

Linking trade and labor standards is understood, in this study, as the adoption of a rule of international law having, in the hierarchy of norms, the same rank and status as WTO rules and ILO standards—without necessarily being established by either of these two agencies. Moreover, since any discriminatory treatment of imports on the grounds of poor labor conditions in the production process of the goods concerned is not allowed under present WTO rules, a link would amend or override these rules.

The Selection of Labor Standards

The selection of labor standards depends on the purpose of the link envisaged. If that link is meant to ensure minimum labor conditions, the selection would have to include standards defining fundamental rights of workers. If the intention is to address other problems such as the effects of poor labor conditions on international trade, the selection would have to include standards which have an impact on trade.

The Conventions on CLS

As far as problems with labor conditions as such are concerned, there is an international consensus on those considered the most important. Indeed, problems appear to be particularly grave where countries violate the standards listed in the 1998 ILO Declaration on Fundamental Principles and Rights at Work. These are the labor standards "expressed and developed" in eight fundamental conventions (not mentioned in the declaration itself), two for each of the four categories. These conventions are:

- C87 on Freedom of Association and Protection of the Right to Organize, 1948;
- C98 on the Right to Organize and Collective Bargaining, 1949;
- C29 on Forced Labor, 1930;
- C105 on the Abolition of Forced Labor, 1957;

- C138 on the Minimum Age, 1973;
- C182 on the Worst Forms of Child Labor, 1999 (adopted after the declaration);
- C100 on Equal Remuneration, 1951;
- C111 on Discrimination (Employment and Occupation), 1958.

The 1998 ILO Declaration on Fundamental Principles and Rights at Work and its Follow-Up explicitly states that these principles and rights are binding, even for countries not having ratified the relevant conventions. Since the adoption of this Declaration, the debate on a possible link between trade and labor focuses on the "core labor standards" laid down in these conventions.

Freedom of Association and the Right to Organize and Collective Bargaining. C83 states that ". . . workers and employers . . . shall have the right to establish and . . . to join organizations of their own choosing without previous authorization." Organizations are defined as "organizations of workers or of employers for furthering and defending the interests of workers or employers." Such organizations "shall have the right to draw up their constitutions and rules, to elect their representatives in full freedom, to organize their administration and activities and to formulate their programs. The public authorities shall refrain from any interference which would restrict this right or impede the lawful exercise thereof."

C98 completes these provisions by stating that

> . . . workers shall enjoy adequate protection against acts of anti-union discrimination in respect of their employment, [in particular against] acts calculated to make the employment of a worker subject to the condition that he shall not join a union or shall relinquish trade union membership [or to] cause the dismissal of or otherwise prejudice a worker by reason of union membership or because of participation in union activities . . .

Collective bargaining is the core of the philosophy underlying the ILO. The conventions on freedom of association and the right to organize and collective bargaining are meant to guarantee the existence and the respect of fair procedures which enable workers to defend their interests and to solve any disputes over labor conditions.

The Elimination of All Forms of Forced or Compulsory Labor. C29 defines forced or compulsory labor as "all work or service which is exacted from any person under the menace of any penalty and for which the said person has not offered himself voluntarily." The same convention lists a number of exceptions including compulsory military service, work which forms part of normal civic obligations or which is requested in cases of emergencies (war, fire, flood, famine, earthquake, etc.), as well as prison labor. While certain provisions of C29 aim at protecting the inhabitants of colonies against exploitation by colonial powers and their companies, this convention does not ban all forms of forced and compulsory labor in colonies.

C105 limits the scope of the exceptions allowed for by C29 by banning forced labor

> as a means of political coercion or education or as a punishment for holding or expressing political views or views ideologically opposed to the established political, social or economic system; as a method of mobilizing and using labor for purposes of economic development; as a means of labor discipline; as a punishment for having participated in strikes; as a means of racial, social, national or religious discrimination.

The two conventions on the elimination of all forms of forced or compulsory labor lay down the very basic principle that employees should be able to freely negotiate their employment and not be forced to make their labor available when they are not paid or when they are unwilling to do so for any other reason.

The Effective Abolition of Child Labor. C138 harmonizes the provisions of a number of previous conventions which since 1919 had established a minimum age for employment in different sectors. Under C138, that age is fifteen years (or fourteen years, in less developed countries). For employment which is hazardous to health, safety, or morals, the limit is eighteen years (sixteen years). The convention provides for exceptions for "limited categories of employment or work in respect of which special and substantial problems of application arise." Similarly, "a member whose economy and administrative facilities are insufficiently developed may . . . initially limit the scope of application of this Convention." C138 recognizes the fundamental right of children below a certain age not to be forced to carry out certain activities, but it does not ban activities such as helping earn pocket money or assisting in a family business outside school hours or during school holidays.

C182 lists a number of activities which children under eighteen should not perform under any circumstances. It bans the worst forms of child labor. According to this convention, these comprise

> all forms of slavery or practices similar to slavery, such as the sale and trafficking of children, debt bondage and serfdom and forced or compulsory labor, including forced . . . recruitment of children for use in armed conflict; the use, procuring or offering of a child for prostitution, for the production of pornography or for pornographic performances; the use, procuring or offering of a child for the production and trafficking of drugs. . . ; work which . . . is likely to harm the health, safety or morals of children.

Most of these activities are illegal and can hardly be considered as "work."

The Elimination of Discrimination in Respect of Employment and Occupation. C100 establishes the principle that "men and women should get equal remuneration for equal work of value." This should be achieved either through "national laws or regulations, a legally established machinery for wage determination or collective agreements between employers and workers." C100 requires that countries promote the "principle of equal remuneration for men and women for work of equal value" and seeks to end discrimination in compensation based on sex. This convention requires not only equal pay for workers doing exactly the same job, but also for those doing different types of jobs having the same value. It intends to avoid structural discrimination, not just obvious bias in the same workplace.

C111 obliges its signatories to "pursue a national policy designed to promote equality of opportunity and treatment in respect of employment and occupation, with a view to eliminating any discrimination in respect thereof." Discrimination is defined as "any distinction, exclusion or preference made on the basis of race, color, sex, religion, political opinion, national extraction or social origin, which has the effect of nullifying or impairing equality of opportunity or treatment in employment or occupation."

C111 recognizes that excluding individuals from jobs for which they do not meet certain specific requirements does not amount to discrimination.

The Wisdom of Selecting these Standards

The designation of certain standards as CLS is the result of a consensus that has emerged over several years. It is indeed the fruit of long and careful reflection. The starting point was "to satisfy the basic need for freely chosen work in humane conditions."[1] However, the selection was not only determined by the nature and importance of certain rights (including their recognition as human rights), but also by practical criteria like the appeal to a large number of stakeholders, the number of ratifications already acquired, and universality, meaning the fact that the standards concerned were unrelated to the level of development and per capita income of countries. Another selection criterion was that all countries are able to implement the relevant standards.[2]

Nonetheless, the list of CLS has been subject to controversy. The standard enjoying virtually unanimous support is that banning forced labor, probably because there is simply no excuse if it is violated. The standard on nondiscrimination is slightly more controversial, perhaps because it is not fully enforced in many countries, including more advanced ones.

Although there is general consensus on the need to eliminate child labor, there is some debate concerning the age limit and the extent to which children should be allowed to contribute to the income of their families. Arguably, a complete ban on child labor would worsen the economic plight of families which can hardly survive without the earnings of their children. Moreover, if children were to lose their jobs, they may either end up on the streets or possibly have to work elsewhere under even more dangerous and exploitative circumstances.

There is more skepticism concerning the standards on freedom of association and the right to collective bargaining. Trade unions have become very powerful in certain countries and some have abused their influence. On the other hand, employers are powerful in most countries and in some countries powerful enough to persuade their governments to send the police against workers on strike. The risk of abuse of power is hardly an argument against the claim that workers should enjoy freedom of association and the right to collective bargaining. When the ILO was created, these rights were regarded as crucial for social protection and political stability. They still are, but this may be overlooked or forgotten in countries where they have been fully implemented for a long time. The ultimate reason why freedom of association and the right to collective bargaining are so important is that they indirectly ensure, indirectly, minimum labor conditions in general.

Other Labor Standards and Wages

While the four CLS are certainly of fundamental importance, working conditions concerning health and safety are hardly less so. The ILO estimates that

> . . . every year, more than 2 million people die from occupational accidents or work-related diseases. By conservative estimates, there are 270 million occupational accidents and 160 million cases of occupational diseases. Death and injury takes a particularly heavy toll in developing nations where large number of people are engaged in hazardous activities.[3]

Some authors therefore make the claim that CLS should include international minimum standards on health and safety.[4]

There is also hard evidence that working hours and wages in certain developing countries are at levels that may be qualified as exploitation. But working hours and wages depend, to a large extent, on the level of development and of productivity in each country. For this reason, there is no international agreement on minimum wages as such. The actual level of wages is not only beyond the scope of CLS, but it is outside that of the ILO altogether.

Rather than adopting legal standards on health, safety, working hours, and wages, these could be fixed through collective bargaining. This would require guarantees of freedom of association and the right to collective bargaining. Arguably, ensuring these rights would provide a sufficient guarantee for reasonable labor conditions in general.

CLS as the Reference for This Study

As mentioned before, the selection of the relevant standards depends on the objective of the link proposed. Thus, the question concerning the selection of standards will have to be revisited once the basic question is answered, whether and for what purpose it would actually be justified to adopt a link, and only if it is actually justified. For now, in order to answer that question, we need a provisional selection of standards—a kind of working hypothesis.

Since the adoption of the 1998 ILO Declaration on Fundamental Principles and Rights at Work, there is an international consensus that the most serious labor problems stem from violations of CLS as defined in this declaration. Since then, these standards have become a kind of "natural" reference and almost unavoidably the starting point for any discussion of the merits of linking trade to labor standards. Moreover, when adopting the 2008 ILO Declaration on Social Justice for a Fair Globalization, the international community recognized the importance of CLS also for trade. The working hypothesis for the following discussion is that a link between trade and labor standards would include at least CLS as a reference.

The Selection of Trade Measures

Theoretically, compliance with labor standards could be linked to a variety of trade measures, including trade bans, quantitative restrictions, tariff quotas, and variable duties.[5] The most severe measure would be a global trade embargo on all exports of a given country, which all other countries would have to respect. A less radical approach would be to authorize trade restrictions on selected products. There are even less stringent trade measures, such as additional trade preferences to countries meeting certain requirements concerning the protection of labor rights.[6]

Whatever the type of trade measure, a link would require applying it in a discriminatory manner, differentiating between imports from countries complying with CLS and others that do not. Anything short of authorizing discriminatory trade measures would not "link" trade to labor standards.

The Meaning of a "Link between International Trade and Labor Standards"

For the purposes of the following discussion, a link between trade and labor standards is understood as *a provision of international law authorizing countries to regulate the access to their market by adopting discriminatory trade measures in accordance with the level of compliance with core labor standards in the country of origin.*

DEFINITIONS, APPROACHES, AND CRITERIA

A link between trade and labor standards can be justified by any problem concerning poor labor conditions, which could be addressed through trade measures and which is serious enough to warrant the application of the latter. Before assessing the existence and importance of specific problems, we have to determine the criteria for doing so.

The Criteria for Assessing Problems Stemming from Poor Labor Conditions

Poor labor conditions may be a problem *per se.* There are internationally agreed standards to determine whether labor conditions are acceptable or not: the ILO standards defined in 189 ILO conventions. Where labor conditions do not meet the most basic standards, it is fair to say that there are real and serious problems.

Another criterion determining the significance of violations of standards is their nature. It is often claimed that certain ILO standards are human rights. Violating these standards would thus appear to be a particularly grave matter.

Poor labor standards may entail further problems, including for international trade. The fact that WTO rules mention only prison labor does not mean that *other* poor labor conditions may not create similar trade-related problems. It is difficult to assess their importance, though, just because WTU rules ignore them. To assess these trade-related problems, we will refer to the general principles that should govern international trade, namely fairness and responsibility.

Actual Problems and the Threat of Problems

There are several GATT provisions (exceptions listed in Articles XX and XXI) that would allow trade restrictions, but which have hardly ever been invoked. They are necessary—"just in case." In fact, sometimes there are good reasons to establish rules to address problems not because they arise, but because *they may arise*. In other words, the threat of a particular problem may be sufficient to justify the adoption of a rule.

The Meaning of "Trade-Relatedness"

Whether problems stemming from poor labor conditions need to be addressed depends first and foremost on their nature and extent, not on their reasons and origins. For the purposes of this study, it is not relevant whether a particular problem is created by corrupt governments, greedy CEOs, capitalism or globalization, or consumer preferences. However, there is one exception: trade. Adopting trade measures to address a specific problem is, as a matter of principle, easier to justify if that problem is trade-related.

The following reflections therefore differentiate between issues that are trade-related and others that are not. An issue may be trade-related in two different ways. The level of compliance with labor standards is trade-related to the extent that it has a bearing on production costs and on the price of exports, which in turn is likely to affect their volume. These effects would be those of labor conditions *on* trade. But it may also be the other way round. Trade and trading opportunities have a feedback on labor conditions, where they encourage investors to go to countries with low standards or motivate governments to lower their standards in order to attract investments. These are effects *of* trade.

In this study, an issue is regarded as trade-related if it would not arise without trade. Accordingly, issues are categorized as non-trade-related if they occur also in the absence of trade. It should be noted, though, that trade-relatedness is *per se* not a reason for adopting WTO rules on the issue concerned.

The Effects of Trade Measures

Problems concerning or stemming from substandard labor conditions can be tackled in two ways. The more radical option is to address the underlying labor problem. The less ambitious is to eliminate their effects without improving labor conditions. Hence, a link between the rules governing international trade and labor standards may pursue two different goals. One would be to *enforce certain labor standards.* The other one would be to *neutralize certain effects of substandard labor conditions* without enforcing the relevant standards.

Trade measures can remove the *effects* of poor labor conditions on international trade. But they cannot achieve *compliance* with labor standards. It has to be kept in mind that trade measures can only exert pressure on governments and employers to comply with the relevant standards.

In practice, it is not always easy to clearly identify what a link should achieve. A human rights activist and a fair trade campaigner may agree on the need to establish a link between trade and labor without realizing that they are trying to solve different problems. Similarly, a country that applies trade measures to imports from countries not respecting certain labor standards may declare that it does so for the sake of the workers concerned, although its real intention is to protect its domestic industries. As both examples show, different motivations, objectives, and intentions may exist at the same time. However, in order to evaluate the importance of a problem or objective, it must be clearly defined. This is what the following chapters will attempt to do.

NOTES

1. L. Emmerij, Contemporary Challenges for Labour Standards Resulting from Globalization, in W. Sengenberger and D. Campbell (eds), *International Labour Standards and Economic Interdependence*, International Institute for Labour Studies, Geneva, 1994, p. 326.

2. In 1978, the European Commission considered the establishment of a link between trade and four labor standards in the framework of EU GSP and the Lomé Convention: non-discrimination, child labor, working hours, and health and safety; European Commission, Development Cooperation and the observance of certain international standards governing working conditions, Commission Communication to the Council: Development cooperation and the observance of certain international standards governing working conditions, COM (78) 492 final of 10 November 1978. In 1984, the Dutch government commissioned the Netherlands National Advisory Council for Development Cooperation to prepare a study on the merits of incorporating minimum labor standards into international agreements on economic cooperation and trade. The minimum labor standards identified in the report of the Advisory Council are virtually identical with core labor standards. The selection used three criteria: A social one related to basic human needs and human rights, a political and legal criterion, related to the level of acceptance of the relevant ILO conventions, measured by the number of ratifications, and an economic criterion meant to ensure that the standards selected would not impose economic hardship or impede economic development; see V. A. Leary, The Paradox of Workers' Rights as Human Rights, in L. A. Compa and S. F. Diamond (eds), *Human Rights, Labor Rights, and International Trade*, Philadelphia, 1996, p. 37.

3. International Labor Organization, The ILO at a glance, Geneva, 2007, p. 19.

4. See J. Hilgert, A New Frontier for Industrial Relations: Workplace Health and Safety as a Human Right, in J. A. Gross and L. Compa (eds), *Human Rights in Labor and Employment Relations: International and Domestic Perspectives*, Labor and Employment Relations Association, Champaign, 2009, pp. 43–68.

5. Studies on a possible link between trade and labor standards frequently refer to "trade sanctions." This term is too narrow as it suggests that a link would necessarily provide for trade restrictive measures. I prefer the term "trade measures," meaning any measure that changes the conditions under which a specific product originating in a given country enters the market of an importing country.

6. The EU has introduced such measures in its GSP.

Chapter Three

Linking Trade to Labor Standards for Non-Trade-Related Reasons

This chapter will examine various reasons which may justify a link between trade and labor standards. It will consider reasons which are not related to trade, starting with the immediate effect of violations of CLS on those enduring them. An assessment will be made of whether the number and seriousness of such violations call for the adoption of a link between trade and these standards.

CLS are binding provisions of international law. Violating them gives rise to a legal problem that will be evaluated in the light of the nature of these norms. To the extent that CLS are viewed as human rights, violations appear particularly grave. This chapter will discuss the question of whether the nature of CLS justifies a link between them and the rules of the multilateral trading system.

Violations of CLS are likely to have other non-trade-related repercussions, such as on the economic and social development of the countries concerned. The question of whether these repercussions warrant a link between trade and labor standards will be studied.

IMPROVING LABOR CONDITIONS IN THE WORLD

Substandard labor conditions are a real and serious problem worldwide. In many countries, they do not even meet CLS. Hence, more should be done in order to ensure compliance with these standards. A link between trade and these standards would allow pressure to be put on the governments of the countries concerned to comply with them. The question discussed in this section is whether the extent and seriousness of violations of these standards would warrant the establishment of such a link.

The Respect of CLS

When the ILO adopted the Declaration on Fundamental Principles and Rights at Work of 1998, it implicitly passed judgment on the question whether the level of compliance with the most important international labor standards was globally satisfactory or not. At that time, the international community clearly saw a need to improve certain basic labor conditions in many countries.

Ratifications of the Relevant Conventions

Number of Ratifications. Since 1998, the number of ratifications of conventions on CLS has risen significantly. As of July 2014, the eight conventions on CLS were ratified by the following numbers of member states (see table 3.1).[1]

Given that the ILO has 185 members, these figures are encouraging. What is less encouraging is the poor record of certain countries. Three countries (Marshall Islands, Palau, and Tuvalu) did not ratify any of these conventions, but these countries joined the ILO only recently. Two countries ratified two conventions (Brunei Darussalam, which joined in 2007, and the United States, which joined in 1934). Myanmar and Somalia ratified no more than three conventions, and five countries (China, India, Republic of Korea, Oman, and Timor-Leste) ratified just four conventions.

Table 3.1. Number of Ratifications of Conventions on CLS

		Number of Ratifications	
Convention		*1998*	*2015*
C87	(freedom of association)	121	153
C98	(right to collective bargaining)	137	164
C29	(forced labor)	145	177
C105	(forced labor)	130	174
C138	(minimum age of employment)	157	167
C182	(worst forms of child labor)	n.a.[a]	179
C100	(discrimination)	136	171
C111	(discrimination)	129	172

[a]Adopted after 1998.
Source: http://www.ilo.org/dyn/normlex/en/f?p=NORMLEXPUB:11300:0::NO:11300:P11300_INSTRUMENT_ID:312327:NO

While the reasons are certainly not the same in all of these countries, it is difficult to understand why twelve countries are unable to ratify not more than half of the eight fundamental ILO conventions. What is even more alarming is that countries such as the United States, China, India, and the Republic of Korea are among them.

Main Reasons for Not Ratifying the Conventions on CLS. According to the most recent report,[2] the reasons hampering the process of ratification as well as compliance with the principles and rights enshrined in these conventions are the following:

- legal incompatibilities with national laws or insufficient provisions of the latter;
- lack of political will;
- lack of consensus on the ratification of the conventions;
- close connection between employers and governments;
- government interference in trade union activities and use of intimidation on trade union members;
- prevailing employment practices;
- precarious employment of workers employed by employment agencies;
- lack of capacity and resources of responsible government institutions;
- lack of labor inspectors and of monitoring and enforcement mechanisms;
- lack of capacity of employers' or workers' organizations;
- lack of tripartite and social dialogue;
- lack of understanding of the content or the implications of the conventions;
- lack of awareness of the requirements of the conventions;
- lack of public awareness and support;
- traditional and cultural barriers;
- reluctance of foreign investors to ensure the realization of core labor standards;
- the security situation;
- lack of data to identify child labor;
- lack of data on salaries.

The most frequently stated reasons for not ratifying the conventions on CLS are a lack either of political will or of capacity and resources. Of course, the fact that a country did not ratify a specific convention does not necessarily mean that it does not comply with the standards concerned. However, the ILO reports show that only a minority of countries that have not ratified all conventions meet the relevant requirements. Some countries explicitly acknowledge that their national laws are incompatible with certain CLS and that they are unwilling to change them.

Compliance with CLS

The 1998 ILO Declaration establishes a follow-up mechanism with an annual review of countries which have not ratified all eight conventions on CLS. It also publishes an annual global report on one of the four categories of fundamental rights.[3] These reports provide a detailed picture of the level of compliance with CLS in the world.

Freedom of Association and the Right to Collective Bargaining. The ILO prepared reports on the application of these rights in 2000, 2004, and 2008. The 2000 report "Your Voice at Work" notes that

> . . . freedom of association and the effective right to collective bargaining are not being universally respected. . . . In many countries, important sectors remain excluded, such as the public sector, agricultural workers, and workers in export processing zones, migrant workers and domestic workers as well as the informal sector.[4]

The 2004 report "Organizing for Social Justice" states that

> . . . serious problems remain. Violations of freedom of association rights of both employers and workers persist in different forms, including murder, violence, detention and refusal to allow organizations the legal right to exist and function. People continue to lose their lives and their freedom for attempting to organize and defend collectively their fundamental rights. Problems range from the tragic and complex case of Colombia to obstacles to extending legislation and protection beyond the sphere of established industrial relations.[5]

The 2008 report "Freedom of Association in Practice: Lessons Learned" confirms that

> . . . there are serious and major cases involving large-scale dismissals, harassment, imprisonment and violence, including killings of trade-unionists. Trade unions and employers' organizations continue to experience obstacles in their day-to-day activities. Problems arise with: restrictions on the establishment of organizations or the right to join them; interference by governments and other parties in the functioning of employers' and workers' organizations; restrictions on collective bargaining; discrimination against union members; and undue restrictions on the right to strike.[6]

In 2011, the ILO estimates that "more than half the world's labor force work in countries that have not ratified both of these instruments [C87 and C98]. Thus, even though their governments may consider that their law and practice are sufficient, millions of workers and employers do not enjoy the protection offered by international law."[7] Currently, there are 146 cases before the Committee on Freedom of Association, in which complaints have been submitted to the governments concerned for their observations. Of course, not all cases are equally serious. Nonetheless, their number illustrates that compliance with this fundamental principle and right is globally a matter of concern.[8]

The Elimination of All Forms of Forced or Compulsory Labor. The ILO prepared reports on the application of these rights in 2001, 2005, and 2009. The 2001 report "Stopping Forced Labor" notes that

> Trafficking of women and children—mainly for prostitution and domestic service but also sweatshop work—has . . . increased dramatically throughout the world in the last ten years. In North America, several high-profile cases in sweatshop industries have resulted in severe penalties and heightened public awareness. In addition, millions of people live and work in conditions of debt bondage in many countries throughout South Asia and Central and South America . . . slavery is still found in a handful of countries in Africa . . . certain post-independence governments perpetuating colonial law and practices.[9]

The 2005 report "A Global Alliance against Forced Labor" notes that

> the warning signals sounded four years ago seem to be even more justified today. Forced labor is present in some form on all continents, in almost all countries, and in every kind of economy. There are persistent cases of . . . bonded labor systems in parts of South Asia, debt bondage affecting mainly indigenous peoples in parts of Latin America, and the residual slavery-related practices most evident today in West Africa. There are also various forms of forced labor exacted by the State for either economic or political purposes. Forced labor today also affects sizeable numbers of migrant workers who are transported away from their countries or communities of origin . . .[10]

The 2009 report "The Cost of Coercion" again notes increases of forced labor in the private economy.[11] In recent years, many cases of human trafficking for labor and sexual exploitation, as well as of exploitation of migrant workers, have been identified as forced labor. The ILO estimates that worldwide at least 12 million people are victims of forced labor, out of which 10 million are exploited in the private sector.[12]

The Effective Abolition of Child Labor. The ILO prepared reports on the application of these rights in 2002, 2006, and 2010.[13] The ILO estimates that 215 million children are engaged in child labor, meaning that they are either under the minimum age for work (176 million children) or above that age and engaged in work that poses a threat to their health, safety, or morals, or are subject to conditions of forced labor (39 million). This number amounts to almost 14 percent of the world population of children between five and seventeen years old (estimated at 1.586 million). Almost half of them work on a full-time basis. Slightly more than half of them—115 million children—are believed to be engaged in hazardous work, while 8 million are trapped in the worst forms of child labor. The majority of children (60 percent) are engaged in the agricultural sector. Overall, two-thirds of child laborers are unpaid family workers. Whereas child labor has diminished in the Asia-Pacific and Latin America and the Caribbean regions, it has increased in sub-Saharan Africa where one in four children is now engaged in child labor.[14]

The Elimination of Discrimination in Respect of Employment and Occupation. The ILO prepared reports on the application of these rights in 2003, 2007, and 2011. The 2007 report "Equality at Work: Tackling the Challenge" acknowledges that "discrimination is an insidious and shifting phenomenon that can be difficult to quantify."[15] According to the 2011 report "Equality at Work: The Continuing Challenge," "capacity does not keep pace with the political will, and a prolonged economic downturn exposes structural weaknesses and even aggravates structural discrimination."[16] Indeed, "discrimination continues to be persistent and multifaceted." The ILO estimates that hundreds of millions of people suffer from discrimination in the area of work.[17]

The Seriousness of Violations

The literature quotes an endless list of instances documenting labor conditions that are often beyond imagination. Recent reports confirm that problems are far from being solved. In an article published on January 25, 2012, the *New York Times* describes

> the human costs that are built into an iPad: Employees work excessive overtime, in some cases seven days a week, and live in crowded dorms. Some say they stand so long that their legs swell until they can hardly walk. Under-age workers have helped build Apple's products, and the company's suppliers have improperly disposed of hazardous waste and falsified records, according to company reports and advocacy groups that, within China, are often considered reliable, independent monitors. More troubling, the groups say, is some suppliers' disregard for workers' health. Two years ago, 137 workers at an Apple supplier in eastern China were injured after they were ordered to use a poisonous chemical to clean iPhone screens. Within seven months last year, two explosions at iPad factories, including in Chengdu, killed four people and injured 77. Before those blasts, Apple had been alerted to hazardous conditions inside the Chengdu plant, according to a Chinese group that published that warning.[18]

The Quality of Labor Conditions in the World Does Not Justify a Link

As shown by the ILO annual reports, compliance with CLS is a matter of serious concern in many countries. Therefore, more should be done to improve it. One possibility would be to authorize trade restrictions against countries not complying with these standards. A link providing for trade sanctions seems a handy tool to enforce CLS.

In my view, however, such a link would not be justified. Violations of labor standards are, *per se*, not more serious than many other problems which could be remedied through trade restrictions, but for which such a solution has never been considered. Arguably, there is a case for the more general use of trade measures in order to promote other policies. If the international community was to agree on such approach, labor standards would certainly be a good starting point. But this would require an overhaul of the present international order, which is not on the agenda of the international community.

Moreover, if labor protection was important enough to justify trade sanctions, it would also justify other measures, such as travel restrictions for members of governments responsible for violations of labor standards or freezing assets of the owners of companies violating these standards. I am not aware of any proposals to sanction violations by such means.

For these reasons, I do not believe that it would be appropriate to establish a link between trade and CLS solely for the purpose of improving compliance with the latter.

PROMOTING HUMAN RIGHTS

CLS are binding rules. Violating these standards means violating international law. Moreover, it is often asserted that these standards are human rights. If CLS are to be classified as human rights, violations would appear particularly grave: "Because human rights entail fundamental values of "superior" moral order, their violation correspondingly entails greater moral condemnation than other wrongs."[19] The classification of CLS as human rights would also imply an obligation to protect these standards adequately. This section attempts to answer the question of whether the very nature of CLS would justify a link with the rules governing international trade.

Are CLS Human Rights?

In its own publications, the ILO states that CLS are human rights.[20] This view is shared by several recent publications.[21]

International Human Rights Instruments Containing Provisions Similar to CLS

Human rights are commonly understood as fundamental rights which are universal and inalienable. Such rights are recognized by a number of international declarations and covenants. Some of them include provisions which wholly or partially overlap with CLS as defined by the eight relevant ILO conventions.

The Universal Declaration of Human Rights (UDHR) of 1948 includes freedom from discrimination, freedom from slavery, as well as freedom of peaceful assembly and association (Articles 20 to 26). UDHR Article 23 explicitly states that "everyone has the right to form and to join trade unions for the protection of his interests." However, this declaration is not binding.

Article 5 of the International Convention on the Elimination of All Forms of Racial Discrimination (ICERD) of 1969 prohibits racial discrimination in the enjoyment of the right to free choice of employment and to equal pay for equal work. This UN convention is legally binding.

In 1966, the UN adopted the International Covenant on Civil and Political Rights (ICCPR) which builds on the rights and freedoms listed in the UDHR of 1946. The rights listed in the ICCPR include freedom of expression, freedom of assembly, and freedom from discrimination. The covenant also prohibits slavery, servitude, and other forms of forced and compulsory labor. It is legally binding international law.

Article 11 of the UN Convention on the Elimination of All Forms of Discrimination against Women (CEDAW) of 1979 states that women are entitled to the same employment opportunities and to equal remuneration, including benefits, and to equal treatment in respect of work of equal value, in terms similar to those of ILO Conventions C100 and C111. This UN convention binds all countries having ratified it.

In 1989, the UN adopted the Convention on the Rights of the Child (CRC), a legally binding instrument for the protection of human rights of children. This convention prohibits discrimination, economic exploitation of children, and work that may interfere with education or be harmful to children's health and well-being.[22]

Arguably, labor standards are human rights to the extent that they *coincide* with certain human rights recognized by these declarations and covenants. However, the latter do not specify the scope and meaning of these rights in the particular context of work relations.

Are CLS as such Human Rights?

It is often claimed that CLS are human rights *per se*. But there is no general agreement on this classification. In fact, nobody is born as a worker. It may therefore be argued that the rights enshrined in labor standards cannot be human rights because they are not rights of all human beings. Nonetheless, "paid employment is central to our current understanding of being a free human being, and . . . in our current social system, it is central to the attainment of all other human rights."[23] CLS may be considered as human rights, which potentially protect all human beings, not just those being employed.

Indeed, the prohibition of discrimination and forced labor seems to be supported by the international human rights consensus. Conversely, the recognition of the other two CLS—effective abolition of child labor and freedom of association and protection of the right to collective bargaining—as human rights is subject to debate.[24]

The Effective Abolition of Child Labor. Several scholars hold that protecting children from being forced to work is a human right.[25] There are two considerations that challenge this view. First, these rights are limited to childhood. A child loses these rights once he or she reaches a certain age. The mere existence of a cut-off age is hardly compatible with the concept of human rights. Moreover, there is no natural or obvious criterion determining the age limit.

The other obstacle to classifying these rights as human rights stems from doubts concerning their scope. It is generally agreed that even below the age limit, children may carry out certain activities for educational purposes or in the framework of a family business, in particular in the agricultural sector. Clearly, it is difficult to determine the extent of these exceptions.

ILO Convention C182, which prohibits the worst forms of child labor, defines the limits of any exceptions. The classification of certain activities as worst forms of child labor suggests that, if protecting children from being forced to work involves a human right, this right is limited to the activities listed in Convention C182. Most of them amount to forced labor. The prohibition of forced labor is widely seen as a human right, not just of children, but of *everybody*. For the essence of the rights mentioned in C182, there is no reason to consider them as particular human rights *of children.*

Nonetheless, one may consider that there are rights, beyond the scope of ILO Convention C182, which are human rights *of children*. Arguably, it is a human right to protect children below a certain age from being forced to carry out *any* activity, when this negatively affects his or her health or schooling.

Freedom of Association and the Right to Collective Bargaining. Human rights are conceived as "inalienable." Yet, the two relevant ILO conventions (C87 and C98) enumerate a number of exceptions concerning armed forces, the police, and other public servants. Arguably, these exceptions rule out that freedom of association and the right to collective bargaining can be classified as human rights.[26] Freedom of association and the right to collective bargaining also differ from other human rights to the extent that they are collective rights. Since the human rights regime established after World War II emphasizes individual rights, collective rights are sometimes viewed as aspirations rather than rights. Some authors also raise the question whether freedom of association includes a right *not* to join a union (although this right is recognized in Article 20 (2) of the Universal Declaration of Human Rights of

1948). Indeed, there are doubts whether this core labor standard is to be classified as a human right.[27]

The Foundations of Human Rights

Many scholars believe that human rights exist even in the absence of any legal texts. Others, on the contrary, regard human rights as a man-made category of rights of fundamental importance.

Human Rights as Natural Rights. A recent publication dealing with this issue in the specific context of labor rights explains that "human rights are literally the rights one has simply because one is a human being . . . they are possessed by every person by virtue of being a human being. . . . Human rights are rights that no government or employer or union or any other body has the moral authority to grant or deny."[28] This concept considers human rights as natural rights which exist independently from any of the commonly acknowledged sources of rights. While the above mentioned declarations and covenants do not provide a definition of human rights, their language suggests adherence to this concept.[29]

The same is true as far as the 1998 ILO Declaration on Fundamental Principles and Rights at Work is concerned. This declaration explicitly states that these principles and rights are binding even for countries not having ratified the relevant ILO conventions. According to the declaration, these obligations arise "from the very fact of membership in the Organization." Since membership requires ratification of the ILO Constitution, members are committed to the rights and principles enshrined therein. But the Constitution does not mention the prohibition of forced labor and discrimination. Membership of the organization alone cannot explain why these rights and principles are binding even in the absence of ratification of the relevant conventions.[30]

There must be other reasons why the prohibition of forced labor and discrimination are binding without being formally adopted. The relevant standards may be regarded as international customary law or natural rights. International customary law is the law accepted by basically all nations. Yet, it can hardly be argued that the provisions of conventions which *require* ratification and which are *not* ratified by *all* nations, represent international customary law and bind even those states that clearly do not want to ratify them. Hence, the view that all states are obliged to prohibit forced labor and discrimination would imply that the corresponding rights are natural rights.[31]

According to the natural rights theory, the existence of such rights flows from the very existence of human beings. However, this assumption is challenged by

> traditional conceptions of the sources of rights, the philosophy and practice of the unregulated market, the long-standing opposition to even the idea of eco-

> nomic rights, the supposed unbridgeable conflict between individual and collective rights, and the wide-ranging consequences of cultural and moral relativism . . . [as well as] . . . the doctrine of national sovereignty.[32]

The reply of the natural rights theory to these challenges is that "a human rights analysis adopts no other philosophical or theoretical disposition beyond the definition of human rights."[33] Yet, this reply does not go unchallenged either. The concept that every person possesses certain rights "by virtue of being a human being" does not determine which rights actually belong to that category.[34] Even if there was agreement on a definition of human rights similar to the one suggested above, this would not answer the question which rights are human rights in the sense of that definition and whether CLS belong to that category.[35]

Apparently, the UN itself encounters difficulties in clearly delimiting the boundaries of human rights. The UN also adopted the International Covenant on Economic, Social, and Cultural Rights (ICECR) which incorporate the rights to work, social security, food, clothing, and housing. These rights which are commonly referred to as "second generation rights" require states to provide certain services. But this requirement is limited "to the maximum of resources available." The UN has recognized certain rights as human rights although it acknowledges that these rights cannot be implemented under all circumstances. This is hardly compatible with the concept of inherent and inalienable rights that would exist even in the absence of written texts.

Besides, a definition is not a proof of existence of what is defined. The idea that every person possesses certain rights "by virtue of being a human being" is similar to the concept of human dignity and the belief that human beings have souls.[36] For my part, I doubt that there are any inalienable and universal human rights which exist *a priori* and independently from any generally accepted source of rights. What we commonly refer to as human rights are rights whose basis is conventional and political.[37] It seems to me that human rights are, rather than natural rights, *cultural* rights created by societies having achieved a certain level of civilization.

Human Rights as Rights of Fundamental Importance. Although there are no valid grounds for assuming the existence of natural rights, there are good reasons for creating a special category of human rights. The rights recognized by the declarations and covenants mentioned above as human rights share one particular criterion: their *fundamental importance for life in any civilized society*. The effective implementation of such rights in all countries is in the interest of all countries. Therefore, all countries have an interest in international cooperation in this area. Such cooperation requires identification of these rights and agreement to enforce them. The ultimate reason for creating a special category of rights called human rights and identifying such rights is to lay the foundations for international cooperation aimed at improving the protection of these rights in all countries. While the 1998 ILO Declaration does not use the term "human rights," the recognition of CLS as "fundamental rights and principles" is tantamount to recognition as rights which are of fundamental importance for life in any civilized society.

The Implications of Classifying CLS as Human Rights

The implications of classifying CLS as human rights depend on whether these rights are understood as natural rights or otherwise.

CLS as Natural Rights

Originally, the human rights theory focused on relations between individuals and the state or government, defining an area of freedom in which the latter should refrain from interfering. Yet, if human rights are understood as inalienable rights, everybody has to respect them, including employers. While non-state actors cannot guarantee human rights, they nonetheless have to respect them. Hence, MNEs are not only bound by the laws of their host countries, but also by human rights.[38] For the same reason, such rights rank high in the hierarchy of legal norms, although views may differ concerning their precise status. On the other hand, natural rights, as such, are not enforceable. The identification of a natural human right basically means an aspiration that it should be respected and possibly protected by international agreements and domestic laws.[39] Such agreements and laws would not *create*, but only *confirm* these rights. Once such agreements or laws are adopted, there are two versions of the same human right: a natural right and a legal one. Accordingly, there may be doubts whether the latter truly reflects the former.

CLS as Rights of Fundamental Importance

On the contrary, if human rights are understood as rights of fundamental importance for life in a civilized society, they exist as rights only where legal instruments *establish* them. In this case, the starting point is not the human being who is entitled to certain rights, but a legal text. The binding force of this text and its place in the hierarchy of legal norms depend on the type of norm establishing them. Human rights, understood as rights of fundamental importance for life in a civilized society, are not, *a priori*, universal, but they should become so. By the same token, they would not bind everybody, but they *should* be respected.[40] Employers should respect them even where governments do not guarantee them.[41]

The Weight of the Human Rights Argument

The weight of the human rights argument as support for the idea of establishing a link between trade and labor standards varies according to the underlying human rights concept. If human rights are conceived as natural rights, the strong point of the argument is the inalienability of the rights concerned. However, natural rights, as such, are not enforceable. For all practical purposes, the strong point of natural rights theory is no more than an imperative to adopt legislation making the corresponding rights enforceable.

The weak point of a human rights argument based on the natural rights theory is the absence of a consensus concerning the very existence of such category of rights. Placing natural rights at the top of the hierarchy of legal norms is meaningless as long as their existence is not commonly accepted. Moreover, any legal definitions of natural rights are just attempts to describe what exists *a priori*. It could therefore be argued that specific legal definitions such as those of CLS do not accurately reflect the natural rights that are invoked to support them. It would probably be more difficult to obtain a consensus on the existence and scope of natural rights than to get agreement on the establishment of a link between trade and labor standards.

Another weak point of the human rights argument based on the natural rights theory is that it is difficult to conceive freedom of association and the right to collective bargaining, but also the prohibition of child labor, as natural rights.

For the reasons mentioned above, I do not consider that CLS are, *per se*, natural rights that are unalienable and universally binding. Conversely, these standards have been recognized by the international community as rights of fundamental importance for life in any civilized society. The strong point of the human rights argument, which understands those rights as rights of fundamental importance, is that it increases the standing of the text establishing these rights, such as ILO declarations and conventions. Recognition as human rights implies that the rights concerned deserve high respect and should be universally observed. But there is also a weak point. The addition of "second generation" human rights has watered down the meaning of "important." If everything is important, nothing is really important anymore.

In essence, there is not much difference between the claim that labor rights are human rights, and therefore *very important*, and the argument that labor standards are very important, and therefore *human rights*. Ultimately, both views reflect the importance that one attaches to the rights concerned.

The Classification of CLS as Human Rights Does Not Justify a Link

Core labor rights may be considered as human rights—either *per se* or because they are included in other, more general rights recognized as human rights by the international community. However, traditionally, CLS have not been the center of attention of the human rights movement. Even if there was general agreement on classifying CLS as human rights, this would hardly further the respect of these standards: "winning the battle over whether labor rights should be classified as human rights will not, by itself, achieve improvements in labor standards."[42]

A link between trade and labor standards may help achieve this. Actually, such a link does exist. As mentioned above, the international community has the possibility of ordering a trade embargo against a country that is found to violate human rights in an endemic and continuous manner, and it has done so.[43] But these are measures of last resort, which the international community is generally extremely reluctant to use unless very serious reasons call for them. The question is whether the recognition of CLS as human rights calls for the establishment of a link authorizing trade sanctions against countries violating them.

In my view, it does not. Authorizing trade sanctions in order to enforce human rights is not on the international political agenda. If it was, such measures should also be allowed against countries still maintaining the death penalty. Authorization of such measures only against countries violating CLS would amount to singling these standards out as a top category of human rights. There is no consensus that they are. Quite the opposite, there are doubts whether CLS are human rights at all. Thus, the recognition that certain labor rights are human rights hardly provides a valid argument in support of a link between trade and labor.

MAKING DEVELOPMENT SUSTAINABLE

When the ILO was founded, certain labor rights were viewed as indispensable elements of what we would call a "developed" country today. Nowadays, these rights are considered not only as part and parcel of development,[44] but as conditions of *sustainable* development. Accordingly, the final report of the Working Party on the Social Dimensions of the Liberalization of International Trade notes that compliance with CLS is a requirement for making development sustainable.[45] The 2008 ILO Declaration on Social Justice for a Fair Globalization expresses the same view. The EU established an incentive scheme in the framework of its Generalized System of Trade Preferences (GSP) with the declared aim of improving labor conditions in order to foster sustainable development.

Sustainable development was defined by the United Nations Commission on Environment and Development (1987) as "development that meets the needs of the present without compromising the ability of future generations to meet their own needs."[46] This notion is based on a compromise between short-term needs and long-term concerns. It attempts to reconcile economic growth with environmental protection and social development.

There is now a wide consensus that development should be made sustainable. The question examined in this section is whether it would be justified to use trade measures in order to ensure minimum labor conditions, with the ultimate aim to achieve sustainable development.

Compliance with CLS and Development

Before discussing this issue, we will examine a preliminary question concerning the relationship between compliance with CLS and development in general: Is it correct to assume that development requires certain minimum labor conditions? To answer that question, we will compare the record of compliance with CLS by developed countries with the record of less developed countries. In order to make that comparison, we will use the Human Development Index calculated by the United Nations Development Program (UNDP). This index divides all countries of the world into four quartiles labeled

- countries having achieved very high human development;
- countries having achieved high human development;
- countries having achieved medium human development;
- countries having achieved low human development.

For the purpose of this discussion, we will divide the world into two: we will consider the first two quartiles as developed countries and the other two quartiles as developing countries.

In order to examine the relationship between the level of development and compliance with CLS, we will study different samples of countries. We will first take a look at the group of countries that have not ratified all eight conventions on CLS. We will then examine which of these countries are facing problems in complying with CLS in each of the four areas covered.[47] Finally, we will consider the situation of countries which have ratified all eight conventions on CLS.

Human Development in Countries Not Having Ratified All Eight ILO Conventions on CLS

Forty-seven countries have not ratified all eight ILO conventions on CLS. Out of this group, the UNDP classifies[48]

- ten countries as having achieved very high human development;
- twelve countries as having achieved high human development;
- twelve countries as having achieved medium human development;

- nine countries as having achieved low human development.

Among the countries not having ratified all eight conventions on CLS, twenty-two have achieved high and very high human development, while twenty-one countries have achieved only medium or low human development. These figures do not suggest that ratification of the eight conventions is a condition for development.

Human Development in Countries Facing Challenges Regarding Compliance with ILO Conventions on CLS that They Did Not Ratify

As mentioned above, the 1998 ILO Declaration establishes a follow-up mechanism with an annual review of countries that have not ratified all of the eight conventions. In the framework of this review, these countries are required to report on progress made toward ratification and compliance with the standards established by the conventions that they have not ratified. The ILO prepares an annual report providing a summary of the statements contained in government reports and comments submitted by national and international employers' and workers' organizations.[49] The terms used in these reports are quite diplomatic: they instead report "challenges" that countries face in the areas covered by the conventions they did not ratify. Although the ILO does not verify the accuracy of the information received, it may be assumed that complaints are not frivolous and that countries facing such challenges actually do not fully comply with the relevant conventions.[50]

Challenges Concerning Freedom of Association and the Right to Collective Bargaining. Twenty-eight of the forty-seven countries which have not ratified all eight ILO conventions on CLS face challenges concerning freedom of association and the right to collective bargaining. The UNDP classifies[51]

- seven of the countries concerned as having achieved very high human development;
- seven of the countries concerned as having achieved high human development;
- seven of the countries concerned as having achieved medium human development;
- five of the countries concerned as having achieved low human development.

Among the countries facing these challenges, the number of countries having achieved high and very high human development (fourteen) is higher than the number of countries having achieved medium or low human development (twelve).

Challenges Concerning Forced Labor. Seven of the forty-seven countries face challenges concerning forced labor. The UNDP classifies

- three of the countries concerned as having achieved very high human development;
- one of the countries concerned as having achieved high human development;
- none of the countries concerned as having achieved medium human development;
- three of the countries concerned as having achieved low human development.

Again, among the countries facing the challenges concerning forced labor, the number of countries having achieved high and very high human development (four) is slightly above the number of countries having achieved medium or low human development (three).

Challenges Concerning Child Labor. Eleven of the forty-seven countries face challenges concerning child labor. The UNDP classifies[52]

- none of the countries concerned as having achieved very high human development;
- two of the countries concerned as having achieved high human development;
- three of the countries concerned as having achieved medium human development;
- three of the countries concerned as having achieved low human development.

Among the countries facing the challenges with child labor, the number of countries having achieved high and very high human development (two) is clearly lower than the number of countries having achieved medium or low human development (six).

Challenges Concerning Discrimination in Respect of Employment and Occupation. Ten of the forty-seven countries face challenges concerning discrimination in respect of employment and occupation. The UNDP classifies[53]

- two of the countries concerned as having achieved very high human development;
- three of the countries concerned as having achieved high human development;
- three of the countries concerned as having achieved medium human development;

- one of the countries concerned as having achieved low human development.

Among the countries facing challenges concerning discrimination in respect of employment and occupation, the number of countries having achieved high and very high human development (five) is nearly the same as the number of countries having achieved medium or low human development (four).

Human Development in Countries Facing Challenges Regarding Compliance with ILO Conventions on CLS that They Ratified

The report of the Committee of Experts on the Application of Conventions and Recommendations prepared on 2014 provides detailed information on compliance with ILO conventions on CLS that were ratified.[54] This report lists cases in which the committee

- has examined the measures taken by governments to give effects to the recommendations of commission of inquiry (complaints under Article 26);
- has examined the measures taken by governments to give effects to the recommendations of tripartite committees (representations under Article 24);
- has examined the follow-up to the conclusions on the Committee on the Application of Standards (2013);
- has requested early reports after an interval of either one, two, or three years;
- has requested governments to supply full particulars to the conference at its next session;
- has requested detailed reports when simplified reports would otherwise be due.

The differences between these lists highlight the different stages of procedures, different degrees of clarification (evidence), and different degrees of gravity of non-compliance. Actually, there are thirty cases, involving twenty-eight countries. The UNDP classifies[55]

- four of the countries concerned as having achieved very high human development;
- five of the countries concerned as having achieved high human development;
- nine of the countries concerned as having achieved medium human development;

- nine of the countries concerned as having achieved low human development.

Among the countries which have ratified all eight conventions on CLS and which are facing challenges concerning compliance with these standards, the number of countries having achieved high and very high human development (nine) is only half the number of countries having achieved medium or low human development (eighteen).

Conclusion

The aim of the above investigation is not to find out whether violations of CLS occur more often in developed or in developing countries, but to answer the question of whether compliance with CLS is *a condition for development.*

Among the countries which have *not* ratified the eight conventions on CLS and which are facing challenges in the areas covered by these conventions, the number of countries having achieved high and very high human development is essentially the same as the number of countries having achieved medium or low human development—with the exception of child labor, where the first group of countries is smaller than the second one. The number of developed countries facing challenges concerning the implementation of CLS suggests that compliance with these standards is not a condition for development.

Among the countries which *have* ratified the eight conventions on CLS and which are facing such challenges, the number of countries having achieved medium or low human development is twice as high as the number of countries having achieved high and very high human development. Nonetheless, there are nine countries having achieved higher development that apparently do not fully implement all CLS. It can therefore hardly be claimed that compliance with these standards is a precondition for sustainable development.

But this does not mean that a link between trade and labor standards could not be justified by the objective of sustainable development. Sustainable development may justify such link if compliance with CLS really helps achieve it.

Labor Conditions and Economic Growth

Enforcing CLS through a link between trade and labor would not help achieve sustainable development if better labor conditions have adverse effects on the economy of countries. The effects of labor protection on economic growth are the subject of heated debate. This debate falls mainly into two camps. One claims that poor labor conditions and the resulting inequalities favor the accumulation of capital and investments and consequently economic growth. The opposite side claims that higher standards improve productivity which in turn has positive effects on growth.

Although there is abundant literature on these issues, there is little empirical evidence proving any specific relation between the level of labor protection and economic growth. Labor conditions in general and the level of compliance with labor standards in particular are an issue of quality rather than of quantity. While the amount of child labor may be assessed by the number of children concerned, any attempt to measure freedom of association or the right to collective bargaining in a given country has unavoidably a subjective bias. Accordingly, it is extremely difficult to evaluate and compare labor conditions in different countries, which is a condition for any inter-country analysis.[56] Moreover, there are great difficulties in identifying all relevant variables, isolating them from each other and determining causal links.[57] It is not surprising that empirical assessments of the effects of labor conditions on the economies of exporting countries remain largely controversial.

The Economic Benefits of Sweatshops

Some renowned economists claim that the economies of developing countries would gain from more sweatshops.[58] The assumption that economic growth benefits from poor standards is plausible to the extent that the latter facilitate the accumulation of capital, which is scarce in developing countries.[59] Arguably, this is what happened during early industrialization in Europe. What is less plausible is the assumption of an antagonism between equity and efficiency. Of course, a policy giving absolute priority to equal distribution will eventually become inefficient. Yet, there are good reasons to assume that a policy committed exclusively to efficiency may yield similarly disastrous results. One hundred and fifty years ago, Bismarck introduced minimum labor protection in order to avoid these consequences. In the end, this legislation had positive economic effects. The assumption that economic growth slows down if labor conditions improve is not supported by empirical evidence.

The Economic Benefits of Better Labor Conditions

More recently, the view is gaining ground that improved labor conditions favor economic efficiency and growth rates.[60] One author finds that ". . . countries that have pursued labor market policies to guarantee worker rights have not only enjoyed greater income equity and faster poverty alleviation but in many cases have grown faster overall than those that have not."[61]

The lack of capital is not the only obstacle impeding development. There are other problems which are equally important, in particular low productivity and internal demand. It has become fashionable to portray these problems as "traps." The image of a trap rather accurately describes the reality in many developing countries. Indeed, there are several obstacles hindering the economic development of low- and middle-income countries, which tend to reproduce themselves.

The Productivity Trap. In general, productivity in developing countries is comparatively low. One of the main reasons for low productivity is a lack of education. People in developing countries are often unable to learn or study because they are forced to work to support their families. As a result, productivity remains low, and so do wages. This is a vicious cycle which could be broken by improving labor standards and labor conditions.[62]

The Demand Trap. Low wages mean low income, which means low internal demand. Low internal demand curbs economic growth. This in turn hampers the increase of wages and the creation of new jobs. To the extent that compliance with CLS would lead to higher wages, it could help to remove this trap.[63]

Conclusion

As stated above, there is no agreement on the effects of poorer or better labor conditions on economic growth. The empirical evidence available remains debatable. Most views rely on theoretical assumptions which ultimately rest on common sense (plus, in many cases, a good deal of ideological prejudice).

Poorer and better labor conditions do not necessarily have opposite effects on economic growth. *Both* could have positive effects on economic growth. The difference is that these effects will not occur at the same point in time. Lower standards may have short-term benefits for economic growth. In the long run, however, the chances of future economic growth without adequate labor protection will probably decrease. On the contrary, with adequate labor protection, developing countries are likely to have better chances to escape certain traps hindering their development. Higher standards are likely to favor growth at a later stage, but in a more *sustainable* manner.

In any event, the claim that poorer labor conditions favor economic growth cannot be made without some qualification. It is simply absurd to portray forced labor and child labor as a recipe for development.[64] By the same token, tolerating any kind of discrimination and banning trade unions are certainly not panacea for the economies of poor countries. While in certain instances, poor labor conditions may benefit economic development, labor conditions below certain standards are unlikely to accomplish this. These standards are the CLS as defined by the ILO.

The Effects of Labor Conditions on Social Development

As mentioned before, the notion of sustainable development attempts to reconcile economic growth with environmental protection and social development. Improving labor conditions would mean progress in terms of social development. It would remove a number of other traps in the way of sustainable development.

The Poverty Trap

The poverty trap is a "self-reinforcing mechanism which causes poverty to persist."[65] For essentially the same reasons that low productivity reproduces itself, poverty, too, tends to persist. According to the ILO, "the key to the eradication of poverty . . . is decent work."[66] Wages in many developing countries do not rise in proportion to economic growth. Accordingly, the number of working poor has hardly decreased over the last fifteen years.[67] But this is not surprising.

Without freedom of association and the right to collective bargaining, the poorest groups of society have no voice to claim their fair share of economic growth. Granting these rights and eliminating forced and compulsory labor is likely to increase wages. Similarly, the elimination of discrimination in respect of employment and occupation would increase chances to get a job and a fair salary. Better wages would allow people to escape from poverty. In essence, compliance with CLS may enable people to get out of the poverty trap.[68]

The Inequality Trap

In their respective 2005 flagship reports, both the United Nations Development Program (UNDP) and the World Bank emphasize the importance of equality for the eradication of poverty and for sustainable development.[69] Both found that countries which have achieved higher than average growth rates did so by ensuring better participation of the poorest groups in the economy. To the extent that compliance with CLS would help to reduce inequalities, development would certainly become more sustainable.[70]

The Demographic Trap

In October 2011, UN agencies reported that the world population has reached 7 billion people. While population growth rates are typically higher in poorer countries, demographic growth is one of the major causes of poverty. It is another vicious cycle, and perhaps the most important one.[71] Curbing population growth is probably the most fundamental condition of sustainable development. Compliance with CLS is likely to result in higher wages and higher income, which typically leads to lower reproduction rates and population growth. It would probably help to escape the demographic trap.

The Unemployment Trap

Population growth is one of the major causes of high unemployment rates. In many developing countries where population growth is high, opportunities for getting a regular job are scarce. "The great mass of world population, which is no longer able to exist in traditional ways, is not able to find a way into the labor market either."[72] In order to find it, workers are forced to accept very low wages. This reinforces the vicious cycles of poverty and population growth.

The Worst Trap of All: Child Labor

Child labor is the result of a combination of several of the traps already mentioned: poverty, low productivity, inequality, population growth, and unemployment. It is itself probably the worst of all traps, not only in terms of human sufferings, but also because it almost inevitably reproduces itself. It is a vicious cycle that puts sustainable development in jeopardy.[73] Indeed, the abolition of child labor is a fundamental condition for sustainable development.[74]

Conclusion

Minimum labor conditions as defined by CLS would remove a number of important obstacles impeding sustainable development. Higher labor standards and better labor conditions are not just an indicator of higher social development, but more importantly a tool to make development sustainable.

The Need to Make Development Sustainable Does Not Justify a Link

Although it is difficult to claim that compliance with CLS is a precondition for sustainable development, the above considerations suggest that compliance with these standards can foster social development and make development more sustainable. One can argue that the pursuit of sustainable development would justify trade measures meant to ensure compliance with CLS.

This would require a global consensus on the basic requirements of sustainable development. It seems to me that there is little chance of achieving such consensus as long as there is no country in the world whose socio-economic system is genuinely sustainable. As far as least developed countries are concerned, the issue is not so much a lack of sustainability, but rather a lack of any development at all. Most other developing countries are engaged in a process of development that is unsustainable both in terms of environmental and labor protection. And developed countries have achieved a level of development that is probably too high to remain sustainable for long. Accordingly, each group of countries has another view on what it takes to make development sustainable.

In contrast, it is quite clear that the requirements of sustainable development go beyond compliance with labor standards. It can hardly be argued that sustainable development starts with CLS. There is no reason why compliance with these standards should be promoted with more energy than other requirements. In my view, the need to make development sustainable does not justify the establishment of a link between trade and labor standards.

CONCLUSION

This chapter examined the question whether there are non-trade-related reasons for establishing a link between trade and labor standards. It started by assessing the need to improve labor conditions in exporting countries. In my view, no violation of CLS is, *per se*, serious enough to warrant a link between trade and labor. By the same token, I do not believe that such link is justified by the fact that CLS are human rights or because they are particularly important for sustainable development.[75]

Although violations of these standards give rise to concern, they are not fundamentally different from violations of other rights and obligations—including other human rights—for which a link was never contemplated. As long as there is neither a comprehensive action plan to enforce labor standards in all countries and by all possible means, nor a global campaign for promoting human rights in all countries (based on a clear understanding of the rights to be promoted), nor a broad program to achieve sustainable development worldwide (based on a clear understanding of its requirements), there is no case for proposing trade measures in order to advance these objectives.

The issues that were examined in this chapter are not related to trade. To solve them, it would not be enough to remove certain effects of substandard labor conditions. Their solution would require compliance with CLS. Trade measures are hardly an adequate tool to achieve that objective. Trade measures themselves cannot improve labor conditions, but only put pressure on governments to enforce labor laws. However, experience has shown that only comprehensive and severe trade restrictions are likely to impress governments in any way. While one may disagree with the foregoing conclusions and argue that the reasons discussed in this chapter would nevertheless justify a link between trade and labor standards, it is clear that none would warrant trade restrictions strict enough to have the desired effects. And it would hardly make sense to authorize trade measures which would be ineffective in any event. Even if there was agreement to allow trade measures in order to enforce labor standards, it is very unlikely that such measures could actually achieve this goal.

NOTES

1. International Labour Organization, Review of annual reports under the follow-up to the ILO Declaration on Fundamental Principles and Rights at Work, Governing Body, 320th session, Geneva, March 2014, document GB.320/INS/4, Appendix 1.
2. International Labour Organization, document GB.320/INS/4.
3. In 2010, these reporting procedures were merged with the follow-up to the ILO Declaration on Social Justice for Fair Globalization. The reports are available on the ILO website.
4. International Labour Office, Your voice at work, Global Report under the follow-up to the ILO Declaration on Fundamental Principles and Rights at Work, Geneva, 2000, p. viii.
5. International Labour Office, Organization for Social Justice, Global Report under the follow-up to the ILO Declaration on Fundamental Principles and Rights at Work, Geneva, 2004, p. 1.
6. International Labour Office, Freedom of Association in Practice: Lessons Learned, Global Report under the follow-up to the ILO Declaration on Fundamental Principles and Rights at Work, Geneva, 2008, p. x.
7. International Labour Organization, Review of annual reports under the follow-up to the ILO Declaration on Fundamental Principles and Rights at Work, Governing Body, 310th Session, Geneva, March 2011, document GB.310/3, paragraph 15.
8. International Labour Organization, 371st Report of the Committee on Freedom of Association, Governing Body, 320th session, Geneva, March 2014, document GB.320/INS/12.
9. International Labour Office, Stopping Forced Labor, Global Report under the follow-up to the ILO Declaration on Fundamental Principles and Rights at Work, Geneva, 2001, p. vii.
10. International Labour Office, A Global Alliance against Forced Labor, Global Report under the follow-up to the ILO Declaration on Fundamental Principles and Rights at Work, Geneva, 2005, p. iv.
11. International Labour Office, The Cost of Coercion, Global Report under the follow-up to the ILO Declaration on Fundamental Principles and Rights at Work, Geneva, 2009.
12. International Labour Organization, The ILO at a glance, Geneva, 2007, p. 10.
13. International Labour Office, A Future without Child Labour, Global Report under the follow-up to the ILO Declaration on Fundamental Principles and Rights at Work, Geneva, 2002; International Labour Office, The End of Child Labour: Within Reach, Global Report under the follow-up to the ILO Declaration on Fundamental Principles and Rights at Work, Geneva, 2006; International Labour Office, Accelerating Action against Child Labor, Global Report under the follow-up to the ILO Declaration on Fundamental Principles and Rights at Work, Geneva, 2010. Figures refer to 2008.
14. These figures must be treated with caution giving the difficulties to gather data, in particular on illegal activities.
15. International Labour Office, Equality at Work: Tackling the Challenge, Global Report under the follow-up to the ILO Declaration on Fundamental Principles and Rights at Work, Geneva, 2007, p. x.
16. International Labour Office, Equality at Work: The Continuing Challenge, Global Report under the Follow-Up to the ILO Declaration on Fundamental Principles and Rights at Work, Geneva, 2011, p. ix.
17. International Labour Organization, The ILO at a glance, p. 12.
18. C. Duhigg and D. Barboza, In China, Human Costs Are Built Into an iPad, *The New York Times*, January 25, 2012. This and similar information may be dismissed as anecdotal, which is why I refrain from using more of it. However, the sheer amount of similar information suggests that the above description comes close to the reality in many places.
19. B. H. Weston, Child Labor in Human Rights Law and Policy Perspective, in J. A. Gross and L. Compa (eds), *Human Rights in Labor and Employment Relations: International and Domestic Perspectives*, Labor and Employment Relations Association, Champaign, 2009, p. 83.
20. International Labor Organization, The ILO at a glance, pp. 8 and 10. However, official ILO declarations rather use the term "fundamental rights."

21. See for instance J. A. Gross and L. Compa (eds), Human Rights in Labor and Employment Relations: International and Domestic Perspectives, Labor and Employment Relations Association, Champaign, 2009; J. A. Gross (ed), *Workers' Rights as Human Rights*, Ithaca, 2003.

22. This convention has been ratified by all countries but two, Somalia and the United States.

23. M. L. Ontiveros, Employment Discrimination, in J. A. Gross and L. Compa (eds), *Human Rights in Labor and Employment Relations: International and Domestic Perspectives*, Labor and Employment Relations Association, Champaign, 2009, p. 197.

24. R. P. McIntyre, *Are Workers Rights Human Rights?* Ann Arbor, 2008, p. 76.

25. B. H. Weston, Child Labor in Human Rights Law and Policy Perspective, p. 74; H. Cullen, The limits of international trade mechanisms in enforcing human right: The case of child labour, *The International Journal of Children's Rights*, 7: 1999, p. 4.

26. On the other hand, rights to protection from anti-union discrimination and protection of public employees' organizations from "acts of interference by a public authority" are granted to public employees by virtue of ILO Convention C151 concerning Protection of the Rights to Organize and Procedures for Determining Conditions of Employment in the Public Service.

27. T. Novitz, Workers' Freedom of Association, in J. A. Gross and L. Compa (eds), *Human Rights in Labor and Employment Relations: International and Domestic Perspectives*, Labor and Employment Relations Association, Champaign, 2009, pp. 123–54; R. P. McIntyre, *Are Workers Rights Human Rights?* Ann Arbor, 2008, p. 53.

28. J. A. Gross, Takin' It to the Man: Human Rights at the American Workplace, in J. A. Gross and L. Compa (eds), *Human Rights in Labor and Employment Relations: International and Domestic Perspectives*, Labor and Employment Relations Association, Champaign, 2009, p. 13.

29. As J. A. Gross, A Long Overdue Beginning, in J. A. Gross, (ed), *Workers' Rights as Human Rights*, Ithaca, 2003, p. 8, puts it: "The United Nations' UDHR, ICCP, and ICESCR, for example, are long on lists of human rights, but short on the foundations of those rights in moral and political thought."

30. The ILO decided that these principles should not be enforced through the complaints mechanisms described above in cases where countries have not ratified these conventions, see Organization for Economic Cooperation and Development, International Trade and Core Labour Standards, Paris, 2000, p. 46.

31. The idea that human rights are natural rights was the main argument challenging the legitimacy of slavery in the eighteenth and nineteenth centuries. Forced labor and discrimination relate to similar situations.

32. J. A. Gross, Takin' It to the Man: Human Rights at the American Workplace, p. 25.

33. See J. Hilgert, A New Frontier for Industrial Relations: Workplace Health and Safety as a Human Right, in J. A. Gross and L. Compa (eds), *Human Rights in Labor and Employment Relations: International and Domestic Perspectives*, Labor and Employment Relations Association, Champaign, 2009, p. 55.

34. B. H. Weston, Child Labor in Human Rights Law and Policy Perspective, p. 89.

35. See J. Hilgert, A New Frontier for Industrial Relations: Workplace Health and Safety as a Human Right, pp. 43–68. The author argues that the protection of health and safety are human rights that are inalienable and universally binding, but he does not explain why.

36. There are other attempts to prove the existence of human rights as an autonomous category of rights. It would, however, go beyond the scope of this study to analyze them further. See D. G. Arnold, Philosophical Foundations: Moral Reasoning, Human Rights, and Global Labor Practices, in L. P. Hartman, D. G. Arnold, and R. E. Wokutch (eds), *Rising above Sweatshops, Innovative Approaches to Global Labor Challenges*, Westport and London, 2003, p. 85.

37. R. P. McIntyre, *Are Workers Rights Human Rights?* pp. 77 and 152.

38. The report "The Corporate Responsibility to Respect Human Rights, An Interpretative Guide," prepared by the UN Special Representative on Business and Human Rights (Geneva, 2011) states that "business enterprises should respect human rights" (guiding principles

11–14); S. R. Ratner, Corporations and Human Rights: A Theory of Legal Responsibility, *The Yale Law Journal*, Vol. 111, No. 3 (2001), p. 443.

39. See the Preamble of the United Nations Declaration of Human Rights.

40. B. H. Weston, Child Labor in Human Rights Law and Policy Perspective, p. 89.

41. This principle is enshrined in the United Nations Global Compact, the OECD Guidelines for Multinational Enterprises, the ILO Tripartite Declaration of Principles concerning Multinational Enterprises and Social Policy as well as in resolutions of the United Nations Human Rights Council such as Resolution 8/7, Mandate of the Special Representative of Secretary-General on the issue of human rights and transnational corporations and other business enterprises of June 18, 2008.

42. S. Herzenberg, In From the Margins: Morality, Economics, and International Labor Rights, in L. A. Compa and S. F. Diamond (eds), *Human Rights, Labor Rights, and International Trade*, Philadelphia, 1996, p. 113.

43. See page 16.

44. R. Hensman, Fine-tuning the Linkage Proposal, in C. Barry and S. G. Reddy, *International Trade and Labor Standards, A Proposal for a Linkage*, New York, 2008, p. 120.

45. International Labor Office, Working Party on the Social Dimensions of the Liberalization of Trade, Country studies on the Social Impact of Globalization, Final Report, GB.276/WP/SDL/1, 276th Session, Geneva, November 1999.

46. United Nations World Commission on Environment, Our Common Future (commonly referred to as the "Brundtland Report"), 1987.

47. As mentioned above, the ILO Declaration on Fundamental Principles and Rights at Work of 1998 establishes, as its follow-up, a special mechanism to monitor compliance with the conventions on CLS. This mechanism requires all ILO members that have not ratified these conventions to report annually their efforts to remove obstacles to ratification.

48. UNDP did not assess four of the forty-seven countries concerned.

49. The latest report was published in February 2014: ILO, Review of annual reports under the follow-up to the ILO Declaration on Fundamental Principles and Rights at Work, Governing Body, 320th session, March 2014, document GB.320/INS/4.

50. The problems underlying these challenges may not be equally important, both in qualitative and in quantitative terms. The available information does not allow determining whether there is a correlation between the importance of problems and the level of development of the countries concerned.

51. UNDP did not assess two of the twenty-eight countries concerned.

52. UNDP did not assess three of the eleven countries concerned.

53. UNDP did not assess one of the ten countries concerned.

54. International Labour Organization, Report of the Committee of Experts on the Application of Conventions and Recommendations, Geneva, Feb. 2014, Document ILC.103/III (1A).

55. UNDP did not assess one of the twenty-eight countries concerned.

56. R. Robertson, D. Brown, G. Pierre, and M. L. Sanchez-Puerta (eds), Globalization, Wages, and the Quality of Jobs, Five Country Studies, The World Bank, Washington, DC, 2009, p. 1.

57. See K. A. Elliott and R. B. Freeman, Can Labor Stands Improve under Globalization? Institute for International Economics, Washington DC, 2003, p. 21.

58. P. Krugman claims that "the overwhelming mainstream view among economists is that growth of this kind of employment is tremendous good news for the world's poor" (In Praise of Cheap Labor, *Slate*, March 20, 1997), while J. D. Sachs believes that "there are not too many sweatshops, but there are too few," cited by A. R. Myerson, In Principle, a Case for More Sweatshops, the *New York Times*, June 22, 1997. See also M. Friedman, The Social Responsibility of Business to Increase Its Profits, *New York Times Magazine,* September 13, 1970, p. 30.

59. In this respect, Myanmar may provide an interesting case to study.

60. International Labour Office, International Institute for Labor Studies, Studies on Growth with Equity, Making Recovery Sustainable: Lessons from Country Innovations, Geneva, 2011; T. I. Palley, The Economic Case for International Labour Standards, *Cambridge Journal of Economics*, Vol. 28, No. 1, 2004, p. 22, footnote 3 believes that "the argument that labour

standards are a source of economic inefficiency that interferes with the realization of the gains of comparative advantage has no merit." Similarly J. Miller, Why Economists Are Wrong about Sweatshops and the Antisweatshop Movement, *Challenge*, Vol. 46, No. 1, Jan.–Feb. 2003, p. 93; D. G. Arnold and L. P. Hartman, Worker Rights and Low Wage Industrialization: How to Avoid Sweatshops, *Human Rights Quarterly*, Vol. 28, No. 3, August 2006, p. 676.

61. S. Polaski, Trade and Labor Standards, A Strategy for Developing Countries, Trade, Equity, and Development Paper, Carnegie Endowment for International Peace, Washington, DC, 2003, p. 4.

62. Organization for Economic Cooperation and Development, International Trade and Core Labour Standards, Paris, 2000, p. 14; W. Martin and K. E. Maskus, Core Labor Standards and Competitiveness: Implications for Global Trade Policy, *Review of International Economics*, 9 (2), 2001, p. 318. Similarly, Article 13.6, paragraph 1 of the FTA between the EU and the Republic of Korea explicitly states: "The Parties recognize the beneficial role that core labor standards and decent work can have on economic efficiency . . ."

63. R. Marshall, Trade-Linked Labor Standards, *Proceedings of the Academy of Political Science*, Vol. 37, 1990, No. 4, p. 71.

64. Ironically, the governments of certain states in which colonial powers had imposed forced labor during the times of colonization did the same after having gained independence, arguing that this was necessary for promoting economic development.

65. C. Azariadis and J. Stachurski, Poverty Traps, in P. Aghion and S. Durlauf (eds), *Handbook of Economic Growth*, Los Angeles, 2002.

66. ILO, The ILO at a glance, p. 4.

67. See also A. Bieler, The Future of the Global Working Class, in A. Bieler, I. Landberg, and D. Pillay, *Labour and the Challenges of Globalization, What Prospects for Transnational Solidarity?* London and Ann Arbor, 2008, p. 9.

68. J. Cavanagh, L. Compa, A. Ebert, B. Goold, Z. Selvaggio, and T. Shorrock, *Trade's Hidden Costs: Worker Rights in a Changing World Economy*, International Labor Rights Education and Research Fund, Ithaca, 1988.

69. United Nations Development Programme, International Cooperation at a Crossroads: Aid, Trade and Security in an Unequal World, Human Development Report 2005, pp. 51–71; World Bank, The World Development Report, A Better Investment Climate for Everyone, Washington, DC, 2005, p. 31.

70. The so-called Kuznets curve predicts that during industrialization, inequality first increases, then stabilizes and eventually falls. Yet, the situation in many developing countries clearly does not reach the second and third stage.

71. J. D. Sachs, *The End of Poverty*, Economic Possibilities for Our Time, New York, 2005, p. 64.

72. S. F. Diamond, Labor Rights in the Global Economy, A Case Study of NAFTA, in L. A. Compa and S. F. Diamond (eds), in *Human Rights, Labor Rights, and International Trade*, Philadelphia, 1996, p. 203.

73. Organization for Economic Cooperation and Development, International Trade and Core Labour Standards, p. 54.

74. S. Polaski, Trade and Labor Standards, A Strategy for Developing Countries, p. 19.

75. J. E. Stiglitz and A. Charlton, *Fair Trade For All, How Trade Can Promote Development*, Oxford, 2005, p. 154, argue that "today, in the absence of alternatives, trade sanctions are one of the few ways that the international community can enforce its will, and though resort to such measures should be carefully circumscribed, the instances enumerated are among those in which sanctions may arguably be justified." According to the authors, sanctions may be justified where the global community is affected. In my view, neither violations of human rights nor unsustainable development could affect the global community in a way that would warrant trade sanctions.

Chapter Four

Linking Trade to Labor Standards for Trade-Related Reasons

The previous chapter examined a number of non-trade-related problems deriving from substandard labor conditions. It concluded that none of these problems would justify a link between trade and labor standards. This chapter will examine the question whether there are other, trade-related problems which require such a link.

As mentioned above, this study considers issues as trade-related if they would not arise without trade. Trade and labor may be related in different ways. Labor conditions may affect and even distort trade by lowering production costs and increasing competitiveness in foreign markets. But trade may also affect labor conditions. Trading opportunities and competition may provide an incentive for exporting countries to opt for a low level of labor protection.

This chapter will examine the effects of imports of goods produced under substandard labor conditions on importing countries and the effects of free trade on the level of labor protection in exporting countries, in order to determine whether these effects would warrant the adoption of a link between trade and labor standards.

The following reflections will be guided primarily by the way the GATT and other international agreements deal with similar trade-related issues. One of the main criteria for assessing the importance of the problems examined in this chapter and the need to deal with them is the analogy with issues addressed by present GATT rules. These rules enshrine the principles that should govern international trade: fairness and responsibility. The following considerations are based on the belief that these principles should also apply where trade meets labor protection.

THE EFFECTS OF LABOR CONDITIONS ON TRADE

This section will consider the effects of substandard labor conditions on trade. Almost seventy years ago, the Havana Charter explicitly recognized that poor labor conditions create problems in the framework of international trade: "The Members recognize that unfair labor conditions, particularly in production of export, create difficulties in international trade, and, accordingly, each Member shall take whatever action may be appropriate and feasible to eliminate such conditions on its territory." More explicitly, the 2008 ILO Declaration on Social Justice for a Fair Globalization states that "the violation of fundamental principles and rights at work cannot be invoked or otherwise used as a legitimate comparative advantage."

The ILO annual reports demonstrate that many countries did not eliminate unfair labor conditions in their territory. According to the 2008 Declaration, this provides them with an illegitimate economic advantage in international trade. This section will examine the question of whether the use of such advantage should be made actionable.

The Impact of Substandard Labor Conditions on Trade

The impact of labor standards (or violations thereof) on trade depends, first, on the costs of implementing them. It also depends on the extent to which these costs (or savings) influence the prices of exports. Finally, the impact depends on how much price variations of exports affect their volume.

The Amount of Savings from Non-Compliance with CLS

Core labor standards are sometimes opposed to "cash standards" meaning those standards which have significant and direct effects on production costs. This criterion is far from being clear—and so is the proposed differentiation. It goes without saying that there are costs associated with the implementation of each and every labor standard, including CLS. Unfortunately, there is little empirical evidence on the costs that employers would have to pay for fully complying with CLS. Besides, it is difficult to calculate these costs before standards are actually implemented. Nonetheless, there is some data that permits an estimate of the amounts that employers may save by not complying with CLS.[1]

Forced Labor. People who are victims of forced labor receive typically very low wages and suffer from poor working conditions like excessive overtime. Moreover, they are often overcharged for accommodation and, in the case of trafficked workers, for recruitment. In its 2009 report "The Cost of Coercion" the ILO offers a "first and provisional estimate" according to which the "total financial cost of coercion to workers affected—excluding the victims of forced commercial sexual exploitation—is approximately $21 billion."[2] The ILO estimates that worldwide 10 million people are victims of forced labor in the private sector.[3] On average, annual wages of victims of forced labor are approximately $2,000 lower than normal wages.

Discrimination. Data provided by the United Nations Development Fund for Women (UNIFEM) show that in certain Asian countries female wages are approximately 60 percent of male wages.[4] In these cases, gender discrimination saves 40 percent of labor costs.

Child Labor. The United Nations Children's Fund (UNICEF) estimates that there are approximately 80 million child workers who are economically exploited. These children typically earn $0.50 to $1.00 per day.[5] Even in the countries concerned, this is only a fraction of what an adult would earn.

Freedom of Association and the Right to Collective Bargaining. The immediate costs of granting freedom of association and protecting the right to collective bargaining may be insignificant. But wages are generally higher and working conditions are typically better where workers are able to freely negotiate them.[6] Denying these rights allows for saving the difference. However, the importance of the difference is unknown as long as those rights are not enforced and wages are not freely negotiated.

The Impact of Saving Labor Costs on Production Costs

The above figures suggest that substandard labor conditions may allow large savings on labor costs. The extent to which such savings influence production costs depends on the share of labor costs. If this share is high, the effects can be quite significant. In certain sectors, however, this share is very low, that is, in the range of 5–10 percent. In these sectors, saving even 50 percent of normal labor costs would lower production costs only marginally. In these cases, savings on labor costs may be only a tiny fraction of production costs in the range of 2.5 to 5 percent.[7]

The Impact of Saving Labor Costs on Trade

Assuming that the producer passes these savings to the exporter, what is the trade effect of a price difference of 2.5 or 5 percent? Both the rules of the multilateral trading system and the tariff schedules of WTO members suggest that a price variation of that range actually makes a difference.

Under the EU tariff scheme, the average duty rate on industrial goods is close to 4 percent. The preferential margin under the EU GSP is 3.5 percentage points. The duties are maintained and these preferential margins are granted because the EU believes that they actually have an impact on trade.[8]

According to Article 5.8 of the WTO Anti-Dumping agreement, "the margin of dumping shall be considered *de minimis* if this margin is less than 2 percent, expressed as a percentage of the export price." Hence, the agreement considers that a margin of 2 percent may have a significant impact on trade. This would also apply to saving on labor costs.

Unfair Competition

The Comparative Advantage from Not Complying with CLS

Many scholars and developing countries argue that non-compliance with international labor standards gives a "comparative advantage." The theory of comparative advantage provides the commonly accepted rationalization of free trade. Comparative advantages are not only those stemming from natural endowments, but any economic advantages, regardless of how they are obtained. Thus, cheap labor provides a comparative advantage, even if it is cheap because labor standards are not complied with.[9]

The Legitimacy of Using This Comparative Advantage

But is it legitimate to use the advantage from not complying with labor standards in international trade? While the WTO has never addressed this question, the position of the ILO has evolved over time. The 1998 ILO Declaration on Fundamental Principles and Rights at Work recalls that "the comparative advantage of any country should in no way be called into question." On the other hand, already in 1997, the ILO Director-General noted that "the comparative advantage that developing countries derive from their lower wages and levels of social protection are legitimate as long as they serve to encourage development and are not maintained artificially as a commercial strategy."[10] Subsequently, the international community joined this position. The 2008 Declaration states that "the violation of fundamental principles and rights at work cannot be invoked or otherwise used as a legitimate comparative advantage."

The Fairness of Using this Comparative Advantage

Indeed, using an advantage from violating rules that are binding international law and that others abide by is a "free ride." Although using the comparative advantage from not complying with labor standards is legal under present WTO rules, it appears to be unfair. The GATT agreements do not provide a definition of fairness in international trade. But they include a number of rules making certain trading practices actionable, which implies that these practices are unfair. Some of these rules authorize trade restrictions for reasons that are similar to the effects of imports of goods produced under substandard labor conditions.

Dumping. One of these rules relate to dumping. Exports of goods produced under substandard labor conditions are often portrayed as social dumping.[11] The situation covered by WTO anti-dumping rules is actually quite similar to the one created by substandard labor conditions.[12] Dumping means selling goods at a price below their "normal value." If goods are produced without paying the costs of complying with certain labor standards, they can be sold below what otherwise would be their normal value.[13] This appears to be as unfair as dumping.

Prison Labor. GATT Article XX (e) allows adopting trade measures "relating to the products of prison labor." However, this provision does not explain why contracting parties may restrict imports of products of prison labor. The purpose may be either to protect inmates in foreign prisons from being abused or to reduce the effects of introducing goods made in foreign prisons into the market of the importing country. As international law does not prohibit prison labor *per se*, it is unlikely that the purpose of the provision is to limit the effects of trade on labor in foreign prisons. The rationale of this provision seems rather to protect against competition resulting from the cost advantage of using prison labor.[14] GATT Article XX (e) implies that this type of competition is regarded as unfair. The same would apply to competition that takes advantage of forced labor, child labor, discrimination, or the absence of trade unions.

The Importance of Fairness in International Trade. The importance of fairness in international trade stems from the rationale of free trade. Theory says that all countries gain from participating in international trade if they use their comparative advantages. Free trade will not be able to keep that promise, though, if exporting countries artificially create cost advantages by paying inputs or by selling goods at a price below their "normal value." Making use of such advantages would distort trade and thus be unfair.[15]

The Situation of Exporters in Countries Not Complying with CLS

Employers in countries that have not ratified the relevant ILO conventions, or do not fully implement them in their territory, may find it difficult to provide labor conditions that meet CLS. This is not so much a problem as far as child labor, forced labor, and discrimination are concerned. Employers should and could respect these prohibitions without being required by domestic labor laws. But employers can hardly comply with freedom of association and the right to collective bargaining if these rights are not granted in their country. One may argue that, in this case, it would not be fair to apply trade restrictions against them. Yet, making use of cost advantages resulting from substandard labor conditions is unfair, regardless of whether the employer concerned is in a position to comply with CLS or not.

Injury to Domestic Producers of Importing Countries

There is no need to provide border protection if there is no victim. This is why trade defense instruments available in the framework of the multilateral trading system can only be used if imports cause injury to domestic producers of like products. Accordingly, the question of whether it would be warranted to restrict imports which enjoy a cost advantage because of substandard labor conditions has to be examined at the level of shipments of specific products from particular exporters.[16]

The Trade-Distorting Effects of Violations of CLS Justify a Link

The whole architecture of the multilateral trading system is based on the concept of fairness. Where trade is not fair, it does not legitimize profits nor can it justify readjustment costs. WTO rules consider dumping and selling goods made by prison labor as unfair practices against which the domestic industries manufacturing like products in importing countries deserve protection. Social dumping is an unfair trading practice that may distort trade in essentially the same way. It would only be consistent to deal with it in a similar manner.[17]

The size of dumping margins depends on the definition of social dumping, in particular of the labor standards used as a reference. Non-compliance with CLS may result in substantial savings on labor costs. Even small dumping margins may distort trade considerably. Hence, social dumping is likely to create serious problems. There is no doubt that social dumping has contributed to driving some industries in OECD countries out of business. Some sectors were swept out and relocated to developing countries. A number of these countries are on the list of the fifty-seven countries facing challenges in the areas covered by the eight conventions on CLS.

One may imagine that this trend has come to an end because industries in OECD countries are now able to deal with the challenge from social dumping. This is an overly optimistic view. Developing countries have shown that they can produce more and more sophisticated and technologically advanced goods and combine high technology with high quality. It is quite likely that in the future, more cases will occur where industries of importing countries require protection against social dumping. There is a need to address this problem.

This claim is not new. In the 1930s, such rules were introduced into the trade laws of several countries.[18] Although Article VII of the Havana Charter expresses similar views, the GATT agreements of 1947 lack any reference to the issue. Only fifteen years later, when Japan started to play a role similar to the one played by China nowadays, did certain GATT contracting parties regret this omission. Some of them made proposals to bridge the gap between trade and labor standards in the framework of that organization. But countries where labor is cheap succeeded in blocking these initiatives. This is what happened in the 1960s and has again been the situation for more than two decades now.

Yet, things are moving, albeit slowly. When adopting the 2008 ILO Declaration on Social Justice for a Fair Globalization, the international community recognized that violations of CLS cannot be invoked as a legitimate comparative advantage. The same governments, gathered in the WTO, should make social dumping actionable in the framework of the multilateral trading system.

THE EFFECTS OF TRADE ON LABOR CONDITIONS

This section will consider the effects of trade on the quality of labor conditions. The preamble of the ILO Constitution adopted almost a hundred years ago explicitly refers to these effects: ". . . the failure of any nation to adopt humane conditions of labor is an obstacle in the way of other nations which desire to improve the conditions in their own countries."

Although this statement does not mention trade, it is clear that the problem arises typically in an environment of free trade like the one that prevailed before World War I and which the founding members of the ILO probably had in mind.[19] In actual fact, free trade may provide an incentive to tolerate poor labor conditions in order to lower production costs.[20] There is more than just a gap between ILO standards and WTO rules: there is actually potential for conflict.

This conflict results from competition at three levels: between workers in exporting countries, between companies, and between exporting countries. The virtually unlimited pool of unskilled workers in developing countries provides employers with the possibility to exploit people. Competition between employers compels them to do so.[21] Indeed, the force of the market makes it difficult for any single company to pay higher wages or to improve working conditions if others do not follow suit. And competition between countries hinders governments to improve their labor conditions as long as others are unwilling to do so.

This section will examine the question of whether it would be justified to establish a link between trade and labor standards in order to solve this conflict.

The Race to the Bottom

Anti-globalization activists claim that developing countries eager to attract investments make strategic use of domestic policies such as labor protection. This is commonly referred to as "the race to the bottom." This term describes a process by which governments lower legal requirements to make their countries more attractive for foreign investors than other countries with higher requirements. A race to the bottom means that countries compete with each other by softening their laws or exempting certain producers from the obligation to respect them. A similar situation would arise where governments decide not to fully enforce their labor laws.[22]

Some governments offer foreign investors particularly advantageous conditions in "Export Processing Zones" (EPZ). These are economically and physically separate enclaves, where it is allowed to import duty free inputs, if they are processed there and subsequently exported. The advantages offered typically include non-application of domestic labor laws. The spread of EPZs clearly is a sign of a race to the bottom.

But is there any general deterioration of labor standards? According to the reports prepared by the ILO on the implementation of CLS,[23] the most disturbing developments occur in the area of forced labor. Yet, the majority of violations of these standards do not concern employment in the export sector but rather of domestic servants. This is not a sector where foreigners would invest. Thus, the situation concerning forced labor does not corroborate the thesis of a race to the bottom. Although the situation also remains very serious as far as child labor is concerned, the ILO reports some progress, not least thanks to the assistance provided under the International Program on the Elimination of Child Labor (IPEC).[24] As for freedom of association and the right to collective bargaining and the prohibition of discrimination, the situation in most countries stagnates, but does not deteriorate.

Although it cannot be ruled out that certain governments tolerate violations of their labor laws in order to attract foreign investment, the findings of the ILO do not support the view that there is a generalized beggar-thy-neighbor policy of softening labor laws. Beyond EPZs, there is no evidence of a race to the bottom.[25]

Trade and the Increase of Violations of CLS

Nonetheless, the conflict between free trade and labor protection is real, to the extent that it *prevents improvements* of labor conditions. This becomes manifest when countries refuse any discussion of linking trade and labor in WTO on the grounds that they want to keep the comparative advantage of cheap labor, and when they declare in ILO that they lack the political will to fully comply with CLS or that foreign investors are opposed to it.

However, keeping labor conditions at the same level does not mean that everything else remains the same too. The ILO reports referred to above show that while the level of labor protection remains basically the same in most countries, the number of violations of CLS is globally increasing. This is not surprising: if exports grow and labor standards are not complied with, the number of violations grows proportionally.

World trade grows at a much higher rate than world production. Over the period between 1950 and 2010, the value of all merchandise exports and imports grew by an average annual rate of slightly over 10 percent.[26] However, the performance of certain countries is far above average. Some of these countries are on the list of fifty-seven countries facing challenges in the areas covered by the eight conventions on CLS. Nineteen countries facing such challenges more than tripled their exports between 2004 and 2013. These surges may have benefited from cost advantages because of substandard labor conditions. What is more important, however, is that in countries not complying with these standards, surging exports signify a massive proliferation of violations of the CLS.

Trade Restrictions for Similar Reasons

Certain GATT rules and international agreements allow for trade restrictions in cases where free trade may act as an obstacle to achieving other political objectives. Would the case of labor protection justify a similar exception?

GATT Article XX

GATT Article XX authorizes a number of "general exceptions" from GATT rules and disciplines. Letter (e) of this article allows the adoption of trade measures "relating to the products of prison labor." As stated above, this provision does not aim to limit the effects of trade on labor conditions in foreign prisons, but the effects of cheap labor on trade. There is no parallel between the situation to which it applies and the issue under consideration here.

Article XX (g) allows for trade measures "relating to the conservation of exhaustible natural resources if such measures are made effective in conjunction with restrictions on domestic production or consumption." As mentioned before, there is a virtually unlimited pool of unskilled workers in developing countries. The situation of labor does not bear any resemblance with "exhaustible natural resources."

Article XX (b) authorizes exceptions "necessary to protect human, animal or plant life or health." This objective is, to some extent, similar to labor protection.

The TRIPS Agreement

A conflict akin to the one between trade and labor exists between trade and intellectual property. Article 51 of the TRIPS agreement authorizes the suspension, by custom authorities, of the release into free circulation of counterfeit trademark or pirated copyright goods, in order to prevent that imports damage intellectual property rights. The protection of these rights compares to labor protection.

Other International Agreements Allowing for Trade Restrictions for Similar Reasons

The GATT agreements are not the only international rules allowing for trade restrictions. For example, the Washington Convention on International Trade in Endangered Species of Wild Fauna and Flora of 1973 (CITES) bans international trade in certain endangered species and the Montreal Protocol on Substances That Deplete the Ozone Layer of 1987 bans imports of certain substances known to deplete the ozone layer. Another example is the Basel Convention on the Control of Transboundary Movements of Hazardous Waste and Their Disposal of 1989. These agreements allow for trade restrictions because trade would make it difficult or even impossible to achieve those objectives. The same may be said, to some extent, of labor protection.

The Effects of Trade on Labor Standards Do Not Justify a Link

Although there is little empirical evidence supporting the thesis of a race to the bottom, there is little doubt that international competition has been an obstacle for many governments to fully comply with CLS. It seems that unless we make concessions on free trade, we are bound to make concessions on labor protection.

Concessions on free trade mean an exception from the rules of the multilateral trading system. Such exceptions are warranted, in general, where trade restrictions are necessary in order to achieve other political objectives that deserve priority over free trade. Hence, when evaluating the merits of introducing an exception to GATT rules, two questions arise. First, does the other political objective deserve priority over free trade? Second, are trade restrictions necessary to achieve it?

CITES and the Montreal Protocol answer both questions themselves by imposing—not only authorizing—trade restrictions. These agreements acknowledge that such restrictions are necessary to protect certain endangered species and the ozone layer and that this protection deserves priority over free trade. Likewise, by authorizing the suspension of release for home consumption of goods infringing intellectual property rights, the TRIPS agreement recognizes that the protection of these rights is more important than free trade and that import restrictions are necessary to provide this protection. In the case of GATT Article XX (b), trade restrictions may be adopted if they are necessary to protect human, animal or plant life, or health. This provision implies recognition that such protection *may* take priority over free trade. Whether it *is* necessary depends on the specific case.

What is the answer to the two questions as far as labor protection is concerned? Is labor protection politically more important than free trade? And are trade restrictions necessary to achieve adequate labor protection? Before trying to answer these questions, it should be recalled that the issue is not whether trade sanctions should be used in order to *enforce* labor standards. The issue under discussion here is whether trade restrictions should be allowed where trade acts as an *obstacle* to improvements in labor conditions.

As far as the question of the importance of free trade versus labor protection is concerned, there is no objective answer. There are no scientific criteria to evaluate costs and benefits of labor protection and of free trade against each other. In any event, this issue goes beyond economic gains and losses. I respect the opinion of those who consider free trade as more important as much as of those who believe that priority should be given to ensuring a minimum level of labor protection. I share the latter position.

If we accept the latter view (and only then), the second question arises of whether trade restrictions are necessary to achieve a minimum level of labor protection. As mentioned above, trade may act as an obstacle to compliance with international labor standards. But are there instances where it would actually be *necessary* to adopt trade restrictions in order to remove this obstacle? It can hardly be argued that without trade restrictions, it would be impossible to achieve compliance with the relevant standards.[27] In other words, trade restrictions would not be necessary.

Moreover, import restrictions imposed by individual countries would not bring about any significant changes to the level of competition in the framework of the global trading environment. They would not suffice to remove the obstacle to achieving compliance. Furthermore, it would not be fair to restrict imports from one country that refuses to improve labor standards in order to keep its competitive advantage, without sanctioning others doing the same. Trade restrictions for the reason discussed in this section would therefore have to be collective ones, adopted by all countries against all sinners. This would require complex machinery. I do not believe that the problems examined here would warrant such efforts.

For these reasons, it would, in my view, not be justified to allow trade restrictions in order to avoid possible negative effects of free trade on labor conditions in exporting countries.

THE ROLE OF IMPORTING COUNTRIES

This section will consider the responsibility of countries importing goods produced under substandard labor conditions. As stated in chapter 3, the number and gravity of violations of CLS are a matter of concern in many exporting countries. However, the conclusion of that chapter was that there is no case for authorizing trade sanctions in order to enforce these standards. This section discusses these violations from another point of view, the role played by countries importing goods from exporting countries not complying with CLS.

By offering "fair trade" goods, fair trade initiatives give consumers a possibility to escape the blame for consuming goods produced under unfair labor conditions. In contrast, importing countries do not have that choice. As WTO members, they have to keep their markets open for imports of such goods. It may be argued that importing countries should be enabled to restrict imports in order to avoid being associated with violations of CLS by countries from which they import goods.

The Responsibility of Exporting Countries

Of course, importing countries can hardly be blamed for violations of CLS in exporting countries if the latter have an excuse for not complying with these standards. Can exporting countries under all circumstances be held responsible if they do not comply with CLS?

Countries May Be Unable to Effectively Implement CLS

Arguably, lack of capacity and resources in exporting countries provide them with such excuse. Effective implementation of labor standards means that a country transforms the relevant standards into domestic laws and enforces them, which requires the capacity to monitor and to sanction violations. Very poor countries may lack adequate labor inspection, judicial systems, or the necessary budgetary resources.

Moreover, certain CLS impose proactive policies. ILO Convention No. 111, for instance, requests governments to pursue a policy aimed at promoting equality of opportunity and eliminating all forms of discrimination in employment and occupation. Under ILO Convention No. 138 countries must adopt a policy aimed at the effective abolition of child labor. Very poor countries may lack the experience necessary to shape and carry out such policies. Moreover, in some countries, the abolition of child labor requires profound social changes and reforms.

Hence, the answer to the question of whether a country is actually in a position to fully implement CLS may differ from one standard to another. Lack of capacity and resources cannot provide an excuse for not granting freedom of association and the right to collective bargaining. It is probably more complicated and expensive to ban trade unions than to permit them.

Lack of capacity and resources may provide an excuse for not enforcing the other three standards. However, countries facing problems in implementing them could get help from the ILO.[28] The ILO is running several programs in order to assist them. Over the last ten years, the agency has spent an average of $130 million annually for eight "InFocus Programs" covering priority issues of technical cooperation. Two of these programs concern CLS: the InFocus Program on Promoting the Declaration on Fundamental Principles and Rights at Work of 1998 and the InFocus Program on Child Labor. The latter includes the International Program on the Elimination of Child Labor (IPEC), launched in 1992, which runs over 1,000 projects worldwide in eighty-eight countries. Approximately half the financial resources available for ILO technical assistance fund the IPEC. In 2001, the ILO adopted a Special Action Program to Combat Forced Labor (SAP-FL).

Considering the amount and quality of technical and financial assistance provided by the ILO, it is fair to say that any country willing to comply with CLS could do so. Indeed, one of the criteria for selecting CLS is that all countries would be able to implement them. Hence, a shortage of skills and budgetary resources are hardly an excuse for not complying with CLS.

Implementing CLS in the Export Sector

The responsibility of importing countries for violations of CLS in exporting countries does not go beyond violations occurring in sectors producing for exports. The ability of countries to enforce CLS in these sectors depends, to some extent, on their export performance and participation in international trade. Countries whose exports represent a considerable share of GDP and increase steadily and significantly will find it easier to mobilize the necessary skills and resources. In these countries, a shortage of skills and budgetary resources are certainly no excuse for not meeting CLS.

The Responsibility of Importing Countries

Both proponents and opponents of a link between trade and labor standards acknowledge that importing countries are responsible for the effects of their trade and trade regimes on the economies of exporting countries. Opponents hint to the possible negative macro-economic effects of trade restrictions. This argument implies that importing countries have a moral obligation to avoid such effects. Proponents argue that importing countries are accountable for the exploitation of workers in exporting countries. This argument considers that importing countries are accomplices of the offenders.[29]

Importing goods and releasing them for home consumption unquestionably involves a certain responsibility of the importing country.[30] There is no doubt that importing countries share the responsibility for violations of labor standards that occurred in the production of goods which they import. They are also responsible for future violations to the extent that each import of goods produced under substandard labor conditions is an invitation to the exporting country to produce the same product under the same conditions, and ship it to the same importing country.

The Big Excuse

Arguably, these considerations would justify trade bans on goods produced under conditions violating CLS. However, such bans would have disastrous consequences for workers employed in the sectors concerned—consequences for which importing countries would be responsible if they ban imports. Hence, importing countries face a dilemma: if they import goods produced under substandard labor conditions, they are responsible for violations of labor standards in exporting countries. If they ban such imports, they are responsible for the loss of jobs and further hardship for those hitherto suffering from those violations. This dilemma provides importing countries with an excuse if they continue to import such goods.

The Automatic Solution

In theory, countries importing goods produced under substandard labor conditions have another excuse. Neo-liberal economists assert that there is no need to worry about violations of labor standards. In their view, time will bring a solution. They contend that poor labor conditions make exports more competitive, that this increases trade, that both poor labor conditions and the resulting increase of trade promote economic growth, and that this in turn leads to an improvement of labor conditions.[31] In other words, they claim that there is an automatic solution. According to this view, importing goods produced under substandard labor conditions would help to improve these conditions.

Is this claim supported by empirical evidence? During the first wave of industrialization, labor conditions did not automatically improve as a result of economic growth, but only after revolution and labor struggles.[32] Moreover, poor labor conditions do not necessarily increase the volume of exports. According to the findings of the OECD "countries with low core labor standards do not enjoy better export performance than high-standard countries."[33] These findings are confirmed by several scholars.[34] They are also corroborated by the fact that among the forty-six countries which over the last ten years were able to triple their exports,[35] nineteen are on the list of those facing challenges concerning the implementation of CLS, while twenty-seven do not face such challenges.

Furthermore, substandard labor conditions do not necessarily foster economic growth, at least not in the long run, as concluded in chapter 3. Even if they do, this will not automatically lead to better labor conditions. Experience has shown that the benefits of economic growth do not necessarily "trickle down" to less advantaged groups of society and that making the pie bigger does not always result in a bigger share for everybody.[36] On the contrary, UNDP and the World Bank found that inequalities are on the rise in most countries.[37] Progress among the poorest 20 percent of the population is far below the national average of many developing countries.[38] By the same token, wages have grown at a substantially slower pace than GDP per capita.[39] Even in countries which have experienced considerable economic growth, labor conditions have not improved accordingly.[40] It is obvious that banning trade unions helps prevent the benefits of growth from trickling down.

While there may be individual cases where labor conditions have improved "automatically," it is not the general rule. The mere expectation that expanding exports would achieve compliance with CLS does not provide an excuse for countries importing more and more goods from countries where these are produced under substandard labor conditions.

It certainly does not in cases where such expectations have been frustrated over a considerable period of time, meaning that labor conditions in exporting countries did not improve although their exports increased steadily and significantly. Nineteen countries that are likely not to meet CLS have tripled their exports over the period from 2004 to 2013. As mentioned above, in countries not complying with these standards, surging exports signify a massive proliferation of violations of CLS. Countries whose imports surge in similar proportions have no excuse for being associated with these developments.

WTO Obligations Do Not Provide an Excuse

Under present WTO rules, the fact that goods are produced under substandard working conditions does not allow importing countries to ban imports. These rules prevent importing countries from taking the steps necessary to escape the blame for participating in violations of CLS in exporting countries. Accordingly, importing countries are in a dilemma. But a dilemma cannot provide an excuse. If countries honor their WTO obligations, they are nonetheless responsible for the labor conditions in countries from which they import goods.

The Responsibility of the Consumer

One may argue that the responsibility for violations of labor standards in countries from which they imports goods lies with consumers, not with the authorities releasing these goods for home consumption. However, consumers do not have sufficient and reliable information on the conditions under which the imports they buy are produced. As long as fair trade covers only a small section of the market, it cannot provide an excuse for governments authorizing imports of goods produced under substandard labor conditions.

The Responsibility of Importing Countries for Increases of Imports of Goods Produced under Substandard Labor Conditions Justifies a Link

Importing countries share the responsibility of exporting countries for violations of labor standards that occur in the production of goods which they import from them. They have an excuse to the extent that a ban on imports would cause hardship for those hitherto suffering from working under poor conditions. And they would, in retrospect, also have an excuse if, after a period of steady and significant growth of exports, labor conditions finally reach the level defined by the relevant ILO conventions. On the contrary, where, over a long period of time, exports increase substantially but labor conditions remain substandard, importing countries have no excuse for continuing imports. If they do, they are to be blamed for the resulting proliferation of violations of labor standards in exporting countries. They are accomplices of the offender, that is, exporting countries violating CLS.

This is a serious matter for several reasons. First, such violations mean serious human suffering. Second, these standards are, if not human rights, at least rights of fundamental importance for life in any civilized society. Moreover, increases in jobs with substandard labor conditions in exporting countries are likely to hamper sustainable development. These considerations demonstrate the moral burden of importing countries associated with the violations of these rights in exporting countries.

The only way to enable importing countries to escape the blame is to authorize them to cap imports of goods produced under substandard conditions.[41] A provision granting such authorization means a link between trade and CLS.

CONCLUSION

This chapter examined the question of whether there are trade-related reasons for establishing a link between trade and labor standards.

It is often alleged that competition between countries has lead to a race to the bottom. With the exception of EPZs, there is little empirical evidence supporting this thesis. Nonetheless, it seems that competition has prevented any significant improvements of labor conditions in the world. There is more than just a gap between ILO standards and WTO rules: there is actually a conflict.

There are international rules solving similar conflicts at the expense of free trade, in particular GATT Article XX, the TRIPS agreement, as well as certain international conventions. For the reasons explained above, I do not believe that it is necessary to solve the conflict between trade and labor standards in a similar manner, that is, by authorizing trade restrictions.

On the contrary, I believe that there are two reasons justifying a link between trade and labor standards. One is to address the trade-related effects of non-compliance with international labor standards on competition, commonly referred to as social dumping. The other is to enable importing countries to escape the blame of being associated with a proliferation of violations of labor standards in exporting countries. Accordingly, there is a need to adopt two links. This study hereafter refers to the first link as "link A" and to the second as "link B."[42]

These links are not meant to enforce international labor standards, but to remove certain trade-related effects of substandard labor conditions. Trade measures are an appropriate tool to achieve their objectives. Reconciling international trade with labor protection would require the adoption of these two links between the rules of the multilateral trading system and CLS.

NOTES

1. Similar calculations are routine in the framework of anti-dumping investigations. Where such investigations lack hard data, they work on the basis of "constructed prices," calculated on the basis of assumptions and comparisons. The savings from not complying with core labor standards can be calculated in a similar manner.

2. International Labour Organization, The Cost of Coercion, Global Report under the Follow-Up to the ILO Declaration on Fundamental Principles and Rights at Work, Geneva, 2009, p. 4.

3. International Labour Office, The ILO At a Glance, Geneva, 2007, p. 10. An ILO press release of June 1, 2012, puts the figure at nearly 21 million, as a result of a revised methodology.

4. United Nations Development Fund for Women, Progress of the World's Women, Biennial Report 2000, p. 93.

5. United Nations Children's Fund, Children at Work, UNICEF East Asia and Pacific Regional Office, Bangkok, 1994.

6. M. Busse, Do Labor Standards Affect Comparative Advantage in Developing Countries? *World Development*, vol. 30, 2002, no. 11, p. 1921.

7. ILO investigations in India estimate that savings from employing children instead of adults are between 5 and 10 percent of the final sales price of the products concerned (bangles and carpets), see H. Lim, *The Social Clause: Issues and Challenges*, International Labor Organization, Bureau for Workers Activities, Geneva, 2001, p. 16. As a proportion of ex factory costs, they are obviously much higher.

8. And so do many entrepreneurs, who lobbied me to maintain the preferences.

9. It seems that some low-wage countries enjoy, for a range of products, an absolute advantage rather than a comparative one.

10. International Labour Organization, Press release ILO/97/10 of April 23, 1998.

11. In the 1930s, the trade laws of Spain and Cuba included substandard working conditions in the exporting country as a case of dumping, see S. Charnovitz, The Influence of International Labor Standards on the World Trading Regime, *International Labour Review*, Vol. 126, No. 5, Sept.–Oct. 1987, p. 569.

12. There are other GATT rules addressing similar issues, but none of them provide guidance on the question of whether it would be justified to establish a link between trade and labor standards. GATT Article XXIII establishes a procedural framework to determine whether nonviolation, nullification, or impairment exist, but it does not define them.

13. In the latter case, the "normal value" would not be defined by economic criteria, but by legal ones, namely international labor standards. The use of such criteria is not uncommon in

the framework of the multilateral trading system. For example, the rules on intellectual property rights refer to legal definitions, not economic ones.

14. E. Alben, GATT and the Fair Wage: A Historical Perspective on the Labor-Trade Link, *Colombia Law Review*, Vol. 101, p. 1441.

15. B. A. Langille, Labour Standards in the Globalized Economy and the Free Trade/Fair Trade Debate, in W. Sengenberger and D. Campbell (eds), *International Labour Standards and Economic Interdependence*, International Institute for Labour Studies, Geneva, 1994, p. 332.

16. Some authors overlook this difference; see, for instance, T. H. Moran, Beyond Sweatshops, Foreign Direct Investment and Globalization in Developing Countries, Washington, DC, 2002, p. 77.

17. J. E. Stiglitz and A. Charlton, *Fair Trade For All, How Trade Can Promote Development*, Oxford, 2005 p. 154, argue that "where countries take actions which unfairly affect costs of production, such as restrictions on collective bargaining, . . . trade sanctions may . . . be justified."

18. S. Charnovitz, The Influence of International Labor Standards on the World Trading Regime, p. 574.

19. F. Maupain, New Foundation or New Facade? The ILO and the 2008 Declaration on Social Justice for a Fair Globalization, *The European Journal of International Law*, Vol. 20, 2009, No. 3, p. 825.

20. J. E. Stiglitz and A. Charlton, *Fair Trade For All, How Trade Can Promote Development*, p. 154.

21. There is little chance for any substantial improvements unless labor becomes scarce, see S. Polaski, Trade and Labor Standards, A Strategy for Developing Countries, Trade, Equity, and Development Paper, Carnegie Endowment for International Peace, Washington, DC, 2003, p. 11.

22. This scenario is different from the one where *companies* race to the bottom. I have met investors who prefer countries without trade unions or where women get very low wages. But this is not what is generally referred to as the race to the bottom. Such race would occur where governments lower legal requirements or decide to not implement them fully.

23. See pages 42–44.

24. See pages 78–79.

25. H. Lim, *The Social Clause: Issues and Challenges*, International Labor Organization, Bureau for Workers Activities, Geneva, 2001, p. 25; Organization for Economic Cooperation and Development, International Trade and Core Labour Standards, Paris, 2000, p. 15; R. Robertson, D. Brown, G. Pierre, and M. L. Sanchez-Puerta, Globalization, Wages, and the Quality of Jobs, Five Country Studies, The World Bank, Washington, DC, 2009, p. 37; D. K. Brown, International Trade and Core Labour Standards, A survey of the recent literature, OECD Labour Market and Social Policy Occasional Papers No. 43, Paris, 2000, p. 23.

26. http://unctadstat.unctad.org/wds/TableViewer/tableView.aspx?ReportId=102.

27. In this respect, there is no analogy with CITES and the Montreal Protocol. These agreements prohibit trade of a very limited number of products for very urgent reasons. There is no similarly urgent need to establish a universal prohibition of imports of goods produced under substandard labor conditions.

28. C. Barry and S. G. Reddy, *International Trade and Labor Standards: A Proposal for a Linkage*, New York, 2008, p. 62.

29. The Interpretative Guide on the Corporate Responsibility to Respect Human Rights, prepared by the UN Special Representative on Business and Human Rights (Geneva, 2011), defines "complicity" as one of the "key concepts" of corporate responsibility: ". . . business enterprises may be perceived as being 'complicit' in acts of another party where, for example, they are seen to benefit from an abuse committed by that party . . . such as when it reduces costs because of slave-like practices in its supply chain . . ." Anyone who subsequently takes advantage from such benefits until they reach the final consumer may also be seen as being "complicit." The same applies, *mutatis mutandis*, to countries and their governments.

30. Sometimes referred to as the "solidarity argument."

31. R. M. Stern, Labor Standards and Trade Agreements Research Seminar in International Economics, Discussion Paper no. 496, Ann Arbor, 2003.

32. R. P. McIntyre, *Are Workers Rights Human Rights?* Ann Arbor, 2008, p. 147; R. J. S. Ross, *Slaves to Fashion, Poverty and Abuse in the New Sweatshops*, Ann Arbor, 2004, p. 284.

33. Organization for Economic Cooperation and Development, International Trade and Core Labour Standards, Paris, 2000, p. 14.

34. R. J. Flanagan, *Globalization and Labor Conditions, Working Conditions and Worker Rights in a Global Economy*, Oxford, 2006, pp. 81 and 135; K. E. Maskus, Should Core Labor Standards Be Imposed Through International Trade Policy? The World Bank Development Research Group, Policy Research Working Paper 1817, Washington, DC, 1997.

35. http://stat.wto.org/StatisticalProgram/WSDBViewData.aspx?Language=E.

36. S. Polaski, Trade and Labor Standards, A Strategy for Developing Countries, p. 10.

37. United Nations Development Programme, International Cooperation at a Crossroads: Aid, Trade and Security in an Unequal World, Human Development Report 2005, p. 55; A. Bieler, The Future of the Global Working Class, in A. Bieler, I. Landberg, and D. Pillay, *Labour and the Challenges of Globalization, What Prospects for Transnational Solidarity*? London and Ann Arbor, 2008, p. 10.

38. United Nations Development Programme, International cooperation at a crossroads: Aid, trade and security in an unequal world, Human Development Report 2005, p. 51.

39. International Labour Office, Global Wage Report 2008/09, Minimum wages and collective bargaining: Towards policy coherence, Geneva, 2008, preface; J. G. Palma notes that in the case of Mexico, "as soon as manufacturing became export-oriented . . . it began to behave as if it were a traditional primary commodity sector: wages immediately stagnated, and all productivity growth was either captures by capital or transferred to consumers in the North." See J. G. Palma, Globalizing Inequality: "Centrifugal" and "Centripetal" Forces at Work, UN Secretariat, Department of economic and social affairs, Working Paper No. 35, ST/ESA/2006/DWP/35, September 2006, p. 17.

40. L. Mosley and S. Uno, Racing to the Bottom or Climbing to the top?, Economic Globalization and Collective Labor Rights, *Comparative Political Studies*, Vol. 40, No. 8, August 2007, p. 923.

41. Similarly R. Hensman, Fine-Tuning the Linkage Proposal, in C. Barry and S. G. Reddy, *International Trade and Labor Standards: A Proposal for a Linkage*, New York, 2008, p. 122.

42. K. A. Elliott and R. B. Freeman, Can Labor Stands Improve under Globalization? Institute for International Economics, Washington, DC, 2003 (pp. 89 and 137) propose a link that combines elements of both links proposed here. However, their proposal does not make it sufficiently clear whether it is justified for human rights concerns or unfair competition.

Chapter Five

Alternative Approaches

The conclusion of the previous chapter was that there are two reasons for linking trade and labor standards. It is commonly accepted that trade restrictive measures should not be used if other, "softer" means are available for achieving the same results. The reasons justifying the two links concern certain trade-related effects of imports of goods produced under substandard labor conditions—unfair competition with domestic producers of importing countries and the responsibility of importing countries for violations of labor standards in exporting countries. The only way to remove these effects is to *restrict* trade accordingly. There is no softer alternative.

Of course, the links proposed in this study would not be necessary if labor conditions meet minimum standards in all countries. It would make any link between trade and labor standards redundant. This gives rise to the question of whether labor conditions could be improved in other and possibly better ways than enforcing CLS.

There are three alternative approaches to the one used by the ILO, that is, international harmonization of norms. The first is to promote ethical behavior of consumers, inciting them to give preference to goods produced under fair labor conditions. The second consists of promoting ethical behavior of companies in relations with their employees. The third way is technical and financial assistance.

This section will examine whether these alternative approaches could improve labor conditions to levels similar to those defined by CLS.[1] It will also examine which lessons can be learned from the practical experiences with these approaches for fine-tuning the links proposed in this study.

FAIR TRADE

An increasing number of consumers feel that they share responsibility for poor working conditions and low wages in exporting countries if they consume imported goods produced under such conditions. More and more often, they give preference to goods certified as produced in compliance with certain minimum standards. Some of these goods are offered under the label "fair trade." In 1998, the four main fair trade networks

- Fairtrade Labeling Organizations International (FLO),
- International Fair Trade Association (now the World Fair Trade Organization),
- Network of European Worldshops (NEWS!), and
- European Fair Trade Association (EFTA)

created FINE, an informal association whose aim is to facilitate the development of common standards and guidelines, to harmonize and improve monitoring systems, and to campaign for fair trade.[2] FINE defines fair trade as follows:

> Fair trade is a trading partnership, based on dialogue, transparency, and respect, that seeks greater equity in international trade. It contributes to sustainable development by offering better trading conditions to, and securing the rights of, marginalized producers and workers—especially in the South. Fair trade organizations, backed by consumers, are engaged actively in supporting producers, awareness raising and in campaigning for changes in the rules and practice of conventional international trade.[3]

The earliest fair trade initiatives date back to the time just after World War II. They were started by religious groups such as the Mennonites. The current fair trade movement, which was shaped in Europe in the 1960s, has its roots in the ideas, popular in those times, that the international order, and in particular international trade, was dominated by Western neo-imperialism and unfair to developing countries. The movement remains committed to ethical principles of social and economic justice. More recently, there has been a proliferation of fair trade initiatives and even of organizations which regroup them. Beside the four organizations listed above, other important fair trade organizations are the Fair Trade Federation and the Fair Trade Action Network.

The Meaning of Fair Trade

Fair trade is a social movement and a way of marketing products. What is at stake here is the latter. Fair trade organizations claim that they are selling goods produced under fair conditions. What these organizations consider as fair or unfair are the conditions of certain transactions that happen before international trades actually take place. In that way, the term fair trade may seem misleading. However, savings from low wages and poor working conditions are likely to benefit anyone else in the chain linking the producer to the final consumer. Each subsequent buyer may take advantage of the unfairly low price (wages) paid to the producer (worker). To the extent that the original lack of fairness "contaminates" all following transactions, trade in such goods may indeed be qualified as unfair.

As a non-binding, market-based approach, fair trade does not challenge the principles of free trade. On the contrary, the consumer has a choice between fair trade products and others *because* both can be freely imported.[4]

The Main Features of Fair Trade

Fair trade organizations certify that their products have been produced, traded, processed, and packaged in compliance with the standards adopted by these organizations. Such products are marketed either by the organizations' own supply chains or by other retailers. In the latter case, fair trade organizations charge a fee for using their label.

Choice of Standards

Fair trade organizations certify products as fair trade products if they meet certain requirements. In the late 1990s, fair trade organizations created a standard-setting body, the "Fairtrade Labeling Organization International" (FLO). The standards set up by the FLO concern essentially the level of income of producers in the country of origin of exports. Accordingly, they focus on the first transaction, that by which the original producer sells his product, typically to a cooperative. Fair trade certification attests that producers obtain fair prices for their products and that the goods concerned are produced in accordance with a number of ethical principles. These include certain CLS, human rights, and environmental protection. However, many producers of fair trade products are not employees, but small independent farmers or self-employed. As far as they are concerned, the labor standards requirement does not apply.

Product Coverage

Fair trade started with handicrafts. Gradually, it expanded to agricultural goods. Fair trade certified products currently include bananas, honey, coffee, tea, oranges, cocoa, cotton, fruits and vegetables, juices, nuts, oil seeds, quinoa, rice, spices, sugar, wine, and others. In 2008, the total value of imports certified with the FLO International's Fairtrade label amounted to nearly $5 billion. In certain countries, some fair trade products reach 20–50 percent of all sales in the sector concerned. Although certified imports are rising annually to be approximately 20 percent, they represent only a tiny fraction of world trade in goods.

Monitoring Compliance

Fair trade refers to specific products, not to exporting countries as a whole. Fair trade products are certified as produced by certified producer organizations. Monitoring starts with the initial certification of producers, who have to meet the agreed requirements. Certification is overseen by a certification body, FLO-CERT, which is also responsible for auditing producers and traders and for monitoring the supply chain.

There are numerous claims that fair trade organizations do not enforce their standards in an efficient manner. Apparently, some producers do not strictly adhere to these standards, and certain products are sold as fair trade certified although they do not meet the requirements. This is not the place to investigate the truth of these allegations. Suffice it to say that the organizations concerned find it difficult to rebut these accusations.

The Objective of Fair Trade

The credo of the fair trade movement encompasses most of the arguments that chapter 3 examined as possible reasons for a link between trade and labor standards. It includes concerns about the hardship of producers and workers, the human rights aspect, and the objective of sustainable development. It also highlights the role of international trade, as well as the responsibility of the final consumer in developed countries for the fate of producers in developing countries. These ideas are similar to the reasons which, in my view, warrant the adoption of a link of type B, explained in the previous chapter.

Chapter 3 found that social dumping amounts to unfair competition. Yet, this has nothing to do with the concept of fairness used by fair trade initiatives. While both fair trade and social dumping regard the conditions of labor in the production process, they focus on different aspects. Fair trade cares about the situation of producers in exporting countries, whereas unfair competition concerns the situation of domestic producers of like goods in importing countries. There is no similarity between the concerns underlying fair trade and those which warrant a link of type A.

Evaluation

Fair trade is a market-based approach that treats labor conditions as a private good for which consumers may be willing to pay a premium. It provides consumers with a choice between goods that are and those that are not produced in accordance with the criteria chosen by the relevant organizations. Fair trade appeals first and foremost to those who have faith in the virtues of the market. Some believe in the merits of fair trade *per se*, while others apparently hope that it would make other solutions redundant, in particular rule-based ones.

Any market-based approach is as good as the information available for the consumer. The information provided by fair trade organizations suffers from poorly defined standards and inappropriate monitoring. The increasing volume of fair trade products marketed in developed countries does not necessarily reflect the real benefits for producers in developing countries. Fair trade initiatives have been unable to provide evidence that the premium paid by consumers actually reaches producers. Fair trade clearly falls short of its ambitions. Although fair trade is growing rapidly, it is not a viable approach for ensuring that labor conditions in all countries meet the requirements of CLS.

CODES OF CONDUCT

Codes of conduct are instruments to promote corporate social responsibility. They provide guidelines for minimum labor conditions which are either prepared and adopted by companies for their own business activities or proposed by entities that do not belong to the business world themselves. The latter include politicians, international organizations, NGOs, trade unions, and a number of multi-stakeholder agencies created for that purpose. Some companies use codes of conduct in combination with product labeling, certifying compliance with the codes concerned. Such codes not only require the respect of certain minimum labor conditions, but also invite the consumer to honor this respect by giving preference to the products concerned, in a way similar to fair trade.

Codes of Conduct Prepared by International Organizations

Already in the 1970s, several international organizations saw the need to provide guidelines for the conduct of business by MNEs in foreign countries which were unwilling or unable to enforce their own labor laws.

The UN Global Compact

As early as the mid-1970s, the United Nations Commission on Transnational Corporations (UNCTC) formulated (but never adopted) a code of conduct on transnational corporations. According to this code, "transnational corporations shall respect human rights and fundamental freedoms in the countries in which they operate. In their social and industrial relations, transnational corporations shall not discriminate on the basis of race, color, sex, language, social, national and ethnic origin or political or other opinion."[5]

In 2000, the UN launched the so-called "Global Compact," which is a voluntary initiative under which companies pledge their adherence to ten "universally accepted principles in the area of human rights, labor, environment and anti-corruption . . . and to align their operations and strategies" with these principles. These principles include:

- the protection of internationally proclaimed human rights,
- avoidance of complicity in human rights abuses,
- freedom of association and effective recognition of the right to collective bargaining,
- the elimination of all forms of forced and compulsory labor.

These principles mention the 1998 ILO Declaration on Fundamental Principles and Rights at Work. More than 6,000 companies, including many big ones, have joined the initiative on a voluntary basis. Global Compact also involves workers and civil society organizations, which may participate in monitoring observance of the commitments made. Adherence to the Global Compact does not create any legally binding obligations.

The ILO Tripartite Declaration of Principles on Multinational Companies and Social Policy

This declaration of 1977 frames a number of principles "in the fields of employment, training, conditions of work and life and industrial relations" which governments, employers' and workers' organizations, and multinational enterprises are recommended to observe on a voluntary basis. It was revised in 2000 to take into account the 1998 ILO Declaration on Fundamental Principles and Rights at Work. It addresses issues such as conditions of work and life, freedom of association and rights to collective bargaining, as well as health and safety in areas like job creation, investment in the local economy, subcontracting, and others. It establishes a complaints procedure involving the "standing committee on multinational enterprises" which may investigate and make specific findings of violations of the principles by individual companies. However, the declaration does not provide for any sanctions to enforce observance of the principles which it enshrines.

The OECD Guidelines for Multinational Enterprises

The OECD first established non-binding Guidelines for Multinational Enterprises in 1976 and revised them repeatedly thereafter. These guidelines comprise "recommendations on responsible business conduct addressed by governments to multinational enterprises." Such enterprises are defined as private or state "companies or other entities established in more than one country and so linked that they may coordinate their operations in various ways." The guidelines should be observed by all parent and local entities within multinational enterprises in or from the thirty member states of the OECD and eleven other, non-OECD countries which joined the initiative. They apply both to enterprises producing in adhering countries and to those established in these countries regardless of where they operate.

Since the comprehensive review of June 2000, the guidelines include recommendations in relation to all CLS. They recognize the rights to organize and to bargain collectively, and require employers to provide facilities and information to union representatives so that they may engage in meaningful bargaining. Moreover, they ban discrimination in employment, require advance notice of layoffs and cooperation with unions to mitigate their effects, and call on management not to threaten plant closures or layoffs to influence contract negotiations or to interfere with the right to organize. However, the guidelines limit the abolition of child labor to "exploitative forms." They do not establish any enforcement mechanism to ensure compliance.

Codes of Conduct Prepared by Private Initiatives

Codes of Conduct Prepared by NGOs and Trade Unions

During the 1980s, NGOs started to be interested in labor conditions worldwide, in particular in the garment and footwear sector. Some of them drafted templates for codes of conduct and systems for monitoring compliance. Such templates may be replicated verbatim or used as a tool for drafting codes of conduct of individual companies.

One of the earliest initiatives is the Clean Clothes Campaign (CCC) of 1989, a European network of labor unions and NGOs, with headquarters in the Netherlands and branches in fifteen European countries. The Ethical Trading Initiative (ETI), a British multi-stakeholder organization created in 1998 whose affiliates include companies, NGOs, trade unions, and government, also established a code of conduct based on ILO conventions.

During the 1990s, European social partners agreed charters and codes of conduct for several sectors. In 1995, the European Trade Union Federation of Textiles, Clothing and Leather (ETUF/TCL) (acting on behalf of workers) agreed a charter on child labor and codes of conducts with the employers' organizations of the footwear sector (1995), the textile and clothing sector (1997), and the tanning industry (2000). In 1999, social partners of the retail sector concluded an agreement on fundamental principles and rights at work, modeled upon the 1998 ILO Declaration.

In 1994, Indian human rights groups and rug producers, together with the UNICEF, created the Rugmark Foundation and prepared a code of conduct in order to eliminate child labor in this industry. Manufacturers and retailers of rugs and carpets bind themselves to this code of conduct, which aims at replacing child labor by adult workers and at providing education to children formerly employed to produce rugs.

FIFA, the world governing body for soccer, also adopted a code of conduct for manufacturers of soccer balls, when reports emerged that balls made for the 1996 European championship had been produced by children in Pakistan.

In 1996, President Clinton created the Apparel Industry Partnership (AIP), a coalition of apparel and footwear companies, consumer groups, NGOs, and universities, meant to improve labor conditions in this sector. In 1997, a code of conduct and monitoring principles for the implementation of this code were adopted. In 1998, the Fair Labor Association (FLA), an NGO comprised of manufacturers and retailers, labor and human rights groups, and universities, was established to monitor compliance with this code. It was the first industry-wide scheme in the United States. When the American garment workers union (UNITE) refused to associate itself with this project, a competitor NGO, the Worker Rights Consortium (WRC), was established and prepared a similar code with tighter monitoring. In 1997, companies in the global fashion and clothing industry founded the Worldwide Responsible Apparel Production (WRAP, now Worldwide Responsible Accredited Production). Also in 1997, the Council of Economic Priorities, a public service research organization, founded the business standards group Social Accountability International (SAI), which also drafted a code known as the SA8000.

Corporate social responsibility created new business opportunities in the field of standardizing codes and monitoring compliance. Some NGOs which are active in this field now look and behave like corporations themselves.

Corporate Codes of Conduct of Individual Companies

In the early 1990s, multinational companies sourcing from suppliers in developing countries faced increasing criticism of working conditions in their suppliers' workplaces. Some reputation-sensitive companies saw a need to self-regulate labor conditions in their supply chains. Rather than adhering to one of the codes prepared by the international organizations or NGOs mentioned above, they opted for drafting their own codes of conduct and supplier standards and monitoring performance of their foreign subsidiaries and suppliers themselves. As a result, there is a proliferation of individual company codes, which look similar but differ nonetheless in some important aspects such as the choice of standards and the form of monitoring.

The Main Features of Codes of Conduct

Choice of Standards

There is no general agreement in the business community about standards to be used in codes of conduct. Hence, these codes vary considerably in terms of both scope and ambition. Some codes commit the company to follow certain standards which they define, while others are just a promise to comply with local legislation. Early codes of conduct put the emphasis on child labor, health and safety, and discrimination, but neglected union rights, overtime, and wages. While an inventory prepared by the OECD in 1998 on codes of corporate conduct found that only 18 percent of the codes mentioned international standards such as ILO conventions or UN declarations,[6] many of the more recent codes include a reference to CLS.

The choice of labor standards also depends on the industry adopting a code. Codes of companies producing and marketing garment and apparel usually deal with child labor and often with bonded labor, working environment, and wages.[7]

The CCC, the FLA, the WRC, the AIP, and the ETI have developed definitions and concepts meant to standardize codes. The FLA code is probably the less ambitious one. The WRC code includes higher requirements, in particular concerning living wages. The SA8000 code and the ETI Basic Code contain explicit references to human rights and CLS. The SA8000 code includes a strong clause on freedom of association that calls for companies to provide "parallel means" for worker representation where governments restrict these rights. It also includes a living wage, with guidance on how to measure it in different countries.

Product Coverage

The bulk of trade to which codes of conduct apply concerns MNEs. Since a large part of world trade takes place within MNEs, a significant part of exports from developing countries is covered by such codes. It is clear, though, that the coverage is far from being comprehensive. Moreover, codes of conduct apply only to the products of the companies that adopted them and not to exporting countries as a whole. On the other hand, they generally also cover inputs from third-party suppliers.

Monitoring Compliance

Some companies undertake systematic monitoring, whereas others carry out ad hoc investigations of complaints. Another approach consists of inspections carried out in factories selected at random. While some monitoring schemes provide for the publication of findings, others (like the Rugmark and the AIP code) keep them confidential. In the latter case, the codes of conduct concerned are less likely to have any meaningful impact on consumers' decisions.

Basically, there are three forms of monitoring. Internal monitoring conducted by brands and retailers is obviously the weakest form of monitoring. External auditing carried out by third-party organizations may be done either by professional auditors or accounting firms or by NGOs. Monitoring by a non-affiliated party may also be performed as an independent evaluation conducted by entities not paid by those being monitored. This is usually referred to as verification and is certainly the most credible form of monitoring.

Companies adhering to the Rugmark code of conduct pay licensing fees to the Rugmark foundation, which employs monitors to carry out inspections of these companies. Hence, monitors are independent from the companies that they inspect. In the case of the FIFA code of conduct, the International Confederation of Free Trade Unions (ICFTU) is monitoring the supply chain of football manufacturers. In 1999, the World Bank, Nike, Gap, and several NGOs created the Global Alliance for Workers and Communities to promote independent surveillance of working conditions credible to the public.

In 1997, the SAI created the Social Accountability Accreditation Services (SAAS) which accredits and trains third-party monitors to conduct audits of compliance with social standards, including SA8000. This standard is implemented by a management system similar to that implementing quality assurance (ISO 9001). The auditing process includes an internal procedure for submitting and investigating complaints about and appeals against decisions made by SAAS concerning accreditation and certification.

The FLA, the WRAP, and SAI established global auditing standards and started to train their own auditors. The FLA now inspects randomly some 5 percent of the facilities of any company each year. Inspections are not announced and results are posted on the FLA website. Nonetheless, the FLA's monitoring scheme is often criticized as unreliable because it depends essentially on internal checks. It is widely viewed as a fig leaf since it is funded by the companies that it monitors. Apparently, the FLA has become part of a corporate social responsibility industry that is "compromised, toothless and cozy with its corporate members."[8]

Apple, one of the world's biggest companies, has adopted a very comprehensive code of conduct, using the standards prepared by SAI and ETI. Their code draws on internationally recognized standards such as the Universal Declaration of Human Rights and ILO labor standards, including all CLS. On February 14, 2012, the *New York Times* reported that "Apple . . . pushes an audit in China. . . . For years, Apple has resisted calls for independent scrutiny of the suppliers that make its electronics . . . the company has asked an outside group—a nonprofit financed partly by participating companies like Apple—to publicly identify specific factories where abuses are discovered." Indeed, although Apple's code of conduct includes an ambitious list of standards and requirements, it is remarkably laconic regarding its own monitoring and auditing. It states that "Apple may visit (and/or have external monitors visit) supplier facilities, with or without notice, to assess compliance with this Code . . ." and mentions "Audits and assessments—Periodic self-evaluations to ensure that the Supplier, its subcontractors, and its next-tier Suppliers are complying with this Code and with applicable laws and regulations."[9] According to the newspaper, Apple entrusted the FLA with the task of inspecting its supplier factories in China.

The Binding Force of Codes of Conduct

Whatever the type or origin of codes of conduct may be, such codes are operational only where companies commit themselves to meet the relevant standards. While they may establish legal and enforceable obligations for suppliers, codes of conduct are usually not intended to create rights for any third party. To the extent that they are non-binding, they may be altered or withdrawn at any point in time. However, codes of conduct may acquire legal status and become binding, through the inclusion of relevant clauses in national or sectoral collective agreements. An example is the code of conduct agreed in 1997 between ETUF/TCL, acting on behalf of workers and the European Apparel and Textile Organization (EURATEX, the employers' organization) for the textile and clothing sector.

The Objective of Codes of Conduct

Companies emphasize that corporate codes of conduct express their commitment to social responsibility and accountability. This suggests that their main objective is to ensure that labor conditions meet certain minimum standards. But codes of conduct may also be motivated by more practical considerations. Companies may feel that self-regulation is superior to governmental control. Alternatively, codes of conduct may be intended to make government regulation and union activities redundant, or simply to limit the legal liability of the company concerned.

Apparently, the motives behind codes of conduct have evolved over time. Earlier codes were part of companies' risk management. They reflected companies' more defensive approach, to protect their brand name. Subsequently, some enterprises discovered that a more proactive approach would give them a competitive edge. They also realized that in some instances better working standards increased the efficiency of management and production. Gradually, codes of conduct have become part and parcel of the management system and strategy of a number of important multinational companies. By and large, social responsibility has become a business objective of its own right.

Evaluation

As stated above, codes of conduct may have two positive effects: one is to impose the respect of certain minimum labor conditions on producers, the other one is to convince consumers to give preference to goods produced under such conditions. Yet, there are serious limitations to the effectiveness of codes of conduct in both respects.

As far as the impact of codes of conduct on consumers' behavior is concerned, it is limited for essentially the same reasons as that of fair trade. The proliferation of different codes makes it virtually impossible to know the quality of labor conditions that a specific company promises to offer. And only few monitoring systems guarantee that this promise is actually kept. In general, codes of conduct are not sufficiently trustworthy as to really influence consumers' choices.

As far as the effects on labor conditions are concerned, results are not much better. While codes of conduct may help to eliminate child labor, forced labor, and discrimination, it is beyond their reach to guarantee freedom of association and to protect the right to collective bargaining. They may require the respect of these rights by the companies concerned, but this is to little avail in countries where governments do not grant them.[10] This is likely to be the weakest point of codes of conduct.

Another important factor reducing the effectiveness of codes of conduct is that they are basically limited to the realm of MNEs. Although the share of imports by MNEs is, in certain sectors, very high, some unbranded products remain outside the scope of this approach. As far as the effects of codes of conduct on the behavior of consumers are concerned, these are limited to the consumption of finished products.

Moreover, voluntary codes of conduct suffer from an inherent dilemma. Stricter codes are unlikely to garner broad support by the industry, while weaker standards, which would be acceptable to a majority of producers and retailers, are unlikely to have any meaningful impact. For this and other reasons, codes of conduct differ significantly. As a result, it is extremely difficult for the consumers to evaluate the impact of their preferences for one or another good claimed to be produced in accordance with specific codes of conduct. This, in turn, limits their effectiveness.

The Achilles' heel of codes of conduct is monitoring compliance. In the case of certain retailers, supplies come from a great number of factories sometimes exceeding a thousand. Monitoring each of them by private auditors would require efforts which are beyond the means available. It is simply impossible to verify whether each and every supplier complies with the requirements every day of the year. But there are also structural problems. Internal auditors have an interest to whitewash their companies rather than to identify real problems. External auditors may not have the necessary expertise to assess compliance with the standards defined in the codes. And even if they do, they may not be sufficiently independent if they belong to commercial audit firms that work for the companies concerned under a broader framework. In general, auditing lacks credibility if it is paid for by the companies that are audited.

In certain instances, the ethical goals of social responsibility and the objective of maximizing profits may coincide. Companies have an interest in providing better labor conditions and wages for the sake of higher productivity and in order to promote their image. There are good reasons to assume that higher standards are more profitable when they motivate consumers to give preference to their goods. But there may be instances of conflict between ethical goals and the objective of maximizing profits. I doubt that companies would, for moral reasons, give preference to higher standards if the costs exceeded the benefits. In the final analysis, codes are not a panacea for achieving social justice. In other words, they cannot replace regulations.[11]

Codes of conduct are based on the erroneous belief that law enforcement can be privatized.[12] It is somewhat bewildering that companies promise to respect *binding laws* on a *voluntary basis.* In my view, morals and markets are no alternative for binding norms. Moral considerations are one of the main foundations and sources of laws, but once they have been codified as laws, they have to be enforced and respected, independently from the scruples and preferences of individual consumers and CEOs.

If companies boost themselves by stating that they comply with the domestic labor regulations of the host country, they actually do what they are obliged to do anyway. Turning these laws into self-imposed obligations suggests that the companies concerned have the choice of whether to respect them or not. Although in fact companies may have that choice in countries where law enforcement is weak, leaving it to them is unlikely to solve the problem of poor labor conditions in developing countries. In sum, codes of conduct are not an adequate means to ensure that all countries comply with CLS.

LEGAL MINIMUM WAGES

As mentioned in chapter 2, the level of wages is beyond the scope of CLS. On the other hand, the implementation of freedom of association and the right to collective bargaining are likely to enable unions to insist on acceptable working conditions and wages. However, governments are often quite reluctant to meet the requirements of the conventions on freedom of association and protection of the right to collective bargaining, for fear that unions may become too powerful. In other countries, unions, although allowed, are not powerful enough to negotiate acceptable pay. Many countries therefore opt for an alternative approach, adopting laws that fix minimum wages.

From the outset, the ILO had endorsed this option by preparing a number of conventions concerning the fixing and implementation of minimum wages. The relevant conventions are:

- C26 on Minimum Wage-Fixing Machinery Convention, 1928;
- C99 on Minimum Wage-Fixing Machinery (Agriculture) Convention, 1951;
- C131 on Minimum Wage Fixing Convention, 1970.

In June 2009, the ILO adopted the so-called "Global Jobs Pact," which encourages governments to consider options such as minimum wages. At present, 90 percent of all ILO member states have a minimum wage policy. However, the ILO conventions do not determine the *actual level* of minimum wages. Governments are free to fix that level. Whether in practice this level is anywhere near what it would be if the level of wages could be freely negotiated remains an open question.

Minimum Wages and Poverty

The ILO provides some guidance on what the level of wages should be. The ILO Constitution of 1919 calls for "a wage adequate to maintain a reasonable standard of life." According to the 1998 Declaration, freedom of association and the right to collective bargaining should enable workers "to claim freely and on the basis of equality of opportunity, their fair share of the wealth which they have helped to generate . . ." The 2008 Declaration promotes "policies in regard to wages and earnings, hours and other conditions of work, designed to ensure a just share of the fruits of progress to all and a minimum living wage to all employed." This declaration also supports "decent work for all" which includes opportunities for work "that is productive and delivers fair income . . . and social protection for families."

This language lacks precise criteria. What is "reasonable," "fair," and "just" is in the eye of the beholder. Arguably, a level that is fair and just is higher than one that is reasonable. The most basic claim seems to be the one for a "minimum living wage."

Although there is no commonly accepted definition of the minimum living wage, there is a threshold below which wages clearly do not provide a living. This threshold is the poverty line. Wages that do not take a family out of poverty are below a minimum living wage.[13] Whether this is the case depends on the level of wages, on the size of the family, the number of earners per household, and the definition of poverty.

Defining Poverty

Basically, there are two methods for measuring and defining poverty. The absolute method takes into account the costs of certain goods and services in the country concerned, while the relative method considers the mean disposable income. There is also an international poverty line which the World Bank defines at $2 (at purchasing power parity) per person per day for poverty and a $1.25 poverty line for extreme poverty.

The ILO claims that wages should take into account the economic situation of the country concerned.[14] Consequently, if poverty is used as a reference for assessing the level of wages, they should be compared to the national poverty line of each country. According to the ILO, wages should also take into consideration "the living standards of other social groups."[15] Therefore, the poverty line should be calculated by the relative method. On the contrary, most developing countries use the absolute one to establish their national poverty lines. In many countries, these amounts are astonishingly low, arguably much too low. For this reason and in order to facilitate comparisons, the following assessment of wages will use the international poverty lines of $1.25 and $2.[16]

The Size of a Family and the Number of Earners per Family

In developing countries, the average size of household exceeds 4, while the average number of children per family is approximately 2.5. Wages should feed a family, but not necessarily a bigger household. If wages do not suffice for a couple and their children, it would be difficult to eliminate child labor. If both parents of a family of four work but earn only very low wages, they could not afford to pay anybody to look after the children. Hence, for the purpose of calculating a minimum living wage, the hypothesis should be that there is only one breadwinner per family and that this person has a job that leaves no time for generating any additional income. Accordingly, wages should feed at least four people.

Minimum Wages in Many Developing Countries Do Not Lift a Family Out of Poverty

The ILO provides statistics on the level of minimum wages for ninety-nine countries.[17] In many countries, these wages are not sufficient to lift a family above the international poverty line, and in some cases, not even above the line of extreme poverty. It takes a monthly income of:

- $150 to provide $1.25 a day, and
- $240 to provide $2 a day for a family of four.

According to ILO statistics, minimum wages are:

- in thirty-three countries — below $150, and
- in seventeen countries — between $150 and 240.

In seventeen countries, minimum wages are not enough to provide a living above the level of extreme poverty. In fifty countries, minimum wages are less than $240 a month, or $8 a day. These wages do not lift a family of four out of poverty.

Minimum Wages Are Not an Alternative to CLS

Minimum wages often do not provide a minimum standard of living. Moreover, there is ample evidence that minimum wages are not fully enforced in all countries. The mere existence of the ILO conventions listed above illustrates that there are problems in this respect. Even if a minimum wage policy could raise wages up to an acceptable level, this would most likely result in a trade-off: employers would try to compensate for the additional costs of higher wages by making savings elsewhere, in particular by offering poorer conditions in terms of safety, etc. In essence, minimum wages cannot be regarded as an alternative to granting freedom of association and the right to collective bargaining. In any event, they cannot ensure that labor conditions in all countries reach the level defined by CLS.

TECHNICAL AND FINANCIAL ASSISTANCE

As mentioned above, one of the main tools used by the ILO in order to promote compliance with labor standards is technical and financial assistance. Financial and technical assistance may be provided either in order to promote compliance with labor standards or as compensation for the implementation costs. Another way to improve labor conditions would be to subsidize wages of poor workers.

Technical Assistance

The ILO runs a comprehensive program of technical assistance.[18] Considering the quality of this program, it is fair to say that any country willing to meet CLS would be able to do so. However, the availability of such assistance is, *per se*, no guarantee that its objective is achieved. Technical and financial assistance would not make the links proposed in this study redundant.

Financial Compensation

Arguably, developing countries should be compensated for the costs associated with the implementation of CLS. The EU shares this view. The additional preferences granted under the GSP special incentive arrangements to countries having achieved a satisfactory level of compliance with labor standards are meant to compensate for the costs thereof.[19] While compensation payments may be an incentive for countries to comply with labor standards, they are no alternative ways to ensure such compliance.

Wage Subsidies

Some authors propose direct income transfers to the working poor which, in their view, are more appropriate than trade restrictions.[20] I fail to see how this could be administered without having the effect of subsidizing employers including MNEs and local employers exploiting labor. Moreover, any compensation scheme tends to maintain the conditions which entitle compensation—in this case, poor labor conditions. Wage subsidies are certainly not an alternative to labor standards.

CONCLUSION

The conclusion of chapter 4 was that there are two reasons for establishing links between trade and labor standards. Arguably, there would be no need to adopt these links if all countries were prepared to fully implement CLS. Since this seems to be out of reach, other approaches have been tried to bring labor conditions up to acceptable levels.

As a result of fair trade and codes of conduct, working conditions are determined, to some extent, by the market on which the products concerned are sold. The effectiveness of such market-based approaches hinges upon the dissemination and reliability of information and the importance that consumers attach to ethical considerations. Under present circumstances, fair trade and codes of conduct suffer from shortcomings in the definition of standards of reference and in monitoring compliance.

Some economists propose to create a market for labor standards that would allow consumers in developed countries to pay for higher standards in accordance to the value that they attach to the latter.[21] I find it difficult to imagine how a "market for labor standards" would function. Even if it worked, the efficiency of any market-based approach is necessarily limited by the fact that it relies on voluntary compliance.

The only approach directly addressing the level of wages is a minimum wage policy, which many developing countries have adopted. However, minimum wages, where they exist, are often very low. In many countries, they are below the amount that a family needs to live above the national poverty line of the country concerned. Moreover, compliance with rules on minimum wages is, in general, hardly better than compliance with other labor norms.

Although technical and financial assistance plays an indispensable role in the framework of international efforts to improve labor conditions in developing countries, it cannot achieve full compliance with CLS. The same applies to proposals for compensation schemes for the benefit of countries or individual workers.

While some of the approaches examined in this chapter have certainly helped to improve labor conditions in the world, none of them is likely to achieve results that would make the links proposed in this study redundant.

NOTES

1. This study does not consider other means—such as readjustment policies of importing countries—meant to cushion the effects of imports of goods produced under substandard labor conditions. Measures that do not remove these effects are no alternative to the links proposed in this study.

2. Much of the information used in this section is provided on the websites of fair trade initiatives.

3. http://www.maketradefair.com/en/index.php?file=21052002111743.htm&cat=4&subcat=1&select=5.

4. Part of the fair trade movement campaigns for changing the rules and practice of conventional international trade.

5. Commission on Transnational Corporations, Report on the First Session 17–28 March 1975, E/5655; E/C. 10/6 Economic and Social Council Official Record, Proposed Text of the Draft Code of Conduct on Transnational Corporations, 31 May 1990, 59th session, supplement no. 12.

6. Organization for Economic Cooperation and Development, Working Party of the Trade Committee, Codes of Corporate Conduct: An Inventory, TD/TC/WP(98)74/FINAL of 29 April 1999, p. 4.

7. Organization for Economic Cooperation and Development, Codes of Corporate Conduct: Expanded Review of their Contents, Directorate for Financial, Fiscal and Enterprise Affairs, Working Paper on International Investment, No. 2001/6, May 2001, p. 2.

8. J. Ballinger, Director of Press for Change, a labor rights group, quoted by C. Duhigg and N. Wingfield, BITS; Apple In Shift, Pushes An Audit Of Sites In China, *The New York Times*, February 14, 2012; T. J. Radin, Levi Strauss & Co.: Implementation of Global Sourcing and Operating Guidelines in Latin America, in L. P. Hartman, D. G. Arnold, and R. E. Wokutch (eds), *Rising Above Sweatshops, Innovative Approaches to Global Labor Challenges*, Westport and London, 2003, p. 254.

9. C. Duhigg and N. Wingfield, BITS; Apple In Shift, Pushes An Audit Of Sites In China, *The New York Times*, February 14, 2012. The move was apparently a response to the allegations made by the newspaper in January 2012.

10. S. Barrientos and S. Smith, Do Workers Benefit from Ethical Trade? Assessing Codes of Labour Practice in Global Production Systems, *Third World Quarterly*, Vol. 28, No. 4, 2007, p. 713.

11. R. J. Liubicic, Corporate Codes of Conduct and Labeling Schemes: The Limits and Possibilities of Promoting International Labor Rights Through Private Initiatives, *Law and Policy in International Business*, Vol. 30, No. 1, 1998, p. 114; T. I. Palley, The Child Labor Problem and the Need for International Labor Stands, *Journal of Economic Issues*, Vol. 28, No.

3, September 2002, p. 602; D. O'Rourke, Outsourcing Regulation: Analyzing Nongovernmental Systems of Labor Standards and Monitoring, *The Policy Studies Journal*, Vol. 31, No. 1, 2003, p. 1.

12. C. Woolfson, The Sense of Measure and Societies "without Limit," in *Dialogue & Debate: Labour, Constitution and a Sense of Measure: A Debate with Alain Supiot, Social & Legal Studies*, 2010, 19(2), p. 227.

13. Similarly R. J. S. Ross, *Slaves to Fashion, Poverty and Abuse in the New Sweatshops*, Ann Arbor, 2004, p. 36; D. Steele, The Living Wage Clause in the ETI Base Code—How to Implement It? Project Archive of the European Initiatives on Monitoring and Verification of Codes of Conduct in the Garment and Sportswear Industry, 2000.

14. The third "general principle" listed in Article 427 of the Treaty of Versailles requires "the payment to the employed of a wage adequate to maintain a reasonable standard of life as this is understood in their time and country."

15. Article 3 (a) of ILO Convention No. C131 concerning Minimum Wage Fixing, of 1970.

16. So does the ILO for calculating the number of the working poor.

17. The statistics available when preparing this study were those for 2007. Where compared to other statistics, the latter refer to the same year.

18. See pages 78–79.

19. Recital 2 of Regulation 1998.

20. C. Barry and S. G. Reddy, *International Trade and Labor Standards: A Proposal for a Linkage*, New York, 2008, p. 37.

21. K. A. Elliott and R. B. Freeman, Can Labor Stands Improve under Globalization? Institute for International Economics, Washington, DC, 2003.

Chapter Six

Links in the Trade Regimes and Arrangements of the EU and the US

The realization that the rules of the multilateral trading system do not adequately address the issue of labor standards led both the EU and the United States to do so within the framework of their own trade policies and laws. Both adopted a number of provisions linking trade and labor in various ways. This chapter will examine those provisions which correspond to the definition of a link used in this study or come close to it. As the United States was the first one to adopt such links, this chapter will start with the US experience. It will include non-preferential trade, non-reciprocal preferential trade schemes such as the Generalized System of Preferences (GSP), as well as bilateral and regional preferential trade arrangements.[1]

Some non-reciprocal trade regimes are determined by laws which expire after a number of years. They are usually reauthorized or replaced by similar laws. This applies, first and foremost, to the GSP. Since the intention is to evaluate the practical experience made with clauses linking trade and labor, the present analysis includes legal provisions which are no longer applicable at the time of writing this study. However, this chapter does not endeavor to present a comprehensive historical account of the different clauses that have been adopted or negotiated over the last twenty years or so. The aim is rather to examine the main features of the approaches used thus far, in order to learn how best to shape the links between trade and labor standards proposed in this study. This chapter will, in particular, examine the question whether the existing unilateral and bilateral provisions linking trade and labor are efficient and how their efficiency could be improved.

PRELIMINARY REMARKS

The Objective of Linking Trade to Labor Standards

As already stated repeatedly, the merits of a link have to be evaluated in the light of its objective. This chapter will try, *inter alia*, to identify the purpose of the links that US and EU legislators and trade negotiators decided to establish. That purpose is not always obvious. While all existing links emphasize the importance of respecting certain labor standards, some seem to do so for the sake of the workers concerned, while others appear be motivated by trade-related concerns. Some of the provisions establishing these links include language stating their purpose. But the declared purpose may not necessarily coincide with the real one.

Where the declared objective is to eliminate certain trade-related effects of substandard labor conditions, there is no reason to assume that this hides another agenda. Of course, such trade measures (or only the threat thereof) may convince the governments of exporting countries to remove the underlying labor problems, but this would only be a byproduct. On the other hand, where the declared objective is to improve labor standards in exporting countries, the real intention may be to remove the trade-related effects of substandard labor conditions for which end the solution (or attenuation) of the underlying labor problem is no more than a means.

Moreover, when trying to determine the objective of a link, it has to be kept in mind that while the effects of trade measures on trade are predictable, the effects on labor conditions are uncertain.

Product Coverage

Ultimately, it is the shape of a link and its particular features which will shed the most light on the real intentions behind it. One important feature is the selection of the products which are covered. It should be noted, though, that the question concerning product coverage has two different aspects.

One concerns the choice of sectors where compliance with labor standards is required (in other words, where violations of these standards justify the application of trade measures). If trade measures may be applied when violations occur in any sector of the economy of the exporting country concerned, including sectors not producing for exports, the rationale of the link is probably not trade-related, but rather to improve labor conditions in that country in general. Conversely, if trade measures may be applied only when violations of labor standards occur in sectors producing for export, it may be assumed that the link is meant to reduce certain trade-related effects of such violations.

The other aspect of product coverage is the selection of products to which trade measures apply. If a link authorizes trade measures on all imports from a given country not fully meeting the relevant standards—even those produced in accordance with these standards—it is probably meant to improve labor conditions in that country across the board rather than to address any trade-related effects of substandard conditions. On the contrary, if trade measures are authorized only on imports of goods produced under such conditions, the purpose of the link is more likely to be trade-related.

Compatibility with WTO Rules

The provisions examined in this chapter link labor standards to trade in the framework of the trade laws and agreements of certain countries. Trade laws of WTO members and trade agreements between them have to be compatible with WTO rules. They do not override them. While links adopted on a unilateral, bilateral, and regional basis may come close to the definition of a link used for this study, they lack one element: they do not adjust the rules of the multilateral trading system.

WTO rules apply to trade between WTO members. As far as imports from non-member countries are concerned, WTO members are free to treat them in a way less favorable than imports from other WTO members. In theory, WTO members could ban imports of goods from non-member countries if these goods are produced under substandard labor conditions. This possibility exists for some forty countries and territories which are still not members of the WTO. It did exist, as far as China is concerned, until this country joined the WTO. Nevertheless, both the United States and the EU used to grant China MFN status before that, while the EU even included it in its GSP.

LINKS IN THE TRADE REGIMES AND ARRANGEMENTS OF THE UNITED STATES

The Relevant Provisions

In the United States, political pressure for trade restrictions on imports from countries not respecting minimum labor standards has been particularly strong. As a result, the United States adopted trade laws linking trade and labor in various ways. Subsequently, it insisted on including provisions on labor standards in trade agreements with other countries.

Non-Preferential Trade

Prison Labor. In 1890, the United States adopted the McKinley Tariff Act, which bans imports of goods made by convicts. This ban was repeated by the Smoot-Hawley Tariff Act of 1930, Section 1307, which forbids imports of goods produced with prison or indentured labor. In 1997, Congress expanded Section 1307 provisions to forced or indentured child labor.[2] To the extent that labor as defined in this legislation amounts to forced labor prohibited by the relevant core labor standard, these provisions are similar to a link as defined above: *a provision of international law authorizing countries to regulate the access to their market by adopting discriminatory trade measures in accordance with the level of compliance with core labor standards in the country of origin.*[3]

Child Labor. In 1999, President Clinton signed an executive order, "Prohibition of Acquisition of Products Produced by Forced or Indentured Child Labor." This order applies only to US government procurement.

Denial of Workers' Rights. In 1988, the United States introduced a reference to labor rights into its non-preferential trade regime. Section 301(a) of the Omnibus Trade and Competitiveness Act of that year applies to cases in which the United States Trade Representative (USTR)[4] determines that "(A) the rights of the United States under any trade agreement are being denied" or "(B) an act, policy or practice of a foreign country—(i) violates, or is inconsistent with, the provisions of, or otherwise denies benefits to the United States under, any trade agreement, or (ii) is unjustifiable and burdens or restricts United States commerce." Section 301(b) applies to an act, policy, or practice which, while not denying rights or benefits of the United States under a trade agreement, is nevertheless "unreasonable or discriminatory and burdens or restricts United States commerce." Section 301(d) (3) (B) provides examples of unreasonable acts, among them the denial of workers' rights. If the USTR determines that an act, policy, or practice is actionable under Section 301 and that retaliatory action is appropriate, he or she may "suspend, withdraw, or prevent the application of, benefits of trade agreement concessions," or "impose duties or other import restrictions on the goods of, and fees or restrictions on the services of, such foreign country for such time as the Trade Representative determines appropriate." These provisions contain the essence of a link between trade and labor as defined for the purposes of this study.

Non-Reciprocal Preferential Trade

The GSP and Regional Non-Reciprocal Preferential Schemes. In the early 1970s, GATT contracting parties decided to adopt a set of provisions allowing for special and more favorable treatment for developing countries. These provisions include a waiver from the principle of non-discrimination authorizing developed countries to grant tariff preferences to developing countries without reciprocity under a "Generalized System of Preferences" (GSP).[5] In 1979, GATT contracting parties adopted the so-called "enabling clause" making the basis of GSP permanent.[6]

The GSP of the United States was first implemented in 1976. It authorizes the president to grant duty-free access to the US market for certain products from developing countries and territories. The program generally has a limited period of validity, but has been reauthorized on a regular basis.

In addition to the GSP, the United States established other non-reciprocal preferential schemes for the benefit of developing countries of particular regions. These schemes include the Caribbean Basin Economic Recovery Act of 1983, the Andean Trade Preference Act of 1991, the African Growth and Opportunity Act of 2000, and the Caribbean Basin Trade Partnership Act of 2000, which adds preferences to those granted under the Caribbean Basin Recovery Act of 1983.

The latter act was the first one to include an eligibility criterion referring to workers' rights, limiting the benefit of trade preferences to countries where "workers enjoy reasonable work place conditions and the right to organize and bargain collectively." A similar criterion was included in the GSP when it was re-authorized under the Trade and Tariff Act of 1984. At present, according to Section 2461 of the Trade Act of 1974 (as amended), a country should not be granted GSP status if it:

- has not taken or is not taking steps to afford internationally recognized worker rights in the country (including any designated zone in that country);
- has not implemented its commitments to eliminate the worst forms of child labor.

Do these requirements establish a link as defined above? In particular, do they authorize discriminatory trade measures? Certainly, there is a difference between import restrictions, on the one hand, and the denial or withdrawal of preferential duties, on the other. But the effects are very similar: both result in less favorable treatment as compared to that previously enjoyed or that enjoyed by other countries. The denial of GSP treatment on the grounds that a country does not meet the eligibility criterion concerning the respect of minimum workers' rights is tantamount to a discriminatory trade restriction. Hence, the eligibility criterion concerning the respect of workers' rights corresponds to the above definition of a link.

The Cambodia Textile Agreement. The United States also applied arrangements offering trade incentives. They date back to the times when there were still textile quotas under the Multi Fiber Agreement. In the beginning of 1999, the United States agreed to increase Cambodia's quota allocation under the US-Cambodia textile agreement annually by 14 percent, provided that Cambodia is in "substantial compliance" with its labor laws and internationally recognized labor standards. This provision, too, links trade and labor in accordance with the definition of a link used in this study.

Reciprocal Preferential Trade

In the early 1990s, the United States started to link trade to labor standards in the framework of its Free Trade Agreements (FTAs). Since then, the United States signed and ratified thirteen FTAs with a total of nineteen countries. The first was the North American Free Trade Agreement with Canada and Mexico (NAFTA). In 1993, a side agreement, the North American Agreement on Labor Cooperation (NAALC), was added. Subsequently, the United States concluded eleven bilateral FTAs (with Jordan, Chile, Singapore, Australia, Morocco, Bahrain, Oman, Peru, Colombia, Panama, and Republic of Korea) and one regional agreement, the Central American Free Trade Agreement (CAFTA), with five countries (the Dominican Republic, Costa Rica, El Salvador, Guatemala, Honduras, and Nicaragua). All of the twelve FTAs negotiated by the United States since 1993 (after NAFTA/NAALC) include provisions on labor in the main body of the text.

The NAALC as well as the other twelve FTAs establish *obligations* on the parties to respect certain labor standards. Some of these obligations are enforceable through trade sanctions. A provision that makes an obligation enforceable is, in essence, tantamount to a link between trade and labor standards as defined above. Some of the FTAs contain provisions under which one trading partner has to pay fines if it does not comply with the relevant labor standards, and the other partner, if such fines are not paid, may collect them by suspending trade preferences foreseen under these agreements. These provisions, too, come close to the definition of a link used in this study.

The Compatibility of these Links with WTO Rules

Non-Preferential Trade

US trade laws prohibiting the import of goods made in prisons benefit from the general exception provided under GATT Article XX (e). Arguably, Article VI of the WTO Agreement on Government Procurement covers the executive order concerning government procurement and child labor. In any event, this is not a major issue as the agreement binds and grants rights only to the signatories.

In 1999, the compatibility of Section 301 with WTO rules has been examined in the framework of the WTO Dispute Settlement Procedure.[7] Traditionally, panels refrain from finding trade legislation incompatible with

WTO rules as long as it is not actually applied in a manner inconsistent with these rules. The panel found that Section 301 could be applied in a manner consistent with WTO rules and has not been applied otherwise. The United States made a commitment to apply the relevant provisions in accordance with the rules of the multilateral trading system and got away with it. However, if the United States was to use Section 301 so as to restrict access to its market for imports from a given country on the grounds that that country denies workers' rights, this would hardly be compatible with WTO rules.[8]

Non-Reciprocal Preferential Trade

When GSP preferences are only available to developing countries, they are incompatible with the WTO principle of non-discrimination. This issue has been addressed by the enabling clause of 1979 which refers to the original GATT waiver of 1971, authorizing special and more favorable treatment of developing countries. The 1971 waiver quotes the agreement reached in the framework of UNCTAD in 1968 on the establishment of a "generalized, non-discriminatory, non-reciprocal preferential tariff treatment in the markets of developed countries for products originating in developing countries." These terms suggest that GSP preferences should not discriminate between beneficiary countries.

While the GSP of the United States includes most developing countries as potential beneficiaries, it contains certain selection criteria which exclude some countries from its benefits. These provisions appear incompatible with the requirement of non-discrimination. This question, too, has been addressed by a WTO panel. In 2002, India challenged the special arrangements under which the EU offers additional GSP preferences to a number of countries committed to combating drug production and trafficking. India claimed that these arrangements include discrimination not authorized by the enabling clause. In 2003, a WTO panel ruled that the tariff preferences provided under the GSP have to be identical for all developing countries.[9] In 2004, the Appellate Body reversed the panel's finding and ruled that GSP preferences may differ and "respond positively" to the specific "development, financial and trade needs" of particular developing countries.[10] The Appellate Body also found that the same treatment must be made available to all "similarly-situated" GSP beneficiaries sharing the same development, financial, and trade needs, and that these needs must be assessed according to "objective and transparent criteria." While the Appellate Body conceded that GSP preferences may be granted on a conditional basis, such conditions must be linked to "development objectives."[11]

Does this mean that GSP preferences may be linked to the level of compliance with labor standards in beneficiary countries? Arguably, the respect of workers' rights is an objective and transparent criterion. And arguably, the requirement concerning the respect of workers' rights has a development objective. Indeed, chapter 3 found that the respect of CLS would foster sustainable development. Yet, the question asked by the Appellate Body is whether a developed country *needs* preferential treatment, not whether it *deserves* it. Development needs of a specific country are determined above all by its level of development, as well as any particular difficulties which it is facing and which may hamper its development. Such needs do not depend on a policy in a specific area such as the protection of workers' rights. Hence, preference-giving countries would not be allowed to select GSP beneficiary countries according to their respect of workers' rights. A selection criteria referring to these rights discriminates in a manner incompatible with the rules of the multilateral trading system.

Reciprocal Preferential Trade

The links established under the US FTAs are compatible with WTO rules to the extent that these rules do not apply to FTAs meeting the requirements of GATT Article XXIV.

The Main Features of These Links

The links between trade and labor standards established under US trade laws and arrangements have evolved significantly over the last three decades. Their scope has increased as more and more standards have been included. But their reach is limited by the fact that violations of labor standards are irrelevant unless they are "trade-related" or "affect trade between the parties."

Choice of Labor Standards and Level of Compliance Required

As a result of the country's poor record in terms of ratification of ILO conventions in general and of those on CLS in particular, the United States faces a problem when it comes to using ILO standards as a reference. Referring to the standards of conventions that the United States has not ratified would give the impression that it considers them nonetheless as binding. US laws and treaties try to avoid that impression by defining labor standards without direct reference to ILO standards. As a result, the scope of the relevant legal requirements and commitments is often not entirely clear.

Non-Preferential and Non-Reciprocal Trade. For the purposes of its non-preferential and non-reciprocal trade regimes, the United States has established a list of "internationally recognized worker rights." Section 2467 of the Trade Act of 1974 (as amended) enumerates these rights:

- the right of association,

- the right to organize and bargain collectively,
- a prohibition on the use of any form of forced or compulsory labor,
- a minimum age for the employment of children, and a prohibition on the worst forms of child labor,
- acceptable conditions of work in respect to minimum wages, hours of work, and occupational safety and health.

This list differs from the list of CLS in that it does not include non-discrimination, while it adds "acceptable conditions of work." Moreover, the Trade Act does not define the workers' rights mentioned in any way similar to the ILO conventions relating to the same rights, except for the worst forms of child labor.[12] Finally, it does not require that these standards be fully implemented. It is enough that a country "has taken or is taking steps to afford the internationally recognized workers' rights" mentioned in the law.[13]

Reciprocal Preferential Trade. The NAALC, as well as all the twelve FTAs negotiated by the United States thereafter, include obligations on the parties to respect certain labor standards. The NAALC and nine of these FTAs limit these obligations to a commitment of the signatories to effectively enforce their *own domestic* labor laws. Dispute settlement procedures only apply to matters concerning this obligation.[14] Labor laws are defined as "a Party's statutes or regulations . . . that are directly related to . . . internationally recognized labor principles and rights." These are the labor rights mentioned above. But the FTAs recognize that the parties have the right to establish their own domestic labor standards. While they shall "strive to ensure" that their domestic labor laws comply with these international standards, they are not obliged to do so.

On the other hand, FTAs concluded after 2000 reaffirm the parties' obligations as members of the ILO and their commitments under the 1998 ILO Declaration. In 2007, political parties in the United States agreed on a bipartisan comprise called *New Trade Policy With America,* according to which all future Free Trade Agreements negotiated by the United States shall include an explicit reference to the 1998 Declaration. This declaration explicitly states that CLS are binding for all member countries of the ILO, whether they have ratified the relevant conventions or not. Arguably, the reaffirmation of the commitments under this declaration implies a commitment to enforce CLS.

The latest three FTAs (the Republic of Korea, Colombia, and Peru) are more explicit in this respect. They do not mention the parties' right to establish their own domestic standards anymore, but stipulate that "each party shall adopt and maintain in its statutes and regulations, and practices thereunder, the rights stated in the 1998 Declaration." However, a footnote inserted into the FTAs states that "the obligations set out in [this provision], as they relate to the ILO, refer only to the ILO Declaration." While this declaration lists the CLS, it does not specify the conventions defining them. Apparently, the purpose of this footnote is to clarify that the FTAs do not commit the signatories to respect the terms of these conventions.[15]

Product Coverage

Non-Preferential Trade. The provisions on prison labor as well as those of Section 301 apply to all products imported into the United States.

Non-Reciprocal Preferential Trade. Since the respect of workers' rights is a condition of eligibility to benefit from GSP treatment, the labor standards concerned have to be met in all sectors of the economy of the beneficiary country concerned.[16]

Reciprocal Preferential Trade. The obligation included in the FTAs to enforce domestic labor laws is not limited to any specific production sectors. But failure to effectively enforce these laws is irrelevant unless it is "trade-related" (under the NAALC) or "affects trade between the parties" (under the other FTAs). Hence, the link established under these FTAs is limited to violations of labor rights in sectors producing for exports to the other party or parties.

Monitoring Compliance

The 1988 Omnibus Trade and Competitiveness Act expanded the obligations of the US State Department to submit periodic reports to Congress on compliance by foreign countries with internationally recognized workers' rights. The State Department assesses labor conditions in most countries of the world when preparing its Country Reports on Human Rights.[17]

In 1992, the United States and China concluded a Memorandum of Understanding on prison labor exports, followed by a Statement of Cooperation in 1995. Under these agreements, US embassy staff has the right, upon request, to visit Chinese prisons suspected of operating factories producing goods for exports.

Monitoring the Cambodia Textile Agreement is based on an arrangement that is noteworthy. At the end of 1999, the United States found that Cambodia was not complying with its labor laws and therefore not entitled to the 14 percent increase of the export quota. However, it recognized that some progress had been made and offered 5 percent on the condition that the situation would be monitored by the ILO. In 2000, Cambodia and the ILO reached a monitoring agreement under which factories in Cambodia are inspected by the ILO. The ILO reports quarterly those factories with inadequate working conditions which did not take measures to improve them.[18]

Complaints and Investigations

Non-Reciprocal Preferential Trade. As far as the GSP is concerned, interested organizations and individuals may bring a petition before the GSP Subcommittee, an interagency group of US trade officials, challenging the situation concerning the eligibility of a country in terms of workers' rights protection. The GSP Subcommittee undertakes an investigation of the country's legislation and its practices, relying on ILO conventions and recommendations as benchmarks for interpreting progress.[19] The GSP Subcommittee either summarily rejects a petition, or accepts it for review and makes a final determination as to whether the country meets the eligibility criterion.

Investigations concerning GSP requirements in terms of workers' rights are difficult undertakings. It seems that occasionally, the ILO has been involved in order to clarify the issue—either because the beneficiary country took the initiative to turn to the organization or because the United States made such a proposal and the beneficiary country accepted.[20] Given the broad expertise of the ILO for assessing compliance with labor standards, this is certainly an elegant solution, but one that requires the consent of the country concerned.

Reciprocal Preferential Trade. Under the NAALC, any party with a recognized interest is allowed to file a complaint or petition with the "National Administrative Office" (NAO). In the case of the other FTAs, such petition may be submitted to the USTR. The NAO or the USTR may present the case to the other party, request consultations, and eventually initiate the dispute settlement mechanism.

Dispute Settlement

Non-Reciprocal Preferential Trade. Disputes in connection with the links established under US trade laws may arise not only because these links are used to apply trade restrictions, but also because they are *not* used. In 1990, the International Labor Rights Fund filed a lawsuit seeking judicial review of the Bush administration's application of the GSP eligibility criterion concerning the respect of workers' rights. The court dismissed the complaint on the grounds that granting or withdrawing GSP benefit is not justiciable.[21]

Reciprocal Preferential Trade. FTAs concluded by the United States create their own institutional structure and dispute settlement mechanism for resolving differences which arise between the parties. NAALC procedures concerning differences over alleged violations of labor standards involve four steps: NAO review and consultation, ministerial consultations, evaluation by a committee of experts, and review by a dispute resolution panel. However, only disputes concerning minimum wages, health and safety, and child labor may reach a panel. More recent FTAs submit labor disputes to the same dispute settlement procedures as commercial disputes.

Trade Measures

Non-Preferential Trade. Under Section 301, a country found to deny internationally recognized workers' rights may lose MFN treatment for all products or for those of a particular sector. Trade restrictions may apply to another sector than that where violations of labor standards occur.[22]

Non-Reciprocal Preferential Trade. If the USTR determines that labor conditions in a beneficiary country of non-reciprocal trade preferences do not meet the required standards, he or she may remove a country from the list of beneficiary countries. Such a measure would apply to all products for which trade preferences are normally available under the scheme concerned.[23] In certain cases, though, the United States suspended GSP eligibility only for the exports of certain sectors.[24]

Reciprocal Preferential Trade. In the case of NAALC, an arbitration panel may impose a monetary fine. If a party has to pay a fine because it does not comply with its labor laws, the proceeds must be used to improve compliance in that country. If compensation is not paid, tariff concessions can be withdrawn to the extent necessary to collect the fine.

If a dispute under any of the other FTAs is not resolved, the affected party shall be entitled to take "any appropriate and commensurate measures," including the suspension of trade benefits. Thus, these FTAs foresee the possibility of withdrawing preferential treatment in response to non-enforcement of domestic labor laws.

The Objectives of these Links

Non-Preferential Trade

The provisions of the Smoot-Hawley Tariff Act authorizing import restrictions on goods produced by prison labor do not apply to goods whose domestic production fails to meet the consumption needs of the United States. This suggests that the intention is to grant protection against imports benefiting from the advantage of cheap labor provided by convicts.

The title of the Omnibus Trade and Competitiveness Act leaves little doubt that the legislator had similar intentions when adopting this law.[25] Section 301 is meant to retaliate to "unreasonable" and "unjustifiable" acts, policies, or practices which burden or restrict US trade. Such burdens may result from imports of goods benefiting from a cost advantage because of substandard labor conditions. The objective of trade sanctions that may be applied under Section 301 against countries denying workers' rights is to provide protection against such imports.[26] Hence, the objective of the links established under the Smoot-Hawley Tariff Act and under Section 301 is to fight unfair competition. This is similar to that of link A.

Non-Reciprocal Preferential Trade

Withdrawal of a country from the list of GSP beneficiary countries means a loss of preferential treatment for all imports from that country, regardless whether they cause trade problems or not. This suggests that the primary objective of the eligibility criterion is the promotion of workers' rights in beneficiary countries. On the other hand, GSP provisions do not require full compliance with minimum standards. All a country has to do in order to avoid the loss of preferential treatment is to take steps "to afford internationally recognized worker rights." Besides, the law provides considerable leeway for indulgence toward violators. Indeed, GSP provisions offer a lot of discretion—both in terms of substance and procedure—to the authority empowered to grant or refuse GSP treatment. If the objective was to promote labor protection in developing countries, the link established under the GSP of the United States would appear to be a half-hearted measure.

In light of these considerations, the real objective of this link remains unclear. It may be to promote compliance with internationally recognized labor standards.[27] But it may also be to avoid or reduce trade problems arising from substandard labor conditions. It may be to prevent beneficiary countries from combining the competitive advantage from substandard labor conditions with preferential treatment under the GSP. It may also be to avoid that the United States, as a preference giving country, is seen as supporting the suppression of workers' rights in other countries by granting preferential treatment to their exports. The rationale of the eligibility criterion concerning workers' rights may even be a combination of various objectives, where different lawmakers had different ideas.

Reciprocal Preferential Trade

The terms of the labor provisions in FTAs concluded by the United States indicate that the goal behind linking trade and labor standards is to promote labor protection. Recent FTAs negotiated by the United States explicitly state that the parties shall adopt domestic legislation in line with "internationally recognized workers rights" (or the 1998 ILO Declaration). Moreover, non-compliance is relevant only in case of a "persistent pattern," not a single instance, of failure to enforce labor laws (NAALC) or where a party "fails to effectively enforce its labor laws, through a sustained or recurring course of action." This implies that the objective of these provisions is to improve labor conditions in countries of origin.

However, earlier FTAs recognize that "it is inappropriate to encourage trade or investment by weakening or reducing the protections afforded in domestic labor laws." By the same token, a footnote in the more recent FTAs clarifies that a party may challenge violations of labor standards by another party "only where such violations affect either trade or investment between the two Parties." Moreover, sanctions apply only where the failure to enforce labor standards is trade-related. Likewise, the criteria for fixing the amount of financial compensation refer, *inter alia*, to "the effects on bilateral trade generated by the failure to comply (with labor standards)" (NAALC). In other words, what is relevant is not a violation of labor standards as such, but its effects on trade (and investment). Hence, the real objective of these links is to remove the trade-related effects of non-compliance with labor standards in the importing country, not to promote compliance in the exporting country.

US Policy Concerning International Cooperation in the Area of Labor Protection

Labor protection was an important item on the US political agenda of the last century. The Clayton Antitrust Act of 1914 states the "labor is not an article of commerce" (a passage repeated in Part XIII of the Treaty of Versailles establishing the ILO) and the Wagner Act of 1935 (passed when the United States joined the ILO) embody the ideals of industrial democracy. The United States has also been one of the most active proponents of adopting international labor standards. The ILO was born out of a US initiative. And the United States has been pushing, for many years, for international rules linking trade to labor standards.

This record contrasts both with the situation of the United States as a member of the international community and with the situation at home. As already stated, the United States did not join the ILO until 1934. In 1977, the United States withdrew from the ILO and rejoined only in 1980. So far, the United States has ratified no more than thirteen ILO conventions and only three of the eight conventions on CLS.[28] The official explanation points to the legal and technical constraints that the United States is confronted with when it comes to ratifying international treaties in areas under the states' jurisdiction. Yet, other countries facing similar problems have much better records in terms of ratifications of ILO conventions.

Of course, the lack of ratification of an ILO convention does not necessarily imply that domestic labor conditions in the country fall short of the relevant standards. The position of the United States is that its own legislation basically satisfies the requirements of international labor standards agreed in the framework of the ILO. Many authors have, however, expressed doubts about this[29] and certain carefully drafted observations made by the ILO suggest that the agency tends to share this view. The United States is mostly criticized for its inadequate implementation of the right to collective bargaining as defined in Convention C98.[30] Labor protection has been a matter of dispute and has, to some extent, been unraveled in the United States over the last six decades.

Indeed, the United States's approach to international cooperation in the field of labor protection, in general, and doubts concerning the compatibility of its domestic legislation with certain ILO standards, in particular, put the country's credibility into question. As one author puts it: there is a "major discrepancy between the US' refusal to submit itself to multilateral accountability (through the ILO) and its preparedness to subject others to a form of accountability in which the US acts as the sole legislator, judge, jury, and enforcement authority."[31]

The Application of These Links

The Number of Cases

Non-Preferential Trade. While the United States threatened to use the link between trade and prison labor in order to ban certain imports from China, to my knowledge, Section 301 has never been applied in order to sanction violations of workers' rights in the framework of non-preferential trade. As long as it is not applied, and so cannot be challenged, the issue of its compatibility with WTO rules remains uncertain. There are good reasons to assume that it will never be applied, precisely because this would be incompatible with WTO rules and principles.

Non-Reciprocal Preferential Trade. Section 2462(b) provides that "the President shall not designate any country a beneficiary developing country (of the GSP) . . . if such country has not taken or is not taking steps to afford internationally recognized worker rights to workers in that country." Similarly, Section 2464(b) states that "the President shall . . . withdraw or suspend the designation of any country if . . . as a result of changed circumstances such country would be barred from designation as a beneficiary developing country." Accordingly, the administration is bound to remove from the list of beneficiary countries all those found not to meet worker rights requirements. This, of course, can be avoided by the country concerned if it "takes steps" to do so.

On the whole, the administration has shown little enthusiasm for withdrawing GSP benefits even if there is hardly any doubt that a beneficiary country does not meet the requirements. In general, the administration makes full use of the discretionary power granted by vague terms of the law. If a country abandons the most egregious violations of workers' rights, this will be seen as taking steps in the right direction and GSP benefits will be maintained, even if the situation remains far from full compliance with the standards. Besides, the GSP Committee found that violence against trade unionists is not a reason for withdrawing GSP preferences because it amounts to "violations of human rights" and not workers' rights.[32]

Reciprocal Preferential Trade. Although there have been cases of ministerial consultations on labor disputes in the framework of the NAALC, none has been evaluated by a committee of experts, let alone been examined by an arbitration panel.[33] The same applies to all other FTAs concluded by the United States. The reason may be that these schemes were designed in such a way as to discourage parties from using them. This is, at least, the message of an exchange of letters between the USTR and the government of Jordan indicating that both parties did not anticipate using the dispute settlement procedures.[34]

The Efficiency of these Links

Non-Preferential Trade. Since Section 301 has never been applied because of a denial of workers' rights, the practical effects of these provisions are somewhat limited. The link between trade and prison labor, on the contrary, has been followed up in practice. Imports of goods made in Chinese prisons were a point of contention when the US Congress had to decide on the renewal of China's MFN status. The available information does not allow passing judgment on the efficiency of this link. On the other hand, there have been cases when the threat of using trade restrictions on imports of goods made in prisons prompted action by the governments of the countries concerned.[35]

Non-Reciprocal Preferential Trade. Since the true objective of the link introduced into the GSP is not entirely clear, it is difficult to answer the question of whether it has been achieved. If the objective is to ensure minimum labor conditions in GSP beneficiary countries, this has not been accomplished in any meaningful manner, although the withdrawal of GSP preferences or the threat thereof seem to have persuaded some countries to improve their labor conditions (e.g., Uganda, in the framework of the GSP, and Guatemala, in the framework of the Caribbean Basin Initiative).[36] If the true objective is trade-related, it has not been achieved either, simply because the eligibility criterion concerning the respect of worker rights has very rarely been used.

Reciprocal Preferential Trade. Whether the NAALC has translated into improved labor laws and practices remains unclear.[37] Under the NAALC, sanctions are restricted to areas where problems are either unlikely to occur or can easily be fixed.[38] Its practical effects are bound to remain somewhat limited.

Some authors believe that the labor clauses in the FTAs concluded by the US are unlikely to have tangible effects on labor conditions in signatory countries.[39] In light of the number of cases where these clauses have been applied, it appears that they are also unlikely to resolve any trade problems arising from substandard labor conditions.[40]

The Risk of Protectionist Capture

Any rule authorizing trade restrictions may be used to restrict imports for other purposes or beyond the limits that it states. This is commonly referred to as the "risk of protectionist capture." If the objective is to remove the trade-related effects of imports produced under substandard working conditions in the US market, then the risk is that trade measures are applied even though the legal conditions are not fully met. If the purpose is to encourage the governments of exporting countries to improve labor conditions on their territory, then the risk is that it is used in order to protect domestic industries. Are these risks real and significant?

Some of the links that exist under the United States's unilateral, bilateral, and regional trade arrangements are undoubtedly motivated by the desire to protect the US market. On the other hand, the US administration has been hesitant to make use of these links even when there was no doubt that the legal conditions were met. The risk that these links are used in cases where the conditions are not fulfilled is very slim.

Other links seem to be motivated by the desire to improve labor conditions in exporting countries. It appears that most complaints alleging non-compliance of foreign countries with the requirements of labor protection under the GSP were motivated by genuine concerns about workers' rights. The reluctance with which the US government has responded to *any* petitions clearly shows that it not inclined to use this link with protectionist intent.[41] The risk that it will do so in the future seems to be remote.

Conclusion

The reason why the United States started to link trade and labor standards in its trade laws was the demand of its domestic industries and trade unions for stronger protection against imports of goods produced abroad under substandard labor conditions. However, the minimum standards required under this legislation are defined in vague terms, allowing the government to easily deny the protection that these links could afford. The United States also introduced provisions linking trade and labor standards in its bilateral and regional trade arrangements. These provisions, too, are meant to address trade-related problems, but turned out to be rather toothless (which, apparently, was the intention, as shown by the letter addressed by the US ambassador to Jordan). While this approach to linking trade and labor standards has the advantage of being more easily accepted by lawmakers and trading partners with little sympathy for such a link, it can hardly yield tangible results, whether in terms of protecting domestic industries and jobs or of protecting workers' rights in exporting countries.

LINKS IN THE TRADE REGIMES AND ARRANGEMENTS OF THE EU

Since the launching of the Uruguay Round, the EU supports initiatives to address labor issues in the framework of the multilateral trading system. Realizing that there is strong resistance in some quarters, the EU decided, like the United States, to adopt provisions linking trade to labor standards in its own trade regime, albeit in a less comprehensive manner than the United States. The EU has adopted a strategy promoting the protection of labor rights in the framework of cooperation on trade and sustainable development. This strategy uses alternatives to trade sanctions.

Trade policy is a common policy of the EU. Trade legislation is adopted by the EU as a whole. This includes regulations on tariffs, conclusion of FTAs, and decisions such as granting or withdrawing GSP preferences. Such legislation and decisions are uniformly applied by all twenty-eight member states. The GSP of the EU is managed by the European Commission.

All EU member states have ratified all of the eight ILO conventions on CLS. As a result, they feel entitled to insist that other countries do the same. And they have no political problem in using these standards as explicit references in their trade laws and agreements.

The Relevant Provisions

Non-Reciprocal Preferential Trade

The GSP. The EU has granted trade preferences to developing countries through its GSP since 1971. Its GSP scheme is implemented over cycles of ten years. At the beginning of each cycle, the EU adopts guidelines which are put into practice through successive regulations applying for periods of three to five years.

In 1978, the European Commission proposed that trade preferences under the EU GSP and under the Lomé Convention be made subject to the implementation by beneficiary countries of certain minimum standards.[42] The Council of Ministers did not adopt these proposals. The guidelines for the period 1995 to 2004 were the first ones to establish that GSP benefits may be withdrawn because of violations of labor standards and export of goods made by prison labor. Subsequent regulations include provisions on withdrawing GSP preferences linking trade to labor in the way defined above.[43]

At the same time, the EU decided to offer "special incentive arrangements concerning labor rights and environmental protection" which became operational in 1998. These arrangements offer, upon request, additional trade preferences to countries proving that they are committed to respect labor rights. This "positive conditionality" represents about the softest approach available to regulate access to markets in accordance with the level of labor protection in the exporting country.[44] Nonetheless, positive conditionality fulfills the criteria of a link as defined above.

The special incentive arrangements may be temporarily withdrawn for the same reasons for which normal GSP benefits may be suspended. In addition, they may be withdrawn if the conditions for granting them are not met anymore, "in particular if the national legislation no longer incorporates the relevant conventions or if that legislation is not effectively implemented."[45] As it allows for trade measures in case of non-compliance with labor standards, this provision, too, establishes a link. This is nothing but the flipside of the positive link, already mentioned, between labor rights and the additional trade preferences granted under the special incentive arrangements. It does not present another link in addition to the two mentioned before.

Thus, there are two links under the EU scheme: withdrawal of general preferences because of violations of labor standards, and granting of additional preferences under the special incentive arrangements. Both links have been revised and amended by each of the successive GSP regulations. Since the introduction of the special incentive arrangements concerning labor rights in 1998, there are in total six different versions: that applying in 1998 and 1999,[46] that from 1999 to 2001,[47] that from 2002 to 2004,[48] that from 2005 to 2008,[49] that from 2009 to 2012,[50] and the present one which entered into force in 2012.[51] These different versions reflect the EU's experience with linking trade to labor standards, to be examined in this section. The different versions will be referred to as Regulation 1998, Regulation 1999, Regulation 2002, Regulation 2005, Regulation 2009, and Regulation 2012.

The Cotonou Agreement. The Cotonou Agreement between the EU and its twenty-eight member states and seventy-nine countries from Africa, the Caribbean, and the Pacific (ACP countries) includes a commitment of the parties to respect CLS, as defined by the eight ILO conventions. Drawing from the 1998 ILO Declaration, the relevant article (Article 50) also states that "labor standards should not be used for protectionist purposes." All issues under the purview of the Cotonou Agreement can by brought to the attention of the Council of Ambassadors or the Council of Ministers. If no agreement is reached, a review panel may be set up. So far, the relevant provisions have not been used to discuss the implementation of CLS by ACP countries. In any event, they do not provide for trade measures.

Reciprocal Preferential Trade

In 1995, the EU decided to include in all FTAs a human rights clause, referring to universal or regional instruments in the preamble and setting out specific rules in the body of the agreement. Egregious violations of human rights may be regarded as a "violation of an essential element" of the FTA concerned. When such violation occurs, the other party may ask for consultations and, if these do not solve the issue, it may take "appropriate measures." Thus, there is a possibility to link violations of CLS to trade measures, but it is most unlikely that this would ever be done.

More recent FTAs that the EU has concluded promote the protection of labor rights in the framework of cooperation on trade and sustainable development.[52] The parties commit themselves to apply their own domestic labor laws and not to weaken or reduce the labor protection afforded by these laws in a manner that affects trade or investment. While the parties reaffirm their international obligations as members of the UN and the ILO, and in particular those under the 1998 ILO Declaration and the ILO conventions that they have ratified, they only seek to ensure that their domestic labor laws reflect the level of labor protection defined by these international standards. Differences concerning labor issues may be settled through an independent panel of experts, but none of the provisions relating to labor protection can be enforced through trade measures. None of these FTAs include provisions coming close to a link between trade and labor standards as defined above.

The Compatibility of These Links with WTO Rules

Temporary Withdrawal of General Preferences

The benefit of any arrangements that the EU offers in the framework of its GSP may be temporarily withdrawn for a number of reasons. Earlier regulations included forced labor and exports of goods made by prison labor. Subsequently, violations of all CLS have been added to the list.

Although the suspension of preferential treatment for goods made by prison labor is a discriminatory measure, it would be justified by GATT Article XX (e).[53] No such justification is available, though, for withdrawal on the grounds of violations of CLS. For the reasons mentioned above, preference-giving countries are not allowed to make GSP benefits conditional upon the respect of workers' rights in beneficiary countries. This means that withdrawing such benefits because of violations of labor standards would be incompatible with the rules of the multilateral trading system.

The Special Incentive Arrangement

When India challenged the special arrangements supporting measures to combat drugs,[54] it initially claimed that the special incentive arrangements concerning labor rights would also be incompatible with WTO rules, for the same reasons as the drug regime. Since the complaint concerning the special incentive arrangements concerning labor rights was subsequently withdrawn, the panel did not examine this aspect. In the light of the Appellate Body's ruling,[55] there is little doubt that these arrangements would also been found incompatible with WTO rules and principles.

In 2005, the EU decided to reshape its GSP in order to bring it into line with the requirements of these rulings. Regulation 2005 replaces the special arrangements to combat drug production and trafficking and the special incentive arrangements concerning labor rights and environmental protection, by merging them into a newly created "special incentive arrangement for sustainable development and good governance."[56] In order to qualify for this arrangement, a country has to ratify and effectively implement a number of "core human and labor rights UN/ILO Conventions" and "conventions related to the environment and governance principles." In addition, a country has to be "vulnerable." Vulnerability is defined by a combination of criteria including income per capita, the concentration of GSP-covered exports to the EU on a small number of sectors in the exporting country concerned, and the share of these shipments in total GSP-covered imports of the EU.

The special incentive arrangement for sustainable development and good governance discriminates to the extent that the additional trade preferences are available only to countries that are vulnerable and have ratified and implemented the relevant conventions. As mentioned above, the Appellate Body found that discriminatory treatment may be justified by the "special development needs of developing countries."[57] Does the special incentive arrangement discriminate in accordance with such special needs?

The European Commission explains that

> multiple international conventions and declarations have acknowledged the link between development and the respect of basic human and labor rights, of the environment and of the principles of governance. The failure to honor these basic standards entails particular problems for developing countries. It is therefore appropriate to address the special development needs positively through granting additional GSP preferences to those countries which have taken on board the major international conventions in these areas.[58]

For these countries, the ratification and effective implementation of the relevant conventions represent a special burden. The additional trade preferences are meant to offset this burden and to promote "further economic growth and thereby to respond positively to the need for sustainable development."[59]

However, the "need for sustainable development" is shared by all developing countries and not a *special* development need. As explained above, the issue is not what a country deserves, but what it needs. Development needs depend first and foremost on a country's current level of development and any particular difficulties, which may hinder its future development. The vulnerability criterion certainly allows assessment of the development needs of specific countries. But I fail to see why the special development needs of countries (that are otherwise similarly vulnerable) differ according to the international conventions that they have ratified and implemented. The compatibility of the special incentive arrangement for sustainable development and good governance with the rules and principles of the WTO remains an open question, as long as no panel has answered it.

The Main Features of These Links

Choice of Labor Standards and Level of Compliance Required

Both links that exist in the framework of the EU scheme refer to specific labor standards which have to be implemented (in the case of the special incentive arrangement) or violated (in the case of withdrawal of preferential treatment). Over time, different labor standards have been selected for these purposes.

Temporary Withdrawal of General Preferences. Any preferential arrangements provided by the EU under its GSP—including the general arrangement as well as the special incentive arrangement—can be withdrawn for a number of reasons specified by the GSP regulations. Under earlier regulations, these reasons include "the practice of any form of forced labor as defined in the Geneva Conventions of 25 September 1926 and 7 September 1956 and International Labor Organization (ILO) Conventions nos. 29 and 105"[60] and "exports of goods made by prison labor." Regulation 2002[61] adds "serious and systematic violations of the freedom of association, the right to collective bargaining or the principle of non-discrimination in respect of employment and occupation, or use of child labor, as defined in the relevant ILO Conventions." This addition brings the provisions on withdrawal into line with the list of CLS.

Since the adoption of Regulation 2005, temporary withdrawal may be decided in reply to serious and systematic violations of principles laid down in a total of twenty-seven international agreements.[62] This list includes the eight ILO conventions defining CLS, other "core human and labor rights UN/ILO Conventions" including the UN covenants mentioned in chapter 2, as well as a number of other, less well-known international conventions.

Another reason for withdrawing GSP preferences are "serious and systematic unfair trading practices including those affecting the supply of raw materials, which have an adverse effect on the Union industry and which have not been addressed by the beneficiary country." Such unfair trading practices are not limited to those which are "prohibited or actionable under the WTO Agreements."[63] Arguably, these provisions allow the withdrawal of GSP preferences from countries that exploit a cost advantage resulting from violations of labor standards.

The Special Incentive Arrangement. In its initial form, this arrangement requires that beneficiary countries implement "domestic legislation incorporating the substance of the standards laid down in ILO Conventions nos. 87 and 98 concerning application of the principles of the right to organize and to bargain collectively and Convention 138 concerning the minimum age to employment." Regulation 2002[64] requires national legislation incorporating the substance of all eight ILO conventions concerning CLS. Since the establishment of the special incentive arrangement for sustainable development and good governance in 2005, additional preferences are available for countries which have ratified and effectively implemented the sixteen "core human and labor rights UN/ILO Conventions" mentioned above, and, in addition, eleven "conventions related to the environment and governance principles." Regulation 2012 requires that a country has ratified the same twenty-seven conventions and that "the most recent available conclusions of the monitoring bodies under those conventions (the 'relevant monitoring bodies') do not identify a serious failure to effectively implement any of those conventions."[65]

Two Different Levels of Compliance. While earlier GSP regulations operate a horizontal division of CLS, considering violations of some of them as reasons for withdrawal and the respect of others as a condition for granting the special incentive arrangement, regulations adopted since 2002 include *all* CLS *both* under withdrawal *and* under special incentives. These regulations operate a vertical division in the sense that they refer to two different levels of compliance with labor standards in beneficiary countries.

Qualification for the special incentive arrangement requires a relatively high level of compliance. This arrangement is available for countries which "effectively apply" domestic laws incorporating the relevant standards or "effectively implement" the conventions concerned. If it turns out that compliance no longer reaches that level, the special incentive arrangement may be withdrawn.[66] On the other hand, any arrangement available under the EU GSP may be withdrawn from countries committing "serious and systematic violations" of the standards concerned.[67] The absence of such violations is the minimum level of compliance that all beneficiary countries of the GSP are required to achieve.

Two different levels of compliance create three different situations: that of countries above the higher level, that of those below the lower level, and that of those in between, countries which neither violate labor standards in a serious and systematic manner nor implement the standards effectively (which is probably the situation of the vast majority of beneficiary countries). It may be difficult, in practice, to determine which situation actually prevails in a given country.

Product Coverage

Temporary Withdrawal of General Preferences. As stated above, the absence of serious and systematic violations of the relevant labor standards is the minimum level of compliance that all beneficiary countries of the GSP are required to achieve. This requirement applies to all sectors. The link established by the provisions on temporary withdrawal of general preferences hence covers all products, including those not covered by the GSP and even those not destined for export.

The Special Incentive Arrangement. Under the initial Regulation of 1998, it was not necessary that, to benefit from the special incentive arrangements, a country fully implemented the relevant labor standards in all sectors of its economy. The earlier versions of these arrangements permitted countries to apply "giving details of . . . the measures taken to implement and monitor (the relevant) legislation effectively, any sectoral limits on their application, any breaches observed and a breakdown of such breaches by production sector." Regulation 2002 maintains that "where the legislation is not applied in certain sectors, a country may request the special incentive arrangements only for those sectors in which it is applied." Subsequent regulations do not provide for this option. At present, in order to qualify for the special incentive arrangement for sustainable development and good governance, countries have to implement the relevant legislation in all sectors of their economy.

Monitoring Compliance

In the framework of its GSP, the EU has to monitor compliance with labor standards in beneficiary countries for two purposes. First, it has to check whether there are cases which justify withdrawal of preferences because of serious and systematic violations of labor standards. This applies to all beneficiary countries of the GSP. Second, the EU has to monitor the situation in countries benefiting from the special incentive arrangement in order to determine whether the conditions for granting the benefit of this arrangement continue to hold.[68]

Since 2002, the point of departure for regular monitoring are reports published by other international organizations. As far as compliance with labor standards is concerned, these are the assessments, comments, decisions, recommendations, and conclusions of the various supervisory bodies of the ILO.[69] "However, such reports may be supplemented by other sources of information, provided that they are accurate and reliable. Without prejudice to other sources, this could include information from civil society, social partners, the European Parliament and the Council."[70]

Temporary Withdrawal of General Preferences. GSP preferences may be withdrawn from any beneficiary country that seriously and systematically violates any of the twenty-seven conventions referred to above. The European Commission does not routinely monitor the application of these conventions by all 178 GSP beneficiaries. It does so only if violations of CLS are brought to its knowledge, either by interested parties or via the activities of international agencies. Since 2005, there is a reference to the "conclusions of the relevant monitoring bodies" meaning, in the case of compliance with labor standards, those of the ILO.[71] The European Commission does not check the situation in specific countries unless the findings of surveillance bodies or the information provided by interested parties suggests that there are reasons for doing so.

The Special Incentive Arrangement. One condition for granting the special incentive arrangement is a commitment by the beneficiary country to maintain the ratification of the conventions and their implementing legislation and to accept and fully comply with the monitoring and review mechanism established under the conventions it has ratified.[72] The European Commission is required to keep under review the status of ratification and effective implementation of these conventions.[73] It shall do so by examining the conclusions and recommendations of the relevant monitoring bodies established under these conventions.[74] In practice, the European Commission heavily relies on these mechanisms—provided that the relevant conventions establish such mechanisms. It also shifts the burden to beneficiary countries, requesting them to present proof of effective implementation of the conventions concerned.[75]

Until 2004, a beneficiary country of the special incentive schemes had to certify that specific exports were produced under conditions meeting the requirements of the relevant ILO conventions. This certification had to be provided in a way and form similar to the certification of origin of the goods concerned.[76] Subsequent regulations did away with this requirement.

Complaints, Applications, and Investigations

There are two different types of investigations concerning compliance with labor standards that the EU may carry out in the framework of its GSP. One concerns complaints. It is meant to assess whether violations of these standards warrant temporary withdrawal. The other one concerns applications for the special incentive arrangements. It is aimed at determining whether countries meet the requirements of the latter. Just as for regular monitoring, the point of departure for investigations in the framework of complaints or applications for the special incentive arrangement are reports published by the relevant international organizations.

Temporary Withdrawal of General Preferences. Regulation 1999[77] explicitly states that "temporary withdrawal is not automatic, but shall follow the procedural requirements laid down in the following articles." According to these provisions, any EU member state, any natural or legal person, or association not endowed with legal personality, which can show an interest in withdrawal of GSP preferences, may provide information to the European Commission to justify temporary withdrawal from a beneficiary country for one of the reasons mentioned in the regulation. After consultations with the beneficiary country concerned, the Commission may decide to open an investigation.

If it does, it first has to publish a notice in the Official Journal of the European Union. Until 2012, this notice invited interested parties to submit relevant information and make their views known in writing.[78] The European Commission shall then seek "all information it considers necessary, *inter alia*, the available assessments, comments, decisions, recommendations and conclusions of the relevant monitoring bodies, as appropriate."[79]

Until 2005, GSP regulations laid down that, in the framework of such investigations, the European Commission could "dispatch its own experts to establish on the spot the truth of the allegations made."[80] Subsequent regulations do not mention this possibility. While the Commission is certainly still free to use its own staff or to hire consultants to carry out field research, this would not be in line with the present approach to investigations.

The Special Incentive Arrangement. As far as withdrawal of the benefits granted under the special incentive arrangements are concerned, the procedure is the same as for withdrawal of the general benefits of the GSP, as mentioned above.

While the procedure for examining requests for the special incentive arrangement has changed considerably over the years, the starting point remains the information provided by the applicant country. Along with its application, a country has to give detailed information concerning ratification of the relevant conventions.[81] Earlier versions also required information on the domestic legislation implementing the latter.[82]

Until 2004, applications were subject to a publication procedure. According to Regulation 1999,[83] the European Commission had to examine applications, seeking whatever information it considered necessary, checking this information with any interested parties, and carrying out checks in the requesting country. Regulation 2002 basically maintained this procedure, clarifying that the point of departure for the examination of applications are the assessments, comments, decisions, recommendations, and conclusions of the various supervisory bodies of the ILO.[84]

Regulation 2005 and subsequent regulations do not require publication of applications. They replace prior evaluations by the European Commission with those carried out in the framework of monitoring schemes established by the relevant international organizations and agencies. When considering applications for the arrangement, the European Commission may verify the information it gathered concerning the qualification of applicant countries for the special incentive arrangements with any relevant source.[85]

Dispute Settlement

Decisions to withdraw GSP preferences or to refuse the benefit of the special incentive arrangement to a country that has applied for it may be challenged in court by any importer who, because of such decisions, pays higher import duties. The same applies to decisions to grant the benefit of the special incentive arrangement. Such decisions can be challenged by an operator who imports goods which do *not* benefit from additional preferences. Conversely, third parties without the commercial interests of importers cannot challenge decisions to grant (or refuse) GSP benefits for imports from a particular country on the grounds that the country complies (or does not comply) with certain labor standards.

Trade Measures

The GSP of the EU uses two types of trade measures. Withdrawal of GSP preferences is a trade restricting measure. Conversely, in the framework of the special incentive arrangements, the GSP offers trade preferences in addition to those available under the regular GSP arrangements.

Temporary Withdrawal of General Preferences. The general provisions on temporary withdrawal allow for the suspension of trade preferences "in respect of all or of certain products."[86] This applies to all arrangements, including the special incentive arrangement. As mentioned above, this arrangement may also be withdrawn if the conditions for granting it are no longer met.

The Special Incentive Arrangement. While the earlier versions of the special incentive arrangements concerning labor rights provided for the inclusion only of those sectors which met the requirements, the present arrangement can only be granted if the conditions are fulfilled in all sectors of a beneficiary country. If this is the case, the special incentive arrangement will be granted to all exports from that country covered by this arrangement.[87] These products are basically the same as covered by the regular GSP.

The margin of the additional preferences granted under the special incentive arrangements has been increased by successive regulations. Initially, the additional preferential margin was defined as a percentage of MFN duty rates and subsequently as a flat rate reduction by 3.5 percentage points off MFN rates. Since 2009, imports benefiting from the special incentive arrangements enter the market of the EU duty free.[88]

The Objective of the Links Established under the GSP of the EU

Temporary Withdrawal of General Preferences

Recital 18 of Regulation 2005 explains why GSP benefits may be withdrawn from countries committing serious and systematic violations of certain labor standards: "The reasons for temporary withdrawal should include serious and systematic violations of the principles laid down in the [sixteen human rights and eleven environmental] conventions . . . so as to promote the objectives of those conventions and to ensure that no beneficiary receives unfair advantage through continuous violations of those conventions." Thus, the objective of the rules allowing withdrawal is twofold: to ensure compliance with the relevant standards and to stop unfair competition. The latter objective is the same as that of link A.[89]

The Special Incentive Arrangement

As far as the special incentive arrangement is concerned, its objective is stated in the title. In their initial version, the arrangements were called "special incentive arrangements concerning labor rights and environmental protection." While the title of the present "special incentive arrangement for sustainable development and good governance" does not explicitly mention labor protection anymore, the latter is now conceived as being part and parcel of sustainable development. It seems that the primary objective of the GSP+ is the promotion of sustainable development, including labor protection.

This reading is confirmed by the requirement that beneficiary countries have to maintain ratification of the conventions concerned and to effectively implement them. Moreover, the fact that the products covered by this arrangement are basically the same as covered by the regular GSP suggests that the selection has not been motivated by trade-related considerations, other than those determining the inclusion of products in the GSP in general. There is no reason to doubt that the objective of the special incentive arrangements is to promote sustainable development by ensuring, *inter alia,* a minimum level of labor protection.

However, after the adoption of the special incentive arrangement for sustainable development and good governance, all beneficiaries of the former drug regime were put on the list of beneficiaries of the new arrangement. This suggests that the selection of countries was somewhat result-oriented, meaning that the objective of the GSP+ is not so much to provide incentives for improving compliance with a number of important international conventions, but rather to provide more favorable treatment to certain trading partners. Moreover, with the addition of conventions beyond those on CLS to the list of those that beneficiaries of the special incentive arrangement are required to comply with, the present version does not promote labor standards in the same specific manner as its predecessors.

The Application of these Links

The Number of Cases

The number of instances in which the EU made use of the links established under its GSP is very limited, both in the case of withdrawal and the special incentive arrangement. Countries on the list of beneficiaries of any of the GSP arrangements are likely to stay there, while those that are not on these lists are unlikely to get enlisted.

Temporary Withdrawal of General Preferences. In 1997, the EU decided to temporarily withdraw GSP preferences from Myanmar because of the existence of forced labor in that country.[90] In 2006, the EU took a similar decision concerning Belarus, because of violations of the freedom of association and the right to collective bargaining.[91] In both cases, investigations were opened upon requests submitted by the International Confederation of Free Trade Unions (ICFTU) and the European Trade Union Confederation (ETUC). In the second case, they were joined by the World Confederation of Labor (WCL).

The very small number of decisions to withdraw GSP benefits because of violations of labor rights could be interpreted as meaning that such violations occur only very exceptionally. This, however, is not the case, as shown by the ILO reports quoted above. The EU is rather reluctant to withdraw GSP preferences, even when it would be quite appropriate.[92]

The Special Incentive Arrangement. In 2005, all countries formerly included in the special arrangements for combating drug production and trafficking were admitted to the special arrangement for promoting sustainable development and good governance. Beyond this group of countries, there are only three other beneficiaries, some of which were already included in the former special incentive arrangements concerning labor rights. In total, there were no more than a handful of applications for these arrangements.

The Efficiency of these Links

Temporary Withdrawal of General Preferences. As stated above, the rationale of this link is twofold: it is labor-related and trade-related. In the two cases in which the EU made use of this link it did so for labor-related reasons. The suspension of GSP preferences for Myanmar, decided in 1997, has been maintained to this day, *because* it had no effect on labor conditions in that country. Thus, the efficiency of this link, as far as its labor-related objective is concerned, appears to be somewhat limited.

The Special Incentive Arrangement. The first version of the special incentive arrangements was intended to "reward countries having achieved a satisfactory level of compliance with labor standards and compensate them for the costs thereof."[93] The first applications were submitted by countries that were certain to meet the requirements. These countries were ex-communist countries[94] with good records in terms of ratifications of the relevant ILO conventions.

But the special incentive arrangements were also expected to provide what their title says, namely incentives: "The additional preferences available to vulnerable developing countries under the special incentive arrangement act as an incentive for them to ratify and effectively implement a set of key international conventions . . . in the field of human rights and labor standards, sustainable development and good governance." This happened at least in one case, when El Salvador ratified certain conventions on CLS in order to become eligible for the GSP+. But on the whole, the arrangements hardly accomplished this mission, as shown by the meager number of applications.

Indeed, the offer of additional trade preferences in exchange for higher labor standards did not trigger much enthusiasm. One reason is certainly the modest margin of the additional preferences. Regular GSP preferences, which are unconditional, are generally used for no more than 50 percent of eligible imports. It is not surprising that preferences which are smaller, and also include some conditionality, do not appeal to potential beneficiaries.

To tell the truth, the additional advantages are less generous than they may appear. They suffer from what is commonly described as the erosion of preferences. For many products, the MFN duty rate is zero or close to it. Moreover, there is no additional benefit for products on which duties are suspended under the regular GSP arrangements. There is no additional benefit either for countries enjoying duty-free access to the EU market under other arrangements, like LDCs do under EBA[95] or ACP countries under the Cotonou agreement.

Another reason for the lack of success of the special incentive arrangements may be that "some beneficiary countries have preferred not to have the content and implementation of their social legislation subjected to the rigors of scrutiny. The length and relative complexity of the valuation procedures have probably made the arrangements even less attractive."[96]

It should also be noted that the immediate benefits of the additional trade preferences available under the special incentive schemes are not for the beneficiary countries concerned, but for importers who would have to pay the duties that are waived under the scheme. The only benefit that an exporting country is sure to reap under the special incentive arrangements is the commercial advantage deriving from the fact that importers have to pay lower duties. Apparently, this is not enough to motivate governments to fully comply with CLS.

The Risk of Protectionist Capture

As stated above, general GSP benefits may be withdrawn for a number of reasons, including trade-related ones.[97] The special incentive arrangements may be withdrawn if the conditions for granting them are no longer fulfilled. Since these provisions have never been invoked in practice, it is unlikely that they will be applied with the intention to protect domestic producers in the future.

It is also noteworthy that EU regulations provide that, if there are reasons for applying anti-dumping or countervailing measures, GSP benefits should not be withdrawn for the same reasons.[98] This provision is meant to avoid double sanctions. The intention is to *prevent* protectionism.

Conclusion

The special arrangements for the protection of labor rights and sustainable development are undoubtedly the most ambitious innovations of the EU GSP. A great deal of persuasion and negotiation was necessary to accomplish them. Much publicity accompanied those efforts. And yet they produced only meager results. Rather than encouraging developing countries to improve labor conditions in order to qualify for the special incentive scheme, the benefits of the scheme were granted to reward countries having already met the requirements. The EU itself implicitly passed judgment on the special incentive arrangements concerning labor rights when it discontinued it as a separate arrangement.

The explanatory memorandum prepared by the European Commission along with its proposal to extend the 2008 Regulation clearly hints to the shortcomings of these arrangements:

> The scheme will place more responsibility for countries and require stricter scrutiny of eligibility by the EU. There will be a more effective and transparent mechanism for monitoring and evaluating the implementation of relevant international conventions, whereby the EU seeks noticeable stability and improvement over time in countries' implementation record. This effectively raises the requirements for beneficiary countries, as they have to provide positive and regular proof that they are indeed implementing conventions.[99]

These remarks suggest that there was and still is much room for improvements.

LESSONS FROM THE LINKS ADOPTED BY THE EU AND THE UNITED STATES

The Compatibility of These Links with WTO Rules

Except in the framework of reciprocal preferential trade arrangements, a link between trade and labor standards as defined for the purposes of this study would be incompatible with GATT rules and principles. Linking trade to labor standards under national trade laws is therefore likely to give rise to challenges by trading partners. So far, neither the EU nor the United States have made extensive use of the links existing in their respective trade laws. If they had done so, they would have been soon reminded that present WTO rules leave very little room for linking trade and labor.

Choice of Labor Standards and Level of Compliance Required

Both the EU and the United States started linking trade and labor standards in their own trade legislation before the adoption of the 1998 ILO Declaration, that is, before the definition of CLS. Thereafter, these standards became the "natural" reference.[100] While US laws and arrangements gradually came closer to that reference—even though they are still differ—the EU immediately used these standards for the purposes of its GSP.

As far as the level of compliance is concerned, the United States is satisfied if countries are "taking steps to improve labor standards," whereas EU laws require that the relevant standards are effectively implemented.[101] Under the EU scheme, withdrawal of GSP benefits requires "serious and systematic violations" of the standards concerned. These are very heavy terms. Apparently, both the United States and the EU are eager to maintain a large margin of discretion when it comes to the practical application of these provisions.

Monitoring Compliance

In its initial shape, the EU special incentive arrangement concerning labor rights established a double conditionality. First, *countries* had to qualify for the benefit of these arrangements. In addition, all *exports* from that country (including all inputs, even imported ones) had to be certified as having been manufactured in accordance with the labor standards concerned. The latter requirement turned out to be not viable for all practical purposes.

The earlier versions of the EU special incentive arrangements concerning labor rights also charged the European Commission to investigate itself whether an applicant country actually fulfilled the conditions for being granted the benefit of the scheme. The lesson learned was that outside the ILO, there is virtually no competent expert to carry out the required field studies and assessments. More recent versions of the EU GSP therefore include references to the activities and findings of the ILO (and other agencies concerned). It seems that the United States, too, is prepared to involve the ILO provided that the country to be investigated agrees.

While the US attempts to monitor compliance with labor standards through its embassies and other means, the EU continues to use a shortcut approach focusing on the question of whether a country has signed and ratified the ILO conventions enshrining the labor standards concerned. This approach grants beneficiary countries a far-reaching benefit of the doubt, as no further questions are asked unless there are obvious reasons to do so. While such an approach has the appeal of being simple, it seems to be somehow disconnected from the real world.

In essence, it appears that there is no alternative to charging the ILO with monitoring compliance with labor standards.

The Efficiency of These Links

Both the United States and the EU have linked trade to labor standards in different ways, but none of these links has proven to be particularly efficient, either as an instrument for resolving trade problems or as a tool for improving labor conditions. In general, the authorities empowered to use these links hesitate to do so. As a result, they are not felt as a threat that might induce governments to improve compliance with labor standards. And even where they were used, they turned out to be rather toothless.

Reluctance to Use the Links

The rules establishing the links in EU and US trade law grant considerable discretionary power to the authority entrusted to decide the application of trade restrictions. A lack of clarity concerning the criteria determining whether the exporting countries actually comply with the relevant labor standards adds even more leeway. More often than not, this leeway is used for not deciding trade restrictions in cases where such a decision would be warranted. This reluctance has various reasons.

One concerns the relations with the governments of the countries concerned. Various scholars have examined the manner in which American presidents exercised their authority to remove developing countries from the list of GSP beneficiaries. In their view, the gravity of violations in certain countries would have warranted a more frequent use of such measures.[102] But the administration has been rather reluctant to use them, not least because of the likely political repercussions.

Another perhaps less obvious reason is the interest and influence of importers. GSP trade preferences which provide preferential treatment to imports from beneficiary countries actually amounts to a gift for importers.

While exporting countries are likely to enhance their exports, they receive no immediate economic benefit. The immediate economic benefit of paying no duties or lower duties remains in the importing country. It is similar to a tax cut. Importers often strongly lobby to keep it. This provides another explanation why the links available under the EU and US GSP have not been used more frequently.[103]

Neither the EU nor the United States have used the links existing in their trade laws and agreements very frequently. Hence, the risk of protectionist abuse seems to be remote. There is rather a risk that the opposite occurs: A link that leaves too much discretion to the executive may not be used often enough.

Lack of Leverage

As a result of the restricted use of the links provided by EU and US trade laws, their effectiveness has been limited. Links may persuade governments to improve labor conditions not only if they are actually confronting trade restrictions, but also if they feel a threat that such restrictions may be applied. On the other hand, if trade restrictions are decided only very exceptionally, there is no reason to fear them.

But even when trade restrictions were decided, they turned out to be rather inefficient. The main reason is the fact that GSP preferences do not provide much leverage. Certain products which are sensitive for the EU and the United States—and which are important for developing countries—are not included in the GSP. In addition, preferential treatment does not apply to products which anyway enter the markets of the EU or the United States duty free. Moreover, GSP treatment is not the only preferential treatment available. Finally, as a result of the Uruguay Round, tariffs have decreased considerably and preferences were eroded accordingly. They have lost a good deal of their economic interest.

Conclusion

Both the EU and the United States address the issue of linking trade to labor standards within the framework of their own trade policies and legislation. However, the policies of the EU and the United States are quite different. While the United States remains attached to sanctions, the EU uses "positive conditionality." Yet, both approaches are not very efficient. As one author puts it: "There is not much room between the dead end track of non-negotiable sanctions and the futility of nominal commitments."[104]

NOTES

1. Some countries like Canada and Chile that negotiated Free Trade Agreements (FTAs) containing labor clauses with the United States subsequently negotiated FTAs with other countries with include similar provisions.

2. Organization for Economic Cooperation and Development, International Trade and Core Labour Standards, Paris, 2000, p. 68.

3. Except that these are not provisions of international law.

4. The USTR is a cabinet-level official serving under the direction of the president. He or she has certain responsibilities which in other countries belong to the Ministry for Trade.

5. Decision of the Contracting Parties of 25 June 1971, relating to the establishment of generalized, non-reciprocal and non-discriminatory preferences beneficial to the developing countries (BISD 18S/24).

6. Decision of the Contracting Parties of 28 November 1979, on differential and more favorable treatment, reciprocity and fuller participation of developing countries ("Enabling Clause") (L/4903).

7. http://www.wto.org/english/tratop_e/dispu_e/cases_e/ds152_e.htm.

8. T. A. Amato, Labor Rights Conditionality: United States Trade Legislation and the International Trade Order, *New York University Law Review*, Vol. 65, 1990, p. 95.

9. With the exception of "least developed countries" and countries which can no longer claim to be developing countries.

10. Appellate Body Report, European Communities—Conditions for the Granting of Tariff preferences to Developing Countries, 128, 173, WT/DS246/AB/R of 7 April 2004.

11. The Appellate Body was criticized for legitimizing the use of GSP preferences as a foreign policy tool, but this was certainly not its intention; see United Nations Conference on Trade and Development, GSP Newsletter, Number 6, November 2005, UNCTAD/DITC/TNCD/MISC/2005/5, p. 4.

12. Section 2467 repeats *verbatim* Article 3 of ILO Convention C182 Worst Forms of Child Labor of 1999.

13. The template of Appendix B to the State Department's annual Country Report states that the flexibility offered by this language covers only standards on "*acceptable conditions of work in respect to minimum wages, hours of work, and occupational safety and health*," which are linked to a country's economic and social development. It is clear, though, that there is no flexibility as far as the worst forms of child labor are concerned. These forms have to be effectively eliminated.

14. As the NAALC limits sanctions to violations of laws concerning child labor, minimum wage, and occupational health and safety, it links trade only to these standards. Only one of them—child labor—is a core labor standard.

15. The provision on "Labor Cooperation and Capacity Building Mechanism" included in these FTAs refers to the principles of the 1998 ILO Declaration and Convention C182 on the worst forms of child labor, singling out the latter. But this may be because it was adopted after the 1998 Declaration.

16. Even in sectors not covered by the GSP such as textiles.

17. United States General Accounting Office, International Trade, Comparison of the US and European Union Preference Programs, Report of the Chairman, Subcommittee on Trade, Committee on Ways and Means, House of Representatives, Washington, DC, June 2001, GAO-01-647.

18. R. Robertson, D. Brown, G. Pierre, M. L. Sanchez-Puerta (eds), Globalization, Wages, and the Quality of Jobs, Five Country Studies, The World Bank, Washington, DC, 2009. pp. 50 and 106.

19. Organization for Economic Cooperation and Development, Trade, Employment and Labour Standards: A Study of Core Workers' Rights and International Trade, Paris, 1996.

20. This information was provided in conversations with ILO officials. A similar arrangement was put in place in the framework of the Cambodia Textile Agreement.

21. US District Court for the District of Columbia, International Labor Rights Education and Research Fund versus Bush, 752, 752 F. Supp. 495 (D.D.C.1990).

22. P. Alston, Labor Rights Provisions in US Trade Laws, "Aggressive Unilateralism"? in L. A. Compa and S. F. Diamond (eds), *Human Rights, Labor Rights, and International Trade*, Philadelphia, 1996, p. 73.

23. In the case of the GSP, this includes roughly half the total number of tariff positions of the Harmonized Commodity Description and Coding System (HS).

24. Pakistan in 1995 for hand-knitted and woven carpets, sporting goods, and surgical instruments because of child labor, Indonesia in 1997 and 1998 for seven products because of non-respect of freedom of association.

25. T. A. Amato, Labor Rights Conditionality: United States Trade Legislation and the International Trade Order, p. 120.

26. P. Alston, Labor Rights Provisions in US Trade Laws, "Aggressive Unilateralism"? p. 84.

27. Most authors take this for granted and evaluate the efficiency of this link on the basis of this criterion.

28. C105, C111, and C182.

29. R. P. McIntyre, *Are Workers Rights Human Rights?* Ann Arbor, 2008, pp. 77 and 107; J. A. Gross, Takin' It to the Man: Human Rights at the American Workplace, in J. A. Gross and L. Compa (eds), *Human Rights in Labor and Employment Relations: International and Domestic Perspectives*, Labor and Employment Relations Association, Champaign, 2009, p. 32; L. Compa, Workers' Freedom of Association in the United States, The Gap between Ideals and Practice, in J. A. Gross, (ed), *Workers' Rights as Human Rights*, Ithaca, 2003, p. 23; J. A. Gross, A Long Overdue Beginning, in J. A. Gross, (ed), *Workers' Rights as Human Rights*, Ithaca, 2003, p. 1.

30. International Labour Organization, Governing Body, 349th report (2008) of the Committee on Freedom of Association, paragraph 805, Case No. 2524 (US), GB.301/8, 301st session, Geneva, March 2008.

31. P. Alston, Labor Rights Provisions in US Trade Laws, "Aggressive Unilateralism"? p. 87.

32. T. Collingsworth, International Workers Rights Enforcement, Proposals Following a Test Case, L. A. Compa and S. F. Diamond (eds), *Human Rights, Labor Rights, and International Trade*, Philadelphia, 1996, p. 233.

33. See table at http://www.naalc.org/public_communications.htm.

34. K. A. Elliott and R. B. Freeman, Can Labor Stands Improve under Globalization? Institute for International Economics, Washington, DC, 2003, p. 87.

35. S. Charnovitz, The Influence of International Labor Standards on the World Trading Regime, *International Labour Review*, Vol. 126, No. 5, Sept.–Oct. 1987, p. 570.

36. H. Lim, *The Social Clause: Issues and Challenges*, International Labor Organization, Bureau for Workers Activities, Geneva, 2001, p. 30.

37. J. McFadyen, NAFTA Supplemental Agreements: Four Year Review, Institute for International Economics, Working Paper 98–4, Washington, DC.

38. K. A. Elliott, Fin(d)ing Our Way on Trade and Labor Standards? Institute for International Economics, Washington DC, Policy Brief 01–5, 2001.

39. R. J. Flanagan, *Globalization and Labor Conditions, Working Conditions and Worker Rights in a Global Economy*, Oxford, 2006, p. 171.

40. K. A. Elliott and R. B. Freeman, Can Labor Stands Improve under Globalization? p. 75.

41. K. A. Elliott and R. B. Freeman, Can Labor Stands Improve under Globalization? p. 80.

42. European Commission, Commission Communication to the Council: Development Cooperation and the observance of certain international standards governing working conditions, COM (78) 492 final of 10 November 1978.

43. Except that it is a provision of EU law. During the preparatory negotiations of Regulation 2002, the Commission proposed a provision linking withdrawal of GSP preferences to decisions taken by the ILO under Article 33 of its Constitution. Member states did not agree.

44. The preference given by the EU to an incentive approach mirrors its predilection for "soft power."

45. Article 26 (3) (a) of Council Regulation (EC) No 2501/2001 of 10 December 2001 applying a scheme of generalized tariff preferences for the period from 1 January 2002 to 31 December 2004, OJ L 346 of 31 December 2001, p. 1.

46. Council Regulation (EC) No 1154/98 of 25 May 1998 applying the special incentive arrangements concerning labour rights and environmental protection provided for in Articles 7 and 8 of Regulations (EC) No 3281/94 and (EC) No 1256/96 applying multiannual schemes of generalized tariff preferences in respect of certain industrial and agricultural products originating in developing countries, OJEC L 160 of 4 June 1998, p. 1.

47. Council Regulation (EC) No 2820/98 of 21 December 1998 applying a multiannual scheme of generalized tariff preferences for the period 1 July 1999 to 31 December 2001, OJEC L 357 of 30 December 1998, p. 1.

48. Council Regulation (EC) No 2501/2001 of 10 December 2001 applying a scheme of generalized tariff preferences for the period from 1 January 2002 to 31 December 2004, OJ L 346 of 31 December 2001, p. 1.

49. Council Regulation (EC) No 980/2005 of 27 June 2005 applying a scheme of generalized tariff preferences, OJ L 169 of 30 June 2005, p. 1.

50. Council Regulation (EC) No 732/2008 of 22 July 2008 applying a scheme of generalized tariff preferences for the period from 1 January 2009 to 31 December 2011 and amending Regulations (EC) No 552/97, (EC) No 1933/2006 and Commission Regulations (EC) No 1100/2006 and (EC) No 964/2007, OJ L 211 of 6 August 2008, p. 1.

51. Regulation (EU) No 978/2012 of the European Parliament and of the Council of 25 October 2012 applying a scheme of generalized tariff preferences and repealing Council Regulation (EC) No 732/2008, OJ L 303 of 31 October 2012, p. 1.

52. See for example the FTA with the Republic of Korea.

53. GSP regulations would allow withdrawing GSP preferences for *all* exports from a country exporting *some* goods made in prisons. This goes beyond the exception granted under GATT Article XX (e).

54. Also referred to as the "drug regime."

55. Appellate Body Report, European Communities—Conditions for the Granting of Tariff preferences to Developing Countries, 128, 173, WT/DS246/AB/R of 7 April 2004.

56. Also referred to as "GSP+."

57. The EU GSP provides for graduation (meaning elimination from the list of beneficiary countries) of countries that have reached certain levels of economic development or trade performance. It is fair to say that the countries meeting the relevant criteria do not have the same development needs anymore.

58. European Commission, Communication from the Commission to the Council, the European Parliament and the European Economic and Social Council: Development countries, international trade and sustainable development: The function of the Community's generalized system of preferences (GSP) for the ten-year period from 2006 to 2015, COM (2004) 461 final of 7 July 2004, paragraph 6.5

59. Originally Regulation 2005, recital 7; at present Regulation 2012, recital 11.

60. These are the two ILO conventions specifying the core labor standard "elimination of all forms of forced or compulsory labor."

61. Adopted after the 1998 ILO Declaration defining core labor standards. Recital 22 of Regulation 2002 explicitly refers to that declaration in the context of withdrawal.

62. Regulation 2012, Article 19 (1) (a) and Annex VIII.

63. Regulation 2012, Article 19 (1) (d).

64. Adopted after the 1998 ILO Declaration defining core labor standards. Recital 18 of Regulation 2002 explicitly refers to that declaration for the purpose of the special incentive arrangements.

65. Regulation 2012, Article 9 (1) (b).

66. Withdrawal of the special incentive arrangements does not necessarily entail withdrawal of normal GSP preferences.

67. This applies also to the special incentive arrangements. The possibility to withdraw the benefit of these arrangements *because of serious and systematic violations* of the relevant

conventions is clearly redundant, since a lack of effective implementation is enough to justify withdrawal.

68. The examination of *applications* for the benefit of the special incentive arrangement is dealt with under the following heading concerning complaints and investigations.

69. Regulation 2002, Article 28 (3). This provision includes a reference to ILO Article 33 procedures, but does not establish a link between decisions taken under that provision and withdrawal of GSP preferences.

70. Regulation 2012, Recital 15.

71. Regulation 2005, Article 16 (1) (a).

72. Regulation 2012, Article 9 (1) (d) and Article 10 (2).

73. Regulation 2012, Article 13 (1).

74. Regulation 2012, Recital 14.

75. Regulation 2012, Article 15 (2).

76. Regulation 1999, Article 14.

77. Article 22 (2).

78. Regulation 2005, Article 19.

79. Regulation 2012, Article 19 (6).

80. Regulation 2002, Article 24 (2).

81. Regulation 2012, Article 10 (2).

82. Regulation 2005, Article 10 (2).

83. Article 12.

84. Recital 19.

85. Regulation 2005, Article 11 (1); Regulation 2012, Recital 15.

86. Regulation 2012 Article 19 (1).

87. Although it may be temporarily withdrawn but only in certain sectors.

88. Until 2008, the additional preferences were also available when countries had lost the benefit of regular GSP preferences, either as a result of a comparatively high level of development or of a comparatively high trade performance. Regulation 2008 does away with this additional benefit, Article 7 (3).

89. Arguably, the concern is competition between different GSP beneficiaries, not with European industries.

90. Withdrawal has been maintained by all subsequent GSP regulations.

91. Council Regulation (EC) No 1933/2006 of 21 December 2006 temporarily withdrawing access to the generalized tariff preferences from the Republic of Belarus, OJ Council Regulation (EC) No 552/97 of 24 March 1997 temporarily withdrawing tariff preferences from the Union of Myanmar, OJEC L 85 of 27 March 1997, p. 8. L 405, 30 December 2006, p. 35.

92. This does not only apply to violations of workers' rights, but to all reasons which may justify withdrawal.

93. Regulation 1998, Recital 2.

94. In the early 1990s, the benefit of the EU GSP scheme was expanded to most transitional economies.

95. "Everything But Arms," which is a special GSP arrangement for least developed countries granting them unrestricted access to the market of the EU for all products but arms.

96. European Commission, Communication from the Commission to the Council, the European Parliament and the European Economic and Social Council: Development countries, international trade and sustainable development: The function of the Community's generalized system of preferences (GSP) for the ten-year period from 2006 to 2015, COM (2004) 461 final of 7 July 2004, paragraph 6.5.

97. Regulation 2005, Recital 18.

98. Regulation 2012, Article 19 (2).

99. European Commission, Proposal for a Regulation of the European Parliament and of the Council applying a scheme of generalized tariff preferences, Explanatory memorandum, COM(2011) 241 final of 10 May 2011.

100. In 2013, two-thirds of all existing trade agreements containing labor provisions referred to ILO instruments. See J. Agusti-Panareda, F. C. Ebert and D. LeClercq, Labour Provisions in

Free Trade Agreements: Fostering their Consistency with the ILO Standards System, International Labour Office, Geneva, 2014, p. 8.

101. However, the flexibility in US trade laws does not apply to all standards. At an early stage, the EU as well used the terms "taken steps to comply with the ILO Conventions in question," see Regulation 1999, Recital 21.

102. P. Alston, Labor Rights Provisions in US Trade Laws, "Aggressive Unilateralism"?, p. 79.

103. This may be the reason why the links under the EU and US GSP have generally not been used with protectionist intentions.

104. K. A. Elliott, Labor Standards and the Free Trade Area of the Americas, Institute for International Economics, Washington, DC, Aug. 2003.

Chapter Seven

The Shape of the Links Proposed in this Study

Chapters 3 and 4 discussed various reasons that may justify a link between trade and labor standards. For the purpose of that examination, we used a basic definition of a link, describing it as *a provision of international law authorizing countries to regulate the access to their market by adopting discriminatory trade measures in accordance with the level of compliance with CLS in the country of origin.* These would be the *essential* elements of a link between trade and labor standards. Yet, the particular features of a link can be shaped in different ways. The present chapter will attempt to determine the most appropriate features of the two links proposed in this study.

The shape of any link between trade and labor depends, first and foremost, on its objective. The rationale of the two links proposed is quite different. Accordingly, their particular features would be different.

This chapter will start with some general considerations that apply to both of them.

GENERAL REMARKS

Special and Differential Treatment Concerning the Level of Labor Protection

The basic definition of a link used so far in this study refers to CLS listed in the 1998 ILO Declaration on Fundamental Principles and Rights at Work. Yet, less developed countries are likely to face more difficulties in fully complying with these standards. Hence, it may be justified to require, in the case of these countries, compliance with fewer standards or a lower level of compliance.

Where necessary, the rules of the multilateral trading system provide developing countries "special and more favorable treatment," also known as "special and differential treatment" (SDT). The ILO, too, has addressed this issue. Part V of the 1944 Declaration of Philadelphia states that ILO principles have to be applied with due regard to the stage of social and economic development of the country concerned. Accordingly, a number of ILO conventions establish different standards for countries with a lower level of economic and social development. ILO working parties have upheld the principle of "flexibility," recognizing that international labor standards cannot be implemented in the same manner by countries with different levels of development.

But there is no flexibility as far as CLS are concerned. These standards were selected because they can be met regardless of the level of development. The ILO found that core standards are actually the very minimum that has to be complied with. As one author puts it, a low GDP cannot justify that "women, men and children are arrested, beaten, tortured, kidnapped and murdered, just because they belong to a trade union, or wish to do so, or because they are struggling for humane conditions."[1]

For these reasons, the two links proposed in this study should not use different levels of implementation of CLS or fewer standards for countries of different economic and social development.

Standing of Countries Not Having Ratified the Relevant ILO Conventions

Another question that arises in this context is whether a country which itself has not ratified or fully implemented all eight ILO conventions on CLS would nonetheless be entitled to apply trade restrictions on imports of goods produced under substandard labor conditions. If such a country applied trade restrictions under link B, this would imply that it attaches more importance to its responsibility for labor conditions in other countries than to those at home. There is no reason for preventing it from doing so, but it seems unlikely that it would actually apply such restrictions.

Link A would apply where substandard labor conditions confer an unfair competitive advantage. That advantage does not exist if labor conditions in the domestic industries of the importing country are also substandard. If the importing country has not ratified or fully implemented all eight ILO conventions, domestic producers of like products would have to prove that they pay normal production costs, including those that would result from full compliance with CLS.

The Role of the ILO and the WTO

As stated above, a link would have to be a rule of international law having, in the hierarchy of norms, the same rank and status as ILO standards and the rules of the multilateral trading system. Moreover, since any discriminatory treatment of imports on the grounds of poor labor conditions in the production process of the goods concerned is not allowed under present WTO rules, a link would have to amend—or override—these rules.

Collective Action or Individual Decisions?

Basically, there are three different ways to decide and apply trade measures under a link between trade and labor standards. There could be a total ban, once and forever, on the imports of products made under substandard labor conditions. There could also be a procedure under which trade restrictions may be decided collectively by the members of the WTO or the ILO and applied by all of them on imports of certain goods.[2] Or a link could give an authorization to importing countries to apply such restrictions individually.

A total ban is clearly out of the question, for the reasons explained in chapter 4. A collective procedure may be envisaged in the ILO. In the WTO, this would truly be an innovation. No rule of the multilateral trading system provides for collective trade restrictions against particular members.

In any event, for the purposes of the links proposed in this study, such a procedure would not be necessary. Both links are motivated by the specific situation of importing countries, which either suffer from unfair competition or are responsible for an increasing number of violations of labor standards in other countries. When the conditions for applying trade measures are fulfilled, importing countries should be free to decide whether to adopt them or not.

The Institutional Framework

As far as the institutional framework for adopting the links proposed in this study is concerned, there are also three options, at least in theory: the ILO, the WTO, and an ad hoc international agreement. Unfortunately, there are problems with each one of them, as we will see below.

Point 4 of the declaration adopted by the WTO at the Ministerial Conference in Singapore in 1996 reads: "We renew our commitment to the observance of internationally recognized core labor standards. The ILO is the competent body to set and deal with these standards." While it is clear that international labor standards should be dealt with in the framework of the ILO, this does not necessarily apply to a link between trade and labor standards. The two links proposed in this study are justified by trade-related considerations. This would rather suggest that the right place to establish them would be the WTO.

The WTO. Since its creation, the GATT and later the WTO have been regarded as the natural place for defining the rules governing international trade, and the organization jealously guards this prerogative. This organization would indeed be the most appropriate forum to adopt rules making the two links operational. But the number of unsuccessful attempts to discuss the issue of trade and labor in the WTO clearly show that there is little chance of getting consensus inside that organization.

The ILO. Establishing the links in the ILO would empower ILO member states to apply trade restrictions against other members not complying with labor standards. Similar proposals were already made back in 1919.[3] Thus, it may not be entirely out of the question to consider a link in the framework of the ILO.

Still, adopting rules authorizing individual members of the ILO to apply trade restrictions on imports from other members would not tally with the institutional architecture of the ILO. Moreover, as a link adopted in the ILO would not override the obligations of countries as WTO members, an authorization to apply trade measures in the framework of the ILO would be incompatible with WTO rules, unless the latter were amended accordingly. Hence, establishing a link between trade and labor standards in the framework of the ILO is not an option.

An Ad Hoc *International Agreement.* The most realistic option may be an *ad hoc* international agreement to be negotiated with the specific aim of establishing the links proposed in this study. This, of course, would sound like heresy to trade negotiators. Nonetheless, it has been used in the past. In specific cases such as the Washington Convention on International Trade in Endangered Species of Wild Fauna and Flora and the Montreal Protocol on Substances That Deplete the Ozone Layer, trade restrictions have been decided outside the framework of the GATT/WTO. This was probably the only way to achieve the political goals of these conventions.

These conventions establish trade bans on certain products and leave no discretion to individual signatories. I am not aware of any *ad hoc* convention that would provide an authorization, outside the framework of the WTO, to adopt individual trade restrictions like the ones proposed in this study. Although, in the light of the number of unsuccessful attempts to discuss the issue of trade and labor in the WTO, the probability of getting consensus seems rather remote, there is, for all practical purposes, no other option than to establish these links in the framework of the WTO.

Prior Authorization?

Prior Authorization by the WTO. In certain instances, WTO members need prior authorization for applying individual trade restrictions. This applies to retaliation measures against countries ignoring the ruling of a panel, which require authorization by the DSB. Another example is GATT Article XXIII (Nonviolation, Nullification, or Impairment) which authorizes (individual) retaliation only provided that it has been determined, by the competent WTO bodies, that the conditions are fulfilled.

In contrast, most other GATT provisions (like general exceptions and anti-dumping rules) enable individual member states to apply trade restrictions, additional or countervailing duties if they satisfy themselves that the requirements are met. The links proposed in this study are similar to these provisions. Hence, they should authorize individual WTO member states to apply trade restrictions under specific conditions, but without prior authorization of the WTO.

Prior Authorization by the ILO. Some proposals for establishing a link between trade and labor suggest that trade restrictions could only be applied subject to prior agreement of the ILO.[4] Such a requirement would have advantages in terms of fact finding and preventing disputes. On the down side, a link having to meet this requirement would probably not be operational. For the same reasons that ILO members tend to refrain from resorting to Article 33 of the ILO Constitution, they would also hesitate to rubberstamp any trade restrictions that importing countries intended to apply. As far as the two links proposed in this study are concerned, there is no need to give the ILO a formal role in this sense.

Product Coverage

As noted above, the question concerning the selection of products is twofold. On the one hand, it concerns the selection of products in respect of which compliance with labor standards is relevant. On the other hand, it relates to the imports to which trade restrictions may apply. The links proposed in this study are both justified by reasons that are related to trade. For both of them, compliance with labor standards is only relevant in sectors producing goods for exports.[5] In contrast, the imports on which trade restrictions may apply are not the same for link A and link B. This question will have to be answered for both of them separately.

Alternatives to Trade Restrictions

It is commonly accepted that trade-restrictive measures should not be envisaged if other, softer means are available for achieving the same results. The reasons justifying the two links proposed in this study concern certain trade-related consequences of imports of goods produced under substandard labor conditions. These consequences can be avoided by restricting trade, and only by doing so. There is no softer alternative.

As stated above, it would not be necessary to establish the links proposed in this study if there were ways to ensure that all countries complied with CLS. Chapter 5 found that there were no such means.

It may also be argued that trade restrictions should only be used provided that the ILO had made serious efforts to secure compliance with the relevant standards in the country concerned, and that these efforts had remained unproductive. Such a requirement makes sense if the objective were to enforce labor standards. Since neither link A nor link B pursues this objective, it is not warranted.

Dispute Settlement

If the links proposed in this study were implemented in the framework of the multilateral trading system and if trade restrictions were applied, under these links, by an importing country, the exporting country concerned might challenge the legality of these measures under the WTO Dispute Settlement Mechanism (DSM). Under present WTO rules, in particular the exceptions of GATT Article XX, the DSM might have to answer questions beyond the scope of the experience of trade panelists. In such cases, they would rely on the judgment of others who are qualified to judge. To the extent that a panel would have to rely on the expertise of the ILO, some cooperation would be required between the WTO and the ILO to establish the latter's responsibility for fact finding. But exporting countries should not be allowed to challenge ILO rulings regarding compliance with labor standards in the framework of the WTO DSM.

LINK A

The Choice of Labor Standards

The definition of the essential elements of a link used in chapters 3 and 4 includes a reference to CLS. The privileged status of these labor standards derives from the 1998 ILO Declaration on Fundamental Principles and Rights at Work and from the 2008 ILO Declaration on Social Justice for a Fair Globalization. The latter declaration states that "the violation of fundamental principles and rights at work [meaning CLS] cannot be invoked or otherwise used as a legitimate comparative advantage." Hence, CLS should be used for link A. Of course, trade negotiators may decide to include other than CLS. But they should refrain from defining labor standards themselves.

The Type of Rule and the Conditions for Applying it

The rationale of link A is similar to that of GATT provisions on anti-dumping and on prison labor. Link A could be adopted by expanding the scope of GATT Article XX (e)—prison labor—to include the entire set of CLS. However, this does not seem to be the most suitable solution.

In general, Article XX authorizes trade restrictions that are necessary to achieve certain political objectives or to comply with certain domestic laws or international obligations. In other words, Article XX allows trade restrictions meant to limit certain effects *of* free trade. In this respect, letter (e) is an exception. The rationale of this provision is not to improve the life of inmates, but to provide protection against unfair competition. It is meant to limit the effects of prison labor *on* trade. In that way, it is similar to the rationale of link A.

In contrast to anti-dumping rules, Article XX (e) would allow trade restrictions even in the absence of material injury to the domestic industries of importing countries. Accordingly, an addition to Article XX covering CLS would have to stipulate that trade restrictions could be applied only if they were necessary to avoid such injury. This would not tally with the architecture of Article XX. This provision would not be the right place for link A.

Link A should rather be shaped along the lines of anti-dumping rules. Trade restrictions would require that (1) certain imported goods are produced under conditions not complying with CLS, (2) the costs of labor in the production of these goods are lower than they would be if these standards were complied with, (3) the domestic industry producing the like product is suffering material injury, and (4) there is a causal link between these elements.[6] The complexity of these rules would require a special agreement like the one on anti-dumping.

Non-Compliance with CLS (Condition 1)

The first condition is that certain imported goods are produced under conditions not complying with CLS as defined by the relevant ILO conventions. These conventions do not directly confer rights nor create obligations for individuals unless the constitution of the country concerned provides for immediate applicability of international law. If a country does not transform the standards into national laws, nobody in that country can comply with them. Yet, in the context of link A, compliance refers to a de facto situation, not a legal one. It is just a benchmark that determines whether competition is fair. The question is whether CLS are met in the production of specific goods, that is, by individual employers, not by exporting countries as a whole.

The Savings from Non-Compliance with CLS (Condition 2)

Implementation of link A requires a calculation of the savings resulting from non-compliance with labor standards. This calculation is certainly not an easy task, in particular when it comes to assessing the savings from denying freedom of association and the right to collective bargaining. But the example of anti-dumping rules shows that there is an answer to all questions, and that the WTO is capable of adopting the most complicated and sophisticated rules if need be.

The "dumping margin" would be the difference between the costs of producing the goods concerned under substandard conditions and those of producing them under normal conditions (meaning under conditions complying with labor standards).[7] In an environment where non-compliance with labor standards is the exception, normal production costs can be more easily determined. This is more difficult, though, where non-compliance is the rule.

It is also difficult to determine the "normal" level of wages for countries not granting freedom of association and the right to collective bargaining. In similar cases, the costs of production under normal conditions could be calculated on the basis of labor costs in another country where similar economic conditions prevail, but where international labor standards were implemented.[8]

Another difficulty may arise when goods imported from one country are produced with inputs imported from another country and made under substandard labor conditions. A link that does not cover this case could be easily circumvented.

There should be a *de minimis* rule according to which any savings of production costs below a certain threshold would not be actionable. This threshold may be fixed at a higher level for least developed countries.

Material Injury to the Domestic Industry of the Importing Country (Condition 3)

The material injury to the domestic industry of the importing country (or threat thereof) could be checked in a manner similar to that used for the purposes of anti-dumping investigations. The criteria to consider would be the volume of imports and the effect of these imports on prices in the domestic market for like products, and the consequent impact on the domestic producers of like products.

Product Coverage

Link A would cover imports of any goods. Thus, compliance with CLS in the exporting country is relevant in sectors producing for export to the importing country and not in any others. Trade restrictions would apply to imports of those products that actually fulfill the above conditions. They may also be applied to imports of goods from countries of origin which otherwise comply with these standards.

The Type of Trade Measures

The rules establishing link A should provide for the possibility to impose variable duties equivalent to the savings resulting from substandard working conditions in the production of the goods concerned or the amount of injury suffered by the domestic industry of the importing country, whichever is smaller.

Monitoring Compliance and Investigations

Such duties would be applied after an investigation opened upon request by the domestic industry of the importing country suffering material injury or threatened to suffer it. The effects of violations of labor standards in one country on the market of another country might also cause injury to the industries of a third country. Other countries indirectly affected should therefore be allowed to request initiation of an investigation.[9]

Requests for an investigation would have to provide sufficient evidence that the conditions for applying trade measures under link A were fulfilled. Whether this is the case has to be investigated by the competent authorities of the importing country. These investigations have to involve the exporters concerned.

While checking conditions 3 (material injury to the domestic industries of the importing country) and 4 (causal link between non-compliance with CLS and material injury) would be routine for authorities entrusted with carrying out anti-dumping investigations, these authorities are likely to lack experience with conditions 1 (determining non-compliance with CLS) and 2 (calculating the savings from non-compliance). For all practical purposes, the only institution capable of carrying out such assessments is the ILO. Therefore, the ILO should be consulted in all cases.[10]

LINK B

The Choice of Labor Standards

CLS as defined by the 1998 ILO Declaration on Fundamental Principles and Rights at Work are, if not human rights, at least rights of fundamental importance for life in any civilized society. This means that the moral burden of association with violations of these standards weighs heavily on importing countries. Hence, these standards, but only these standards, should be used for link B.

The Type of Rule and the Conditions for Applying It

If link B were to be adopted as a new WTO rule, the most suitable solution would be an addition to the general exceptions listed in GATT Article XX, together with an agreement spelling out the details.

Link B would authorize trade restrictions provided that (1) goods had been imported, over a number of years, from a country not having complied with CLS during that period of time and that (2) imports from that country had steadily increased, at a considerable rate, over the same period.

Non-Compliance with CLS (Condition 1)

The first condition is that an exporting country has not complied with CLS over a certain period of time. In the context of link B, compliance means that countries respect the obligations defined in the eight conventions on CLS. International treaties and agreements create obligations for states that have ratified them and only these states can "comply" with them. Conversely, the eight conventions on CLS are binding even in the absence of ratification. Accordingly, all states have to comply with them.

Compliance requires effective implementation of the relevant standards. Implementation means that a country has transformed them into domestic laws and has put in place enforcement procedures. This includes monitoring the application of the relevant domestic laws and providing adequate complaint and dispute settlement mechanisms. Thus, non-compliance with international labor standards may result from two different scenarios. Either a country has not *adopted* national legislation transforming ILO standards into the law of the land. Or it has transformed them, but does not effectively *enforce* them.

Of course, there will always be cases of non-compliance with these domestic laws, in any country. As long as these are sporadic, they are irrelevant. But if there are frequent and serious violations of the laws implementing labor standards in a given country or a particular sector of its economy, this country has not complied with the international obligations under the ILO conventions concerned.

Implementation may be used not only as an absolute benchmark, but also as a goal toward which a country should move. For example, US trade laws use a relative and dynamic criterion defined as "steps that countries have taken or are taking" toward effective implementation. It may be argued that trade measures would not be warranted if the country concerned could demonstrate that it is making serious efforts to comply with the standards concerned. But this argument loses weight over time. It becomes irrelevant if after a long period of time, countries still do not reach that goal of effective implementation. This is the situation where trade restrictions are justified.

The Rate of Increase (Condition 2)

Condition (2) requires that exports have steadily increased, at a considerable rate, over a number of years. A considerable rate would be a rate significantly above the average of world trade growth. Between 1950 and 2010, the annual average growth rate of the value of world trade was slightly over 10 percent.[11] Condition 2 would be fulfilled if exports of a country grow over a period of five years by an annual average in the range of 15 percent.

Other Requirements

If link B were to be adopted as an addition to GATT Article XX, trade restrictions would have to satisfy the requirements mentioned in the *chapeau* of this provision. In particular, they should not be applied "in a manner that constitutes arbitrary or unjustifiable discrimination." This means that if an import country makes use of link B, it should do so in regard to imports from all countries fulfilling the requirements mentioned above. This would require monitoring compliance with CLS in all countries from which it imports.

Article XX permits trade measures "provided that they are necessary." Link B would apply in a situation where trade restrictions were the only way to escape the blame of being associated with violations of CLS in exporting countries. This situation arises where imports increase while labor conditions remain the same. In that case, importing countries would have no excuse. They would be fully responsible for the consequences of keeping their markets open. Where the conditions of applying link B were fulfilled, trade restrictions would indeed be necessary to escape the blame.

Product Coverage

As noted above, the question concerning product coverage is twofold: on the one hand, it concerns the sectors in which compliance with labor standards is relevant. As far as link B is concerned, this is the case in all sectors producing for exports to the importing country concerned.

The other question concerns the products to which trade restrictions might apply. Link B is meant to address a situation where importing countries share the responsibility of exporting countries tolerating an increase of violations of CLS on their territory. Exporting countries may do so only in certain sectors or areas, such as Export Processing Zones. Link B should therefore be implemented on a sectoral basis.[12] Accordingly, if the conditions mentioned above are fulfilled in a particular sector of the economy of the exporting country concerned, they could be also applied to imports of goods of this sector.

Trade restrictions should be permitted only when the volume of the trade concerned is sufficiently important. Importing countries may restrict imports of goods of a specific sector from a particular country, if these imports amount to at least 5 percent of total imports from that country.

The Type of Trade Measure

The rationale of link B could be attained by using quantitative restrictions or quotas above which additional duties would be applied. It is commonly accepted that, if various trade measures are available, preference should be given to the least trade-restrictive alternative. Arguably, tariff quotas are less trade restrictive than quantitative restrictions. However, since the justification of link B is the responsibility of importing countries for the proliferation of violations of CLS in exporting countries, there is a strong case for applying quantitative restrictions. Imports should be limited to the volumes imported during previous years. This could be implemented in the same way as GSP or textile quotas used to be managed.

Monitoring Compliance and Investigations

Governments eager not to be blamed for violations of CLS in countries from which they import goods would have to regularly screen labor conditions in these countries, as well as the volume of their exports. The starting point should be information provided by the ILO. In addition, the WTO could request its members to provide information on compliance with CLS in the framework of its Trade Policy Review Mechanism (TPRM).[13]

Trade restrictions under link B would only be decided after appropriate investigations. Investigations may be requested by anybody who, as a consumer, feels responsible for an increase of violations of CLS in the exporting countries concerned and is able to produce evidence that suggests the existence of such violations and a significant increase of imports of the goods concerned.

Determinations concerning condition (1), mentioned above, could not be made without consulting the ILO. But the ILO may hesitate to provide the required input. It seems that in some instances, the perspective of losing trade preferences motivated exporting countries to ask the ILO to certify them. Link B may provide similar incentives. If asked, the ILO would have no reason for refusing an assessment of a country's performance in terms of labor protection.

No final determinations would be made without prior consultation with the exporting country concerned.

CONCLUDING REMARKS

This chapter attempts to define the most appropriate features for the two links proposed in this study. With these features, both links would easily fit into the multilateral trading system. Their scope is much more limited than imagined by many participants in the discussion of linking trade to labor standards. Neither of the two links proposed would lead to an unpredictable proliferation of trade restrictions. In essence, introducing the two proposed links into the WTO system would not turn it upside down. It would not, as predicted in 1999 by the Egyptian trade minister Boutros-Ghali, be "the end of the multilateral trading system."[14] On the contrary, it would significantly increase the system's coherence and legitimacy.

NOTES

1. H. Lim, *The Social Clause: Issues and Challenges*, International Labor Organization, Bureau for Workers Activities, Geneva, 2001, pp. 9 and 26.
2. In this sense T. H. Moran, Beyond Sweatshops, Foreign Direct Investment and Globalization in Developing Countries, Washington, DC, 2002, p. 68; D. S. Ehrenberg, From Intention to Action, An ILO-GATT/WTO Enforcement Regime for International Labor Rights, in in L. A. Compa and S. F. Diamond (eds), *Human Rights, Labor Rights, and International Trade*, Philadelphia, 1996, p. 163.
3. In those days, the ILO was the only option, since the GATT did not yet exist.
4. European Commission, Commission Communication to the Council: Development cooperation and the observance of certain international standards governing working conditions, COM (78) 492 final of 10 November 1978, paragraph III.
5. Sectors such as agricultural production for home consumption (where the bulk of child labor exists) or domestic work in households (where most victims of forced labor work) thus remain outside the scope of these links.
6. Other requirements of the anti-dumping agreement should be applied *mutatis mutandis*, for example, the condition that dumped imports represent a meaningful share of all imports of the same products in the importing country concerned.
7. P. Alston defines the dumping margin as the difference between production costs under substandard conditions in the exporting country and those in the importing country, where "producers would not be permitted to tolerate such low standards," see P. Alston, Labor Rights Provisions in US Trade Laws, "Aggressive Unilateralism"? in L. A. Compa and S. F. Diamond (eds), *Human Rights, Labor Rights, and International Trade*, Philadelphia, 1996, p. 90, note 2. However, this definition of the dumping margin overlooks the fact that production costs are likely to be different in the exporting and importing country, even if both fully comply with labor standards. It may make exporting countries lose a legitimate comparative advantage of low labor costs.
8. K. E. Maskus (Should Core Labor Standards Be Imposed Through International Trade Policy? The World Bank Development Research Group, Policy Research Working Paper 1817, Washington, DC, 1997) argues that it would be virtually impossible to calculate a meaningful "social dumping margin." Although I disagree, for the reasons explained above, with the proposals made by K. Bagwell and R. W. Staiger (The Simple Economics of Labor Standards and the GATT, National Bureau of Economic Research Working Paper, no. w6604, 1998), I agree with them that it is feasible to calculate the advantage provided by lower labor protection.
9. Along the lines of Article 14 of the WTO anti-dumping agreement.

10. The ILO may assist in different ways; see J. Agusti-Panareda, F. C. Ebert, and D. LeClercq, Labour Provisions in Free Trade Agreements: Fostering their Consistency with the ILO Standards System, International Labour Office, Geneva, 2014, pp. 20–26.

11. http://unctadstat.unctad.org/wds/TableViewer/tableView.aspx?ReportId=102.

12. In the latter case, the provisions may use a standard classification of sectors such as the one provided by the GSP of the EU.

13. It seems that such proposals were already made, but did not succeed.

14. S. Greenhouse and J. Kahn, U.S. Effort to Add Labor Standards to Agenda Fail, *New York Times,* December 3, 1999.

Chapter Eight

Objections to Linking Trade and Labor Standards

Many scholars, politicians, and trade negotiators oppose a link between international trade and international labor standards. The most radical voices contest the wisdom of having internationally binding labor standards, or even of providing any labor protection at all. Some trade officials claim that linking trade to labor standards would open the door to protectionist abuse. Certain authors oppose a link on the grounds that it would entail considerable economic nuisance. Finally, some scholars object to a link with arguments related to rationale of free trade and the philosophy of the multilateral trading system.

This chapter will examine the most frequently made objections against linking trade and labor and assess whether and to what extent they apply to the two links proposed in this study.

OBJECTION (1): TRADE RESTRICTIONS SHOULD NOT BE USED TO ENFORCE CLS

Many scholars are of the view that trade sanctions should not be used to enforce labor standards. I share this view, for the reasons explained in chapter 3. But I believe that there are good reasons—presented in chapter 4—to use trade restrictions in order to prevent certain trade-related effects of noncompliance with CLS. For the two links proposed in this study, these standards serve only as a *reference*. There is no intention to *enforce* them.

The purpose of link A is to stop the *effects* of social dumping, but not the underlying violations of labor standards. Social dumping is an unfair trading practice. Compliance with CLS is used as a criterion to determine whether competition is fair. Of course, this implies a judgment, that is, that these standards should be respected. But link A is not meant to promote, let alone to achieve, compliance.

The rationale of link B is that importing countries deserve the same moral blame as exporting countries not complying with CLS, if they import goods from them beyond certain limits. These standards are used, in the framework of link B, in order to determine the *existence* of the original offense—the violation of these standards—not to *sanction* it.

Hence, the above objection does not apply to these proposals. On the other hand, the mere existence of the two links proposed in this study may convince employers or governments to improve labor protection and conditions. Whether this provides a reason for opposing them depends on the effects of improved labor conditions. These effects will be examined in the following pages.

OBJECTION (2): THE RISK OF PROTECTIONIST CAPTURE

Protectionism is a recurrent argument presented by opponents to a link between trade and labor standards. The Singapore Declaration adopted by WTO in 1996 rejects "the use of labor standards for protectionist purposes," whereas both the 1998 and the 2008 ILO Declarations state "that labor standards should not be used for protectionist purposes."[1] However, this language is not really an argument against a link, but rather a reminder that the multilateral trading system leaves no room for it. It rather seems that those invoking protectionism against proposals to link trade and labor standards use trade arguments to protect themselves from being accused of tolerating exploitative use of labor.

The term "protectionism" may refer to the use of existing rules allowing for trade restrictions, but also to proposals for the adoption of new rules. Protectionist abuse of existing rules occurs where trade restrictions are used although the conditions are not fulfilled, or where trade restrictions authorized for non-trade-related reasons are used in order to protect markets. A proposal to adopt new rules allowing for trade restrictions would appear protectionist if it is not supported by valid reasons or if non-trade-related reasons are invoked, even though the real intention may be to increase border protection.

Would the Establishment of a Link Amount to Protectionism?

Link A would protect domestic producers against unfair competition from countries violating labor standards. The reasons for adopting such a rule are as valid as those justifying similar existing ones. The purpose of link B is to limit the responsibility of importing countries of being associated with an increase of the number of violations of CLS as a result of the creation of new jobs with substandard labor conditions in exporting countries. These are valid trade-related considerations. Hence, there is no reason to oppose them on the grounds that they are "protectionist."

Would a Link Open the Door to Protectionist Abuse?

Of course, once adopted both links may be captured for protectionist purposes, just like any existing GATT rules authorizing trade restrictions. As far as link A is concerned, there is a risk that trade restrictions are adopted beyond the limits permitted. On the contrary, link B implies the risk that countries declare that they wish to escape the blame for association with violations of labor rights in exporting countries, while their real intention is to restrict access to their markets.

As mentioned in chapter 6, practical experience with existing unilateral and bilateral schemes linking trade to labor suggests that the risk of protectionist capture is rather remote. The reaction of most governments to the decision of the ILO authorizing trade restrictions against Myanmar was not very enthusiast. Moreover, the United States is on record as having been very reluctant to remove countries from the list of those eligible for GSP preferences.[2] Similarly, the EU has taken a very cautious stance when it comes to suspending GSP treatment.

When negotiating the rules of the GSP of the EU, I have found that EU had more interest in granting trade preferences than in protecting its market. The EU granted GSP treatment to China at a time when trade flows provided good reasons for suspending that treatment. And various OECD countries decided unilaterally to give duty-free market access to products from LDCs. On the whole, the mood is not for more market protection.

The main supporters of a link between trade and labor are high-income OECD member states. They would probably also become the main users of a link. The EU and US experience with their links does not prove that all other countries would apply similar policies if the links between trade and labor proposed in this study were to be adopted. Countries facing huge and growing trade deficits may be tempted to apply any possible trade restriction even when the conditions are actually not fulfilled.

In order to prevent this risk, the rules establishing that link would have to clearly define the conditions under which trade measures were justified. With a clear definition of these conditions, the risk of protectionist capture would only be marginal. Obviously, there will always be a residual risk that a new rule might be used for protectionist purposes. This risk exists, though, in respect of any rule of the multilateral trading system allowing exceptions from GATT principles and disciplines. In the case of a link between trade and labor, this risk would not be greater than in that of other WTO rules, such as anti-dumping. The risk of protectionist abuse does not provide a valid argument against a link.[3]

OBJECTION (3): CLS ARE NOT AN APPROPRIATE REFERENCE

Some authors oppose the idea of linking trade to international labor standards because they have some basic reservations about these standards. It should be noted that most of these objections have lost their weight since the adoption of the 1998 ILO Declaration on Fundamental Principles and Rights at Work.

Labor Conditions Should be Determined by the Labor Market

Certain economists believe that wages, working hours, and working conditions should be determined solely by the labor market.[4] In their view, any regulation of labor conditions unduly interferes in that market. However, where weakness meets violence, there is no market.[5] A market supposes free decisions and agreements. Forced labor (and probably child labor in the majority of cases) is not something that is freely agreed by those who are obliged to carry it out. In general, the bargaining power of employers and employees is not the same, and increasing mobility of capital has reduced the bargaining power of labor even further. In many developing countries workers do not have enough options to make labor markets function.

This situation requires corrective measures. Even free market enthusiasts acknowledge that "no country has been willing to permit market forces to be the sole arbiter of national employment conditions."[6] All countries seem to recognize that the labor market, if it was to function without basic rules and safeguards, is bound to fail. These basic rules are defined by CLS.

The Level of Labor Protection Should Be Country-Specific

One may ask whether the same references should be used in respect of all exporting countries. Some scholars oppose international harmonization of labor protection through international minimum standards. They contend that such standards should be country specific or context sensitive, meaning that labor protection should be set at levels reflecting a country's level of development.[7] This question has been discussed above under two different headings: the selection of the appropriate standards and the merit of providing special and differential treatment. The conclusion was that there is no reason for making exceptions from CLS.

Some Countries Are Unable to Implement CLS

Some authors fear that less developed countries are unable to implement CLS. If a link between trade and CLS had no other consequence but to make these countries suffer from trade restrictions, it would not make much sense. However, one of the selection criteria of CLS was that all countries were able to implement them.[8]

As mentioned above, some countries may lack capacity and resources. The ILO runs a comprehensive program of technical assistance to help these countries. It is fair to say that it is quite feasible to overcome these challenges. The claim that in some countries it may be impossible to comply with CLS is unfounded.

As far as link A is concerned, the issue is not effective implementation by exporting countries, but compliance by employers and exporters. Companies producing for the export sector usually have to abide by strict quality standards, which are controlled with utmost efficiency. Where this is possible, compliance with labor standards should also be feasible.[9]

CLS Do Not Bind All Countries

Another argument opposing the use of CLS contends that they are not universally binding. It is true that a number of countries did not ratify all eight relevant conventions. Nonetheless, the 1998 ILO Declaration on Fundamental Principles and Rights at Work clearly states that conventions are binding for all countries, including those not having ratified them. Moreover, using norms as references does not require that they are ratified by all countries.

CLS Are Not Precise

Another objection against CLS claims that they are not precise enough.[10] ILO conventions are drafted in the traditional style of continental legislation, with abstract definitions, rather than according to the Anglo-Saxon habit of providing lengthy enumerations of all possible hypotheses to which the law may apply. Although such definitions may leave some specific questions unanswered, this does not put into question the appropriateness of CLS as a reference for a link.

International Labor Standards Are Incompatible with State Sovereignty

Some authors oppose international labor standards on the grounds that they are incompatible with the principle of state sovereignty. While the UN Charter confirms the principle of state sovereignty, it puts limits to its exercise. Only sovereign states can join the organization but, if they do, they have to accept these limits. These limits include the respect of human rights, together with that of CLS.[11] In any event, using these standards as a reference in the framework of the two links proposed would not limit the sovereignty of exporting countries or would hamper its exercise.

CLS Are Western Values

Certain countries justify their reserve against CLS (and, more generally, the idea of human rights) by invoking "cultural relativism."[12] And certain scholars support this position.[13] Considering the genesis of labor standards, it would appear that they were originally invented by the United States and European countries. Arguably, these countries are the sinners of the past whose early industrialization benefited from poor social conditions. Meanwhile, most countries of the world have become states, albeit many of them of a pre-democratic nature. Most states have adopted the economic system developed in Western countries and are eager to reap the benefits from participating in a global economic order based on this system. If they claim that they should now have their chance by denying the values and norms that are needed to make this system human, they are looking for a free ride.

The issue is whether we consider that individuals have a value or not. Those who do not recognize the value of human beings are outside the consensus on civilization defined in 1919 by the founding members of the ILO. They are also outside the consensus defined by the 1998 ILO Declaration, accepted by all 185 member states of that organization (out of 193 states that are members of the UN).

OBJECTION (4): THE COSTS OF LINKING TRADE TO LABOR STANDARDS

The allegation that a link between trade and labor standards would have significant economic costs for exporting countries is one of the most frequently invoked arguments of opponents. There are two versions of this objection. One focuses on the effects of trade restrictions. It argues that *restricting trade* would harm the economies of developing countries. The other version considers the scenario that governments would decide to improve labor conditions in order to avoid trade restrictions. It claims that *better labor conditions* would slow down the economic growth of the exporting country concerned. However, the economic effects both of free trade and of poor labor conditions are far from evident, and so are those of trade restrictions and improved labor conditions. Both objections are quite controversial, indeed.

It is noteworthy that opponents raising this objection apparently take it for granted that only developing countries would feel the effects of linking trade to labor standards. Although I did not find a correlation between the level of development of countries and compliance with ILO conventions, the discussion of the objection under consideration here will focus on the situation of developing countries.

Opponents also seem to take it for granted that linking trade to labor to labor standards would have devastating economic consequences for these countries. This view relies on two assumptions. One is that the situation of labor conditions in certain exporting countries is actually very bad. This is the case, as shown in chapter 3. The other assumption is that a link would stop all imports of goods produced under substandard conditions. The proposals made in this study are much more limited. Their effects would compare to those of anti-dumping duties and textile quotas.

The Macro-Economic Effects in Exporting Countries

The Effects of Trade Restrictions

Some economists oppose a link between international trade and labor standards on the grounds that trade restrictions would reduce the welfare gains of free trade.[14] Chapter 7 specified the type of trade restrictions that the two proposed links would authorize: quantitative restrictions and variable duties. As a result of quantitative restrictions applied under link B, certain exports would no longer increase. Additional duties decided under link A might even stop all imports of the goods concerned.

What would be the further consequences for the economy of the exporting countries concerned? While there is a general consensus that trade favors economic growth, increasing exports are unlikely to have long-lasting positive effects on the rate of economic growth unless they result in higher productivity.[15] By the same token, as long as shrinking exports do not lower productivity, trade restrictions are unlikely to have long-lasting negative effects on economic growth.

The Effects of Compliance with CLS

Although the links proposed in this study are not meant to improve labor conditions, they may well have this result. Trade restrictions on imports from countries violating CLS may actually prompt these countries to fully comply. Some economists predict that this will have adverse effects on trade and economic growth and also deter foreign investments.[16]

The Effects on Trade. Developing countries fear that compliance with labor standards would reduce the comparative advantage of cheap labor and adversely affect exports. However, according to the findings of the OECD, "countries with low core labor standards do not enjoy better export performance than high-standard countries."[17] These findings are confirmed by several scholars.[18] Moreover, even though compliance with labor standards may reduce the competitive advantage of cheap labor, it will not take it away entriely.[19] Labor is cheaper in developing countries, even in those complying with labor standards. Where products from developing countries compete with products from developed countries, the loss of competitiveness from compliance with labor standards is unlikely to have a major impact on trade.[20]

The Effects on Economic Growth. Many opponents to a link between trade and labor standards are convinced that low labor conditions favor economic growth and that a link, to the extent that it would promote higher standards, would have a negative impact on growth rates. For the reasons explained in chapter 3, I disagree. While lower labor conditions may favor economic growth in the short run, higher labor protection is likely to promote sustainable growth and development. Any short-term economic benefits of poor labor conditions are certainly less important than the long-term economic benefits of sustainable development.

Even if it were true that low labor conditions favor economic growth, it would still not justify a policy of low labor standards. The costs of such policy would be borne by workers.[21] Substandard labor conditions amount to subsidizing inefficient companies.[22] In economic terms, this makes little sense. Whether it does in political terms is a question outside the scope of economics.

The Effects on Foreign Investment. Opponents to a link between trade and labor standards also argue that improving labor standards would discourage foreign investment in countries that so far do not meet these standards. This would certainly have adverse effects on the economic development of the exporting countries concerned. But there is no empirical evidence suggesting that foreign direct investment is attracted by countries where standards are particularly low.[23] With the exception of China, countries which do not implement CLS receive only a small share of global investment flows.[24] Accordingly, if these countries improve labor conditions, they would not lose much anyway.

The Effects on Companies in Exporting Countries

The Effects of Trade Restrictions

Although the global effects of trade restrictions resulting from the links proposed in this study are probably insignificant, individual companies may feel them to be harsh. This is less likely as far as link B is concerned, since this link would not reduce exports below previous performance. Trade restrictions applied under link A may be more painful.

Link A would authorize trade restrictions when unfair competition causes injury to domestic industries of importing countries. This is an economic concern. Trade restrictions may, of course, have negative effects on producers in exporting countries. This, too, is an economic concern. However, retaliation against unfair competition is justified, whereas unfair competition is not. Hence, the likely impact of trade restrictions on companies in exporting countries does not support an objection against link A.

The Effects of Compliance with CLS

In order to avoid trade restrictions, governments, in the case of link B, or companies, in that of link A, may decide to meet CLS. This would raise production costs by the amounts estimated in chapter 4. Would companies be able to bear these costs?

The Competitive Advantage of Cheap Labor. Paying the costs of fully complying with CLS would remove only part of the competitive advantage provided by cheap labor. Some authors suggest that "there is room to at least triple real wages of workers in the South without there arising any possibility of the cost advantage of Southern production being lost."[25] Accordingly, it is unlikely that companies could not bear the costs of meeting CLS.[26]

Labor Costs and Sales Prices. Labor costs in certain production sectors like textiles are typically only a tiny fraction of the price paid by consumers in developed countries. The cost of labor for a non-brand-name garment product is often in the range of 3 or 4 percent of the final sales price. For brand-name products, it may be even much lower.[27] Moreover, companies in this sector generally use sales strategies based on extremely flexible pricing. There is no reason to assume that there is no margin for paying higher wages in the producing countries.

Labor Costs and Profits. By the same token, the profits realized by many MNEs suggest that labor costs could increase substantially without driving them out of business. On January 24, 2012, the *New York Times* reported:

> Apple's Profit Doubles. . . . Apple said its net income for the (past quarter) rose 118 percent to $13.06 billion, or $13.87 a share, compared with net income of $6 billion, or $6.43 a share, a year earlier. Revenue rose 73 percent to $46.33 billion, from $26.74 billion a year ago. The rosy results sent Apple shares soaring more than 7 percent in after-hours trading to more than $450 each.[28]

This information, along with the report on working conditions published in the same newspaper the following day,[29] suggests that the company was able to increase its profits because its Chinese suppliers grossly neglected workers' rights. Indeed, the company's profit levels confirm that there is some headroom for increasing wages and improving working conditions in factories in countries like China.

Not all suppliers are locals. There are also foreign investors who attempt to take advantage of low labor costs in developing countries. During the years that I was managing the EU GSP, I met European businessmen who own textile producing sites in Nepal and Bangladesh. They told me that setting up one such site requires an investment of roughly $200,000, and that they expect a net return of 40 percent p.a., basically because of low wages. There is no doubt that they would be able to pay decent wages.

The Effects on Workers in Exporting Countries

The Effects of Trade Restrictions

The possible negative effects of trade restrictions on individual workers in exporting countries depend on the macro-economic effects of such restrictions, as well as on the effects on the companies which employ them. For the reasons mentioned above, the macro-economic effects of both links and the effects of link B on individual companies are likely to be anodyne, while trade restrictions decided under link A may have more painful effects for the companies concerned. They may be forced to layoff some or all of their workers. Still, these consequences would be justified for the same reasons as those justifying these restrictions.

The Effects of Compliance with CLS

It goes without saying that individual employees stand to benefit if their working conditions improve. However, a general improvement of labor conditions does not necessarily benefit all workers. To the extent that it raises production costs, compliance with CLS may drive some companies out of business, with the result that the workers concerned lose their jobs. This is quite unlikely, though, for the reasons mentioned before.

Certain employers who are able to meet the costs of compliance and would still remain adequately competitive may nonetheless prefer to go out of business, because they regard the remaining profit margin as not sufficiently interesting. The likelihood that employers take that view depends, above all, on the costs of compliance with labor standards. The more important the savings from non-compliance, the more likely it is that employers forgoing these savings decide to close their shop. Savings are generally more important where labor standards are particularly poor. Thus, employees suffering from very poor working conditions and low wages are more likely than others to lose their jobs.[30]

Labor Costs and Productivity

Some economists warn that "wages should not rise above the level of productivity," as this would lead to a loss of jobs.[31] It is true that any factor of production faces the risk of being replaced by another that is cheaper or more productive. Cheap labor in developing countries may be replaced either by labor (when it is even cheaper or more productive) or by capital.

Over the last two centuries, capital has replaced an enormous amount of labor in developed countries and still does. The same is likely to happen in developing countries, in the long run. However, this will be a slow process because capital is generally scarce in countries where labor is cheap. It will even be slower in certain sectors such as textile, footwear, and others where mechanization has reached technical or economic limits (or both).[32] These industries will, for some time, remain labor intensive. Cheap labor attracts foreign investment, in particular in these sectors, but instead of replacing labor, such investment creates jobs. As long as labor remains comparatively cheap in developing countries, there is no reason to replace it with capital. Although compliance with CLS would lead to higher wages and higher production costs, there is no imminent risk that jobs are replaced by capital.

Labor in developing countries has replaced labor in developed countries because it is generally much cheaper. Many economists believe that the ratio of wages between developed and developing countries essentially reflects the ratio of productivity. Some claim that differences in terms of labor productivity account for 90 percent of differences between wages in developing and developed countries.[33] This is certainly not the case in labor-intensive sectors using little capital and much unskilled labor.[34] MNEs invest in developing countries because differences in wages are much more important than differences in productivity. This suggests that wages in developing countries are "below productivity."

One reason is that in the absence of freedom of association and the right to collective bargaining workers have no voice to claim their fair share of the growth which they help to generate.[35] It is therefore not surprising that, for several years, wages in many countries have not increased as much as productivity.[36] Giving labor a voice may bring wages up to the level of marginal productivity. But there is no reason to assume that wages would go beyond that level. There is hardly any risk that as a result of compliance with CLS, jobs go back from developing to developed countries.

On the other hand, labor in one developing country may be replaced by labor in another developing country where it is either cheaper or more productive. Labor is likely to become more expensive in a country which decides to meet CLS. Wages in that country may then exceed the level of productivity in other countries which do not comply with these labor standards. As a result, jobs may go to these countries. This would certainly be a serious negative consequence. It could be reduced, though, if the links proposed in this study are equally applied to all exporting countries.

The Effects of Slower Economic Growth

The previous discussion concluded that neither trade restrictions (taken under one of the links proposed in this study) nor compliance with CLS (decided in order to avoid such trade restrictions) would have significant negative effects on the economic growth of exporting countries. For the sake of argument, it shall be assumed that both scenarios would result in slower economic growth. What would individual employees lose if, as a result of establishing the links proposed in this study, the rate of economic growth of their countries slowed down?

For workers, economic growth does not matter unless it improves their overall living standards.[37] Neo-liberals are confident that the benefits of economic growth will "trickle down" to less advantaged groups of society and "that a rising tide lifts all boats." They attempt to justify intolerable working conditions with the promise of better ones for tomorrow. For the reasons explained in chapter 4, it is naive to believe in any automatic solution. In countries with very poor labor conditions, tomorrow never comes just *because* of these conditions. Individual workers stand little to lose if growth slows down because governments decide to comply with CLS. On the contrary, implementation of these standards would raise their chances of getting a fair share of the growth that they have helped create.

Conclusion

The adoption of the two links proposed in this study would allow trade restrictions on imports from certain countries. These countries could avoid them by complying with CLS. Although the economic consequences of both scenarios are probably insignificant, it cannot be ruled out that they negatively affect the countries' export performance or economic growth, certain companies or their employees.

For some scholars, this is a reason for categorically opposing the idea of linking trade to labor standards. This position is based on the view that economic efficiency and growth deserve priority over all other concerns. It treats labor as a commodity.[38] Moreover, it makes little sense even in economic terms. The costs of substandard labor conditions are borne by workers.[39] Such conditions amount to subsidizing companies.[40]

The rationale of link A is basically an economic one. It would allow retaliation against unfair competition. The negative economic effects of unfair competition on the domestic industries of importing countries justify trade restrictions *and* their negative economic effects on exporting countries and their industries. But there is no justification for unfair competition. Quite the opposite, it contradicts the rationale of free trade. Hence, the economic consequences of trade restrictions on exporting countries cannot provide an argument against link A.

Link B would allow for trade restrictions when, in spite of growing exports, labor conditions have not improved and workers do not get a fair share of the wealth that they help to generate. If this is the case, the loss of the blessings of free trade and economic growth can hardly be invoked as an argument against link B. In any event, the rationale of this link is not economic, it is political. Link B would allow importing countries to escape the blame of association with violations of CLS in exporting countries. This can only be achieved by restricting trade, which may have adverse economic effects on exporting countries. From the point of view of the rationale of this link, these considerations are secondary, though economists may disagree.

Even if the links proposed in this study would affect the economic growth of exporting countries, individual workers would lose very little. However, these links may, in the short run, lead to the creation of fewer new jobs or even to a loss of jobs in exporting countries that do not fully comply with labor standards. The possibility that they would entail a loss of jobs is probably the most serious objection against them.

The question, then, is whether, in order to avoid a loss of jobs in exporting countries, importing countries should be forced to endure unfair competition and to share the responsibility for violations of labor standards in exporting countries.[41] The matter is particularly controversial in the case of child labor. It is also a question of short-term versus long-term benefits, and thus of sustainable development of exporting countries.

Many authors believe that these countries should be able to answer that question for themselves. But then it would only be fair that importing countries too may chose whether they are prepared to suffer the effects, both on their domestic industries and in terms of their responsibility for labor conditions in exporting countries. Adopting the two links proposed in this study would give them that choice.

OBJECTION (5): LABOR PROTECTION SHOULD NOT BE LINKED TO THE MULTILATERAL TRADING SYSTEM

The Division of Labor between the International Organizations Involved

Point 4 of the declaration adopted by the WTO at the Ministerial Conference in Singapore in 1996 reads: "We renew our commitment to the observance of internationally recognized core labor standards. The ILO is the competent body to set and deal with these standards." Opponents to a link between trade and international labor standards frequently bring into play the architecture of the present international order. They underline the fact that there is one international organization—the ILO—that is in charge of adopting and implementing these standards, while another international organization—the WTO—is responsible for the multilateral trading system and negotiation of new trade rules and disciplines. International labor standards, so they say, should be dealt with where they belong, that is, in the framework of the ILO. This argument implies that issues concerning labor standards should be dealt with in the way the ILO usually does, that is, without applying sanctions. It also suggests that where two different agencies are responsible for two different areas, they should ignore each other.

The latter argument is clearly mistaken. The first argument is correct to the extent that issues should be addressed by the international agencies which are competent. It is also true that the ILO is the agency responsible for the adoption of labor standards and the surveillance of their implementation. However, although they refer to standards defined by the ILO, the links proposed in this study are not meant to promote compliance, but to address certain trade-related effects of non-compliance. This is an issue for which the WTO is responsible. Obviously, the organization has, so far, little experience in this area. But similar difficulties in other areas have not prevented trade negotiators from making new rules.

WTO Rules Should Not Be Extended to Workers' Rights and Social Protection

Another standard objection against a link between trade and labor contends that WTO rules should not be extended to workers' rights and social protection. A similar argument was used by developing countries opposing the adoption of new rules on services and intellectual property rights during the Uruguay Round. According to them, WTO's mission is to discipline the use of trade measures and to reduce barriers to trade, not to establish new ones.

As far as labor protection is concerned, this objection is erroneous for several reasons. In the first place, it cannot be denied that labor conditions have an impact on trade. Thus, opponents have to explain why this impact should be ignored by the multilateral trading system. What is more, this objection implies that free trade prevails over labor protection. This position cannot go unchallenged. From the beginning, the multilateral trading system has included rules limiting unfair trading practices. Opponents should explain why trade should be free although competition is unfair because certain labor standards are not met. From the beginning, GATT rules have included exceptions from the principles of free trade for the sake of certain other policies. Opponents would have to explain why free trade deserves unconditional priority over the responsibility of importing countries for labor protection in exporting countries. Undoubtedly, there is a conflict between the objectives of the ILO—labor protection—and those of the WTO—free trade. This conflict cannot be solved unless WTO rules address the issue of workers' rights and social protection.

No More Exceptions from WTO Rules?

Opponents also argue that there should be no more exceptions from WTO rules and principles. It is true that, as a result of a proliferation of new rules, the multilateral trading system has become more complicated, and not necessarily more efficient. But this is not a valid argument against the adoption of new rules and exceptions, if they are justified.

Nonetheless, linking trade to labor conditions may be unwise as it may dilute one of the basic concepts of the multilateral trading system: the distinction between production and trade. As stated above, the principle of non-discrimination applies to "like" products. Basically, products are alike if they compete with each other. The traditional view is that products are alike even if PPMs—methods and conditions of production and processing—are different. Yet, there are exceptions which allow trade-restrictive measures because of production methods and conditions. GATT Article XX (e) allows restriction of imports of products of prison labor. Other exceptions can be found in the SPS code (on sanitary and phytosanitary measures), the TBT code (on technical barriers to trade), and the code on government procurement. The two links proposed in this study would add to the list of exceptions from, but not dilute, the principle of non-discrimination.

Labor Costs Should Not Be Equalized

Some opponents of a link between trade and labor standards claim that it would result in equalizing labor costs among producers of like products in all countries. To the extent that equalization annihilates comparative advantages, it removes the benefits of free trade.

Equalization of labor costs can be achieved either *a priori* by enforcing the same labor standards in all countries or *a posteriori* by applying additional duties on imports of goods produced under substandard labor conditions. As the two links proposed in this study are not meant to enforce CLS, they would not result in equalizing labor costs *a priori.*

While link B would only cap imports which has no impact on costs and prices, link A would authorize additional duties on imports enjoying a price advantage because of poor labor conditions. Such duties would indeed equalize differences in labor costs *a posteriori*. But they would only compensate for illegitimate comparative advantages. They would not reduce the benefits of free trade.

On the other hand, both links proposed in this study may indirectly and in the long run help to establish a minimum level of labor protection in all countries. This may result in some *a priori* equalization of labor costs. But again, it would only level the playing field and prevent the use of unfair advantages. Moreover, it would not imply that labor laws in all countries are the *same*. It would only mean that they would meet certain minimum standards. National standards could be higher and no country would be obliged to lower them if they are stricter than those set by ILO conventions. Besides, CLS do not establish minimum wages. Quite the opposite: freedom of association and the right to collective bargaining provide a mechanism to determine wages in accordance with productivity, purchasing power, and the supply of skilled and unskilled labor on the labor market of each country. Compliance with CLS does not lead to equalizing labor costs.

Too Many Disputes and a Lack of Expertise of the DSM

Some scholars hint to the lack of expertise of the WTO DSM in determining whether countries comply with international labor standards. This question arises if these links were to be adopted in the framework of the multilateral trading system—which, for the reasons explained above, would be the most appropriate solution. Under present rules, in particular the exceptions of GATT Article XX, the DSM may have to answer questions beyond the scope of the experience of trade panelists. In such cases, they rely on the judgment of others who are qualified to judge. They could also do so when it comes to determining whether certain labor standards are respected in a given country. As suggested above, fact finding in the framework of dispute settlement should be left to the ILO.

Opponents also point to the likelihood that the adoption of new rules in the framework of the multilateral trading system would increase the number of disputes. This, however, is hardly an argument for refuting new rules which are otherwise justified.

CONCLUSION

This chapter discussed the main objections raised against the proposals to establish links between trade and labor made in this study. These links are not meant to improve labor conditions, but to address certain trade-related effects of violations of labor standards. Hence, the standard objection that trade should not be linked to labor standards for the purpose of enforcing the latter does not apply.

A number of other objections against linking trade to labor are based on an opposition to the idea of harmonizing labor standards. Since for the two links proposed in this study, compliance with CLS is only a reference and not a goal, these objections are not relevant.

In my view, none of the technical objections against linking trade to labor standards overrides the arguments in support of these links. And I fail to see any valid trade-related objection either. Likewise, for the reasons explained above, I do not believe that the possible negative economic effects of the proposed links provide a valid argument against them.

NOTES

1. This language is somewhat redundant, though. The rules of the multilateral trading system do not allow using labor standards for just any purpose. On the other hand, there are rather obvious reasons for linking trade and labor, and some WTO members have already done so unilaterally. The sentence may be meant to remind these countries of the limits imposed by relevant WTO rules and principles.

2. R. J. S. Ross, *Slaves to Fashion, Poverty and Abuse in the New Sweatshops*, Ann Arbor, 2004, p. 317.

3. K. A. Elliott and R. B. Freeman, Can Labor Stands Improve under Globalization? Institute for International Economics, Washington, DC, 2003, p. 74.

4. F. Hayek, *Law, Legislation and Liberty: A New Statement of the Liberal Principles of Justice and Political Economy*, London, 1980.

5. See C. B. MacPherson, Elegant Tombstones, A Note on Friedman's Freedom, *Canadian Journal of Political Science*, Vol. 1, No. 1 March 1968, pp. 95–106.

6. R. J. Flanagan, *Globalization and Labor Conditions, Working Conditions and Worker Rights in a Global Economy*, Oxford, 2006, p. 147.

7. K. Bagwell and R. W. Staiger (The Simple Economics of Labor Standards and the GATT, National Bureau of Economic Research Working Paper, no. w6604, 1998) accept the idea of a link between trade and the degree of labor protection, but propose adjusting it to the level of development of each country and linking variable custom duties to variable labor standards. It seems to me that using variable standards as a reference for variable duties turns the race to the bottom into a rule-based mechanism. I see little chance that the international community would agree on such a scheme. And I do not believe that it would be feasible. I do not see any criteria to objectively determine a country's level of development, the corresponding level of labor protection and the level of the duty. At least one country would disagree: the one that is concerned.

8. Besides, this view is incompatible with the claim that core labor standards are human rights: such rights are binding independently from the level of development of a given country.

9. It happened, apparently, at the occasion of quality checks that the FIFA discovered that footballs were produced by children.

10. T. H. Moran, Trade Agreements and Labor Standards, Policy Brief 133 from the National Academy of Science, Washington, DC, 2004.

11. B. H. Weston, Child Labor in Human Rights Law and Policy Perspective, in J. A. Gross and L. Compa (eds), *Human Rights in Labor and Employment Relations: International and Domestic Perspectives*, Labor and Employment Relations Association, Champaign, 2009, pp. 82 and 87.

12. H. Lim, *The Social Clause: Issues and Challenges*, International Labor Organization, Bureau for Workers Activities, Geneva, 2001, p. 15.

13. See for example J. Bhagwati, Policy Perspectives and Future Directions: A View from Academia, Proceedings of a Symposium, in International Labor Standards and Global Economic Integration, United States Department of Labor, Bureau of International Labor Affairs, Washington, DC, 1994, pp. 57–62.

14. R. J. Flanagan, Globalization and Labor Conditions, Working Conditions and Worker Rights in a Global Economy, pp. 81 and 185.

15. J. E. Stiglitz and A. Charlton, *Fair Trade For All, How Trade Can Promote Development*, Oxford, 2005, p. 195.

16. See, for example, D. K. Brown, A. V. Deardorff and R .M. Stern, Pros and Cons of Linking Trade and Labor Standards, Paper prepared for the Murphy Institute Conference on "The Political Economy of Policy Reform," Nov. 2001, p. 13.

17. Organization for Economic Cooperation and Development, International Trade and Core Labour Standards, Paris, 2000, p. 14.

18. D. K. Brown, International Trade and Core Labour Standards, A Survey of the Recent Literature, OECD Labour Market and Social Policy Occasional Papers No. 43, Paris, 2000, p. 16; R. J. Flanagan, Globalization and Labor Conditions, Working Conditions and Worker Rights in a Global Economy, pp. 81 and 135; K. E. Maskus, Should Core Labor Standards Be Imposed Through International Trade Policy? The World Bank Development Research Group, Policy Research Working Paper 1817, Washington, DC, 1997.

19. C. Barry and S. G. Reddy (*International Trade and Labor Standards: A Proposal for a Linkage*, New York, 2008, p. 94) estimate that "the multiple by which labor costs must be increased across the board to eliminate the cost advantage of Southern production is usually very large, and it is at least three under a highly conservative assumption."

20. See the empirical analysis provided by C. Barry and S. G. Reddy, International Trade and Labor Standards: A Proposal for a Linkage, pp. 89–99.

21. D. K. Brown, International Trade and Core Labour Standards, A Survey of the Recent Literature, p. 21.

22. R. Marshall, Trade-Linked Labor Standards, *Proceedings of the Academy of Political Science*, Vol. 37, 1990, No. 4, p. 70.

23. D. Kucera, Core labour standards and foreign direct investment, *International Labour Review*, Vol. 141 (2002), No. 1–2, p. 32.

24. Organization for Economic Cooperation and Development, International Trade and Core Labour Standards, Paris, 2000, p. 139.

25. C. Barry and S. G. Reddy, *International Trade and Labor Standards: A Proposal for a Linkage*, p. 94.

26. A case study on Indonesia finds that there is no evidence that higher minimum wages have "a negative employment impact for large firms, both foreign and domestic, but some evidence that workers in small, domestic firms may lose their jobs," V. Alatas and L. A. Cameron, Should Nike And Reebok Pay Higher Wages? The Impact of Minimum Wages On Employment In a Low Income Country, Research Paper of the Department of Economics of the University of Melbourne.

27. T. H. Moran, Beyond Sweatshops, Foreign Direct Investment and Globalization in Developing Countries, Washington, DC, 2002, p. 79; C. Barry and S. G. Reddy, *International Trade and Labor Standards: A Proposal for a Linkage*, p. 91.

28. N. Wingfield, Apple's Profit Doubles on Holiday iPhone 4S Sales, *New York Times*, January 24, 2012.

29. See page 44.

30. It is, of course, difficult to determine at what point employers would consider that profits are insufficient. There is no empirical evidence showing the amount of additional costs that employers are ready to pay. According to my personal experience, employers are prepared to close their shop rather sooner than later.

31. J. D. Sachs, *The End of Poverty, Economic Possibilities for Our Time*, New York, 2005, p. 12.

32. As R. J. S. Ross (*Slaves to Fashion, Poverty and Abuse in the New Sweatshops*, p. 2) puts it: "A robot may bring a stiff fender to a hard chassis, but as yet only a human hand can guide two limp pieces of fabric to be machine-sewn together in an arc or a tight corner."

33. R. J. Flanagan, Globalization and Labor Conditions, Working Conditions and Worker Rights in a Global Economy, p. 38. Differences in terms of productivity may explain differences in wages, but they do not necessarily justify them. If productivity could justify the level of wages in developing countries, it would also justify sweatshops in developed countries.

34. The examples provided by T. H. Moran (Beyond Sweatshops, Foreign Direct Investment and Globalization in Developing Countries, p. 78) clearly show that differences in wages are a multiple of what differences in productivity could possibly be.

35. D. Rodrik, Democracies Pay Higher Wages, *The Quarterly Journal of Economics*, Vol. CXIV, Issue 3, August 1999, p. 707.

36. International Labour Office, Global Wage Report 2008/2009, Minimum Wages and Collective Bargaining: Towards Policy Coherence, Geneva, 2008, p. 14; ILO, Report of the Working Party on the Social Dimension of Globalization, Governing Body, 310th Session, Geneva, March 2011, document GB.310/16, paragraph 16.

37. G. Fields, The Role of Labor Standards in US Trade Policies, in A. V. Deardorff and R. M. Stern (eds), *Studies in International Economics: Social Dimensions of US Trade Policies*, Ann Arbor, 1999, p. 179.

38. K. D. Ewing (The Sense of Measure: Old Wine in New Bottles, or New Wine in Old Bottles, or New Wine in New Bottles?, in *Dialogue & Debate: Labour, Constitution and a Sense of Measure: A Debate with Alain Supiot*, *Social & Legal Studies*, 2010, 19[2], p. 231) puts it this way: "Labor law has been deep down a blind alley for at last 15 years or so, seeking to find self-justification in economic efficiency or economic competitiveness. This has allowed the debate to be fought on the territory of neo-liberals, and for justifications to be sought which are implausible, unsubstantiated, and unconvincing."

39. D. K. Brown, International Trade and Core Labour Standards, A Survey of the Recent Literature, p. 21.

40. R. Marshall, Trade-Linked Labor Standards, *Proceedings of the Academy of Political Science*, Vol. 37, 1990, No. 4, p. 70.

41. This issue is similar to—and overlaps, to some extent, with—what is known as the "dilemma of the informal sector": the informal sector has an important potential to create jobs, but these jobs may not necessarily provide decent work. While attempts to regulate the informal sector are likely to reduce the number of new jobs, they will nevertheless improve their quality.

Chapter Nine

Additional Benefits of Linking Trade and Labor Standards

Establishing the links proposed in this study would have further benefits of a global nature.

PREVENTING UNILATERAL ACTION

Rules linking trade and labor standards in the framework of the WTO would help to prevent unilateral action. Certain countries have adopted unilateral measures in the area of intellectual property rights before the TRIPS agreement was signed. Some countries like the United States, the EU, as well as a number of other countries, have also taken unilateral action or regional initiatives in the area of international labor standards because they believe that such actions were justified and required. Without a constructive agreement on the issue of how to link trade and labor standards, individual countries are left to adopt measures which may turn out to be incompatible with GATT and WTO rules. Adopting the links proposed in this study would prevent unilateral action.

REBALANCING THE MULTILATERAL TRADING SYSTEM

It is often argued that there is a lack of balance concerning the rules of the multilateral trading system. Over the years, these rules were expanded to a number of new areas, while others like the environment and labor protection, which have equally close ties with trade, have been left out. Adopting the links proposed in this study would rebalance the system.

The TRIPS Agreement

The lack of balance is particularly obvious if we consider intellectual property rights. Although there is also an agency in charge of protecting them, the World Intellectual Property Organization (WIPO), the TRIPS agreement itself defines the intellectual property rights which WTO members have to respect. And it authorizes trading partners to use the WTO DSM for disputes over the respect of these rights. In other words, it does in respect of intellectual property rights exactly what the Singapore Declaration of 1996 prohibits in respect of international labor standards: that the WTO sets and deals with them. Nonetheless, labor standards remain "off WTO's radar screen," as a representative once observed in a GATT meeting. This suggests that the multilateral trading system considers intellectual property rights, which are private rights (as specifically underlined by the preamble of the TRIPS agreement) as more important than CLS, which are widely acknowledged as human rights. The links proposed in this study would rebalance this position.

WTO and the Environment

In the framework of the WTO, labor standards play an even less prominent role than the protection of the environment which, at least, is *discussed* in that forum. Attempts to put the environment on the agenda of the Uruguay Round in 1986 failed. Finally, in 1990, it was agreed to establish a working group on the environment.[1] The first item on the group's agenda was the basic question of how to accommodate the rules of the multilateral trading system and the provisions of multilateral environmental agreements. Twenty-five years later, the WTO has still not been able to fully answer that question.

One of the reasons why the WTO decided to include the environment in its agenda is because the protection of the environment has global implications. But so do violations of labor standards. It is difficult to understand why the WTO continues to snub the issue of labor standards. On the other hand, the lack of any substantial progress in the framework of WTO work on the environment has been blamed, *inter alia*, on the absence of a worldwide organization for the protection of the environment. For labor, such an organization exists: it is the ILO.

Improving the Image of the WTO

Apparently, the priorities of the multilateral trading system are somewhat biased. For many years, trade negotiators have managed international trade as a merely commercial function that should be dealt with in isolation from social concerns. The explanation that comes readily to mind is that the system is shaped for a world economy based on capitalism. While it includes sophisticated rules to protect the interests of capital, it almost entirely ignores the environment and social protection. This is why the WTO has come under heavy attack by a number of NGOs who have asserted that the WTO favors unfair trade rather than sustainable development. Linking trade and labor standards in the way proposed in this study would improve the image of the WTO.

REBALANCING RELATIONS BETWEEN DIFFERENT GROUPS OF WTO MEMBERS

There are three classes of WTO members: developed countries, developing countries, and least developed countries. In general, developed countries have to respect more trade disciplines than others, and developing countries more so than least developed countries. Where developing countries do not comply with international labor standards, this actually accentuates the differences between the three classes of WTO members. Linking trade to labor standards would help to rebalance the relations between the different groups of WTO members.

IMPROVING GLOBAL GOVERNANCE

Both the ILO and the WTO are cornerstones of the international order. Unfortunately, their rules are not entirely consistent. From the perspective of the ILO, it is not legal to violate CLS although they are universally binding, even on (the few) countries that are not member states of the ILO. No state should ignore them, whether in the framework of domestic policies or at the international level, that is, as a member state of the WTO. From the perspective of the WTO, compliance with these standards is nonetheless irrelevant. Linking trade to CLS would remove this inconsistency. Both the architecture of the international order and global governance stand to benefit from the links proposed in this study.

CONCLUSION

Adopting links between trade and labor would have a number of additional advantages. It would prevent unilateral action. It would rebalance the multilateral trading system. It would improve the equilibrium between different groups of trading partners. And it would advance global governance, by removing a major inconsistency of the global international order. It should be recalled, however, that these are bonuses, which, *per se*, do not provide a justification for linking trade to labor standards.

NOTE

1. After the 1972 United Nations Conference on the Human Environment in Stockholm GATT Contracting Parties agreed to establish a working party on trade and the environment in 1975. However, this working party has met only once.

Chapter Ten

Getting Agreement on Linking Trade and Labor Standards

If there are, as this study suggests, plausible reasons for establishing links between international labor standards and the rules of the multilateral trading system, and if there are also ways and means, as shown in chapter 7, to shape these links to ensure that they can achieve their objectives, and not more than that, why then has it been so far impossible to adopt them? This chapter attempts to answer this question, with a view to assess the chances that the links proposed here or any similar rules may be adopted in the future.

THE LOST CHANCE

Arguably, there was a window of opportunity, at the end of the past millennium, to put the issue of labor standards on the international trade agenda. During the 1990s, industries in developed countries became increasingly exposed to cheap imports from developing countries, whose labor costs were low, whose production capacities had surged, and whose trading opportunities had greatly benefited from trade liberalization. Workers in developed countries realized that they did not necessarily stand to win from globalization, while consumers started to notice that the amazingly low prices of many imported goods were a blessing for them just because they were not a blessing for those who had produced these goods. Several governments realizing that more should be done in order to improve labor protection in countries from which they imported goods tried to put the issue on the international political agenda.

The Copenhagen UN World Summit on Social Development of 1995, the WTO Ministerial Declaration adopted in Singapore in 1996, the 1998 ILO

Declaration on Fundamental Principles and Rights at Work, and the WTO Ministerial Meeting in Seattle in 1999 illustrate the importance that certain governments attached to the issue of trade and labor standards. The Seattle meeting provided an opportunity to open a real discussion in the competent international forum. Unfortunately, that opportunity was lost, for several reasons.

Bad Timing

The proposals made by the EU and the United States to discuss trade and labor standards in the 1990s suffered, first and foremost, from bad timing. They came shortly after the conclusion of the Uruguay Round, whose results left many developing countries with a feeling of having gotten a bad deal. During that round, developed countries had insisted on adopting new rules on services and intellectual property rights, areas in which developing countries had little or no interest. They had accepted the results of the round because they were promised more access to the markets of OECD countries, in particular for agricultural products, and an end to textile quotas. Thereafter, OECD countries did not have many bargaining chips left, at least not enough to put labor standards on WTO's agenda.

The Proposals Were Not Presented as Trade-Related

Above all, the rules of the multilateral trading system are meant to fix trade-related problems. Thus, it would seem less difficult to convince trade negotiators of the merits of adopting new rules if these are intended to solve *trade-related* issues. However, proposals from OECD countries to take up labor standards in the framework of the WTO did not present the issue as primarily trade-related. While the proposals used very careful language in order to avoid the impression of protectionist intentions, President Clinton's comments made in Seattle offered a welcome pretext for some governments to refuse any discussion of the issue at all. They were probably aware that a discussion would have soon reached the conclusion of this study: that there are obvious trade-related reasons for establishing a link between trade and labor standards. As one scholar comments: "Ironically, it may be that international fair labor standards would have advanced further if they had been motivated more by protectionism than by moralism."[1]

Lack of Clarity of the Objective Pursued

Furthermore, proposals from OECD countries for putting labor on the WTO agenda lacked clarity about their real objective. Perhaps the authors of these proposals were not completely clear about their own intentions. They were driven by the political desiderata of various stakeholders pursuing different objectives. Some of them felt pity for workers suffering from inhuman labor conditions, others feared for the jobs in developed countries, and yet others found that the rules of the multilateral trading system were not fair. The agenda of proponents included several of the reasons for establishing a link between trade and labor standards examined in chapters 3 and 4, but did not always sufficiently differentiate between them. As a result, the main objective of the proposals remained unclear. This weakened them considerably.

As shown above, a link between trade and labor standards has to be shaped in accordance with its objective. Since the purpose of linking trade to labor was ambiguous, there was no clear idea of how a possible link would look. Thus, opponents were free to imagine that a link would have the features and consequences that they would not accept under any circumstances.[2] In other word: the lack of clarity also opened the door to objections which a clear proposal might have countered more easily.

Lack of Coordination among Proponents

Last but not least, the proponents of a discussion of trade and labor standards in the WTO did not sufficiently coordinate their efforts. In the run up to the Seattle WTO Ministerial Meeting of 1999, Canada proposed the establishment of a WTO working group to report to the next Ministerial Meeting on the "relationships between appropriate trade, development, social and environmental policy choices in the context of the experiences of and challenges faced by all WTO members in adjusting to globalization." The EU proposed a "joint ILO/WTO Standing Working Forum on trade, globalization and labor issues." And the United States proposed the adoption of a "work program to address labor-related trade questions and the establishment of a Working Group on Trade and Labor, to operate under the supervision of the WTO General Council."[3] It is easy to imagine that a common proposal would have gained greater support.

THE POSITION OF STAKEHOLDERS

The view that a link between trade and labor is warranted is shared, in general, by the left, trade unions and human rights and other labor activists as well as the governments of many OECD countries, while the right, employers, many trade economists and the governments of major developing countries oppose it.

Workers in Exporting Countries

In general, workers participate in a discussion like this with the help of trade unions. In countries which do not grant freedom of association, workers are, to a large extent, prevented from participating in the debate. Thus, we know very little about their position.

Trade restrictions may result in a loss of jobs in exporting countries. Yet, for the reasons mentioned above, the links proposed are not likely to produce major job losses. But they are likely to improve working conditions in the long run. It may be assumed that the likely positive effects of the links proposed in this study outweigh their possible negative effects. Workers in exporting countries would be well advised to support these links.

Workers in Importing Countries

Workers in importing countries suffer the effects of imports produced in other countries under substandard working conditions or the consequences of relocation of their industries to countries where such conditions prevail. There is empirical evidence that wages in certain sectors in developed countries such as the garment and apparel industry have been put under considerable pressure as a result of that competition. This has even led to the reappearance of sweatshops in some OECD countries.[4] There is also evidence that a significant amount of jobs have been lost in these countries due to relocation of production sites to developing countries.

However, wages in most OECD countries are much higher than in developing countries, regardless of whether the latter comply with international labor standards or not. A link would, at best, bring wages in countries not respecting labor standards up to the levels of countries that fully implement them. But this would neither lessen the pressure on wages in developed countries nor reduce the incentives for relocation. In other words, workers in developed countries do not stand to gain from the links proposed in this study. Nevertheless, there may be instances where individual companies in developed countries would not survive without the trade restrictions that link A would permit. That link might help some workers in OECD countries to keep their jobs.

Trade Unions

Trade unions in developed countries used to favor the idea of linking trade and labor standards. As this position is seen to reflect protectionist motives, it is not endorsed by trade unions in developing countries, which fear that a link would put jobs in their countries in jeopardy. Unions of the North and of the South are divided on the issue.[5] I imagine that they would be just as divided on the links proposed in this study.

In most developing countries, the level of membership in trade unions is low. Moreover, their influence is limited where freedom of association and the right to collective bargaining are not granted. On the other hand, in developed countries, union membership has significantly declined over the last fifty years.[6] As a result, unions have lost part of their influence.[7] It seems that they have also lost interest in the issue under consideration.

Employers

Employers in exporting countries exploiting labor obviously have little sympathy for the idea of linking trade to labor standards. The same is likely to be true as far as other participants in the supply chain are concerned who take advantage of the savings that substandard labor conditions produce. Some of them have enough political influence to ensure that their governments give priority to their interests.

Link A would help to protect the domestic industries of importing countries against imports of goods produced under substandard labor conditions. While employers in developed countries asked for protection for many years, more recently there has been a shift of interest. Many companies were driven out of business by imports from countries not meeting CLS. The industries which survived are those able to compete with imports of goods from countries where labor is cheap, whether the reason is non-compliance with labor standards or some other. These companies do not need the protection that link A would provide.

Some industries which disappeared in developed countries went to low wage developing countries. For them, poor labor standards are not a problem, but rather a business opportunity. They now lobby the governments of OECD countries to keep their markets open. Linking trade to labor standards in the way proposed in this study would certainly not be in their interest.

Governments of Developing Countries

Freedom of association and the right to collective bargaining are, in some developing countries, much more than a labor issue. Their denial is part and parcel of an authoritarian system that does not tolerate any opposition and combats the formation of any forces that may undermine the government's authority or threaten its survival.

Other governments are eager to keep the competitive advantage of cheap labor, including the part that derives from substandard labor conditions. C. Barry and S. G. Reddy attempt to identify a type of linkage that would stand up to any objection. Their reflections are based on the assumption that everybody endorses the objective of "improving the level of advantage of less advantaged persons in the world to a greater extent." In fact, this assumption appears unrealistic: there are reasons to believe that some governments do not care about "improving the level of advantage of their less advantaged citizens." These governments not only object to a link, but more generally to any proposals to improve labor conditions. Their position basically reflects the economic interests of a minority that behaves in a way similar to former colonial powers.[8]

Governments of Developed Countries

Some OECD countries have established links between trade and labor standards in their own trade regimes. Yet, these links have not been used as frequently as they could have been. By the same token, the reaction of many governments to the decision of the ILO authorizing a trade embargo against Myanmar was rather lukewarm. The lack of interest in making use of existing links suggests that there is actually little real interest in establishing the links proposed in this study.

Meanwhile, both the United States and the EU seem to have put the issue on the backburner of their international trade agenda. The Bush administration was not interested in linking trade to labor as much as the previous one, while the EU opted for promoting CLS by development cooperation and policy dialogue.

Consumers

To the extent that the savings from substandard labor conditions in the production of exports reaches the consumer, the latter has an economic benefit. With a link between trade and labor, this benefit may be foregone. But many consumers feel that it is unfair in the first place. An increasing number gives preference to goods sold by fair trade organizations. If sufficiently informed, consumers are likely to support links of the kind proposed in this study.

International Organizations

The two international organizations primarily concerned with trade and labor standards are the ILO and the WTO. Since their membership overlaps to a large extent, both have adopted similar lines of action, as shown by the declarations they adopted in the late 1990s. Of course, it is only consistent that governments do not accept in the WTO what they refuse in the ILO. However, the purpose of the two links proposed in this study is not to enforce CLS, but to address certain trade-related effects of non-compliance with these standards. For the reasons explained above, the most appropriate place to do so would be the WTO. But there is no agreement that the issues *need* to be addressed. The right place to achieve this basic consensus may be the ILO.

Other international agencies participating in the debate of trade and labor standards are the OECD and the World Bank. Both organizations favor policies that improve the respect of labor standards. The OECD has carried out a number of comprehensive studies of the issue and surveys of the academic literature in this field. Yet, these papers do not conclude that there is a need to link trade to labor.[9] A stronger focus on the trade-related aspects discussed in this study may bring about a change in this respect.

NGOs and Activists

While the stakeholders who are most directly concerned—workers in developing countries—are often unable to voice their concerns and to defend their interests, others do it on their behalf. There is a strong lobby of NGOs supporting better implementation of labor standards, motivated by compassion for those who suffer from poor labor conditions. The most active support for a link between trade and labor currently comes from human rights activists. They have shown that, by drawing on a network of partners and like-minded informants around the world, they are able to uncover violations of labor rights even in areas such as the informal sector which is difficult to reach. Their understanding of the importance of labor rights in the broader context of sustainable development has influenced both public opinion and the international policy agenda. The rationale of link B may convince human rights activists and fair traders to lend their support to this proposal.

Academics

On the other hand, there is also a group of people, among them renowned economists, who oppose a link without having any personal interests. For most of them, the main issue is a choice between efficiency and equity. Since equity is basically beyond the scope of their studies, they tend to give priority to efficiency. They claim that low labor standards are justified by efficiency gains and higher economic growth.

Giving preference to growth over labor standards is certainly in the interest of those who profit from poor labor standards, but not of those who endure them. Some trade economists actually seem to be motivated by the desire to promote the special interests of the former rather than to carry out objective scientific research.[10] Although their advice, for the reasons explained above, fails to convince, it continues to dominate the debate and helps to block any substantive discussion of trade and labor in the framework of the multilateral trading system. They remind me of those who tried to justify colonization and slavery on religious grounds.

THE STATE OF THE PRESENT DEBATE

Just like the discussion of trade and the environment, that of trade and labor was dramatized before it even began. As a result of the economic interests at stake and the appalling working conditions in some countries, the debate has become heavily politicized. Due to an intransigent attitude of certain trade negotiators and the partisanship of many academics it has also become emotionally charged. Occasionally, the debate even took to the streets.

The Debate is Deadlocked

Over the last quarter of a century, efforts were made to solve the problems discussed in this study *without restricting trade*. The EU endeavored to improve workers' rights in exporting countries by offering them additional trade preferences. The ILO concentrated its activities on the promotion of fundamental principles and rights at work, the ratification of the relevant conventions, and their implementation. NGOs and academics insisted on the importance of these rights as human rights, hoping to convince governments to enforce and companies to respect them. MNEs committed themselves to codes of conduct which include basically the same principles and rights. And fair trade initiatives tried to convince consumers to set aside products made in violation of these rights.

At the same time, the discussion focused on the human rights aspect, globalization, and private labor governance. Many academics acclaimed self-regulation in the form of fair trade and corporate codes of conduct as a better alternative to state intervention and the normative approach of the ILO. Neoliberal economists declared that there is no need to address the problems examined in this book, claiming that globalization would produce acceptable working conditions anyway. Although this belief lacks supporting empirical evidence, it has acquired virtually doctrinal status.

As a result, the discussion of trade and labor is trapped in deadlock. The partisans of one view (or the other) seldom listen to anybody arguing the opposite. While those responsible for violating labor standards are by and large immune to ethical considerations, those invoking the latter are seldom impressed by economic arguments.

The Debate Lacks a Frame of Reference

As stated above, a link is a tool to achieve a political objective. Hence, the starting point for discussing the merits of linking trade to labor standards ought to be the political objective that such links would help attain. Anything else amounts to putting the cart before the horse. Nonetheless, many scholars evaluate the economic effects of a link without clearly identifying its objective and shape. As a result, much of the discussion of a link has taken place in a vacuum. Indeed, in spite of a huge number of publications, the discussion has not advanced very far.

Trade, Labor Standards, and Globalization

A number of recent studies on the interrelation between labor protection and trade liberalization examine this issue in the broader context, which is commonly referred to as globalization. Many scholars assume a conflict between the predominant economic and political driving forces of our times and certain legal provisions on labor protection, which they consider as more or less obsolete.

Globalization enthusiasts compare the situation of countries that have participated in globalization to those that have not, and find that the former had faster economic growth and better labor conditions. *Per se*, these conclusions seem to be plausible. However, globalization enthusiasts seldom ask whether labor conditions are truly satisfactory, whether in absolute terms or in comparison to the level of economic development of the country concerned, and whether it would have been easier or more successful to improve them through specific policies (other than *laissez-faire*).

The anti-globalization movement blames globalization for the spread of sweatshops in the third world. This claim, too, is plausible to the extent that globalization amounts to the application of the principles of capitalism to economic relations and transactions beyond state boundaries. Indeed, unfettered capitalism, as prevailed in Europe at an early stage and which globalization now replicates in many developing countries, tends to put heavy pressure on labor conditions.

In my view, approaching the issue of trade and labor standards under the angle of globalization is not very helpful. The commonly offered definition of globalization—liberalization of trade and capital movements together with advances in transport and communication technology—combines several elements. Hence, claims that globalization is responsible for labor conditions, good or bad, are not very meaningful. A more pertinent question is whether the results of globalization actually legitimize the policies that made it possible in the first place. As far as certain effects of free trade are concerned, there are valid reasons to adopt corrective measures—such as the links proposed in this study.

THE CHANCES OF LINKING TRADE TO LABOR STANDARDS IN THE NEAR FUTURE

Just like any other successful policy, globalization has produced undesirable side effects. The same happened during the early days of industrialization. Governments eventually reacted and corrected these effects by adopting labor laws and others such as anti-trust legislation. In 1919, minimum standards of social protection were supported by a coalition between those who wanted socialism and those who feared it: both hoped that establishing such standards would further their respective agenda.

From the outset, there were proposals to combine international labor standards with rules on international trade, but no concrete measures were adopted. More recently, when a number of developing countries achieved a higher level of participation in world trade, the idea gained support again. There was a window of opportunity, in the late 1990s, to put the issue on the international trade agenda, but that opportunity was lost. Accordingly, the latest round of multilateral trade negations, the Doha Development Agenda, does not include the issue of labor standards. In the worst case, we have to wait for the conclusion of this round and the launching of another before we can discuss the matter in the WTO.

Meanwhile, some supporters of a link have lost interest. Both for governments and trade unions in OECD countries the issue seems no longer a political priority. Corporations in developed countries, which initially had asked their governments to protect them against cheap imports from developing countries, are now lobbying them to keep their markets open for goods that they themselves produce in these countries. Today, a coalition between MNEs and other employers in developing countries, the governments of these countries, and importers and retailers in importing countries opposes a link between the rules of the multilateral trading system and international labor standards. The chances for linking the rules of the multilateral trading system to ILO labor standards are now probably slimmer than any time before.

On the other hand, the United States and the EU continue to push for better labor protection in the framework of their bilateral and regional trade arrangements. This has reached a point of no return both in the United States and the EU, since neither their legislative bodies nor their public opinion would accept doing away with this policy. It could provide the basis for multilateral rules. It goes without saying that the chances of establishing a link in the framework of the multilateral trading system would be greater if the United States and the EU reached similar positions. The EU and the United States should agree on a common approach.

The United States prepared their request for the inclusion of new rules on worldwide protection of intellectual property rights by taking unilateral measures, some of which were not compatible with the rules of the multilateral trading system. In the end, the WTO adopted the TRIPS Agreement. The United States started with similar initiatives in order to push its agenda on trade and labor standards. Countries which are convinced that a link between the two is required should not hesitate to apply unilateral trade restrictions even if these are incompatible with WTO rules. Under the present circumstances, this seems to be the only way to start a discussion in the WTO. It would also provide a bargaining chip for negotiations—just as in the case of intellectual property rights.

As shown in chapter 6, the links adopted by the EU, the United States and their respective trading partners in their domestic trade laws and trade agreements are motivated by considerations similar to those underlying the two links proposed in this study. They try to avoid the worst through bilateral and regional arrangements. This would suggest that there is nonetheless some interest in dealing with the issue that link A would address. The chances of adopting link B are better, to the extent that it is based on moral considerations which are likely to gain support over time. Maybe one day a coalition will emerge between consumers, human rights activists, trade unions, and the governments of some developed countries to fight for the establishment of such a link.

In the history of the GATT and WTO, several new rules were introduced which a decade or two prior to their adoption would have looked like non-starters. They became law because they were supported by strong arguments—and by strong negotiators. If we really want to link trade and labor, we could get it.

NOTES

1. Charnovitz, The Influence of International Labor Standards on the World Trading Regime, *International Labour Review*, Vol. 126, No. 5, Sept.–Oct. 1987, p. 581.

2. See e.g., D. K. Brown, International Trade and Core Labour Standards, A Survey of the Recent Literature, OECD Labour Market and Social Policy Occasional Papers No. 43, Paris, 2000, p. 34, who seems to take it for granted that a link would necessarily be a trade *ban*.

3. WTO, WT/GC/W/383, of 5.11.1999, WT/GC/W/382, of 1.11.1999, and WT/GC/W/360, of 12.10.1999

4. R. J. S. Ross, *Slaves to Fashion, Poverty and Abuse in the New Sweatshops*, Ann Arbor, 2004

5. R. Hensman, Fine-Tuning the Linkage Proposal, in C. Barry and S. G. Reddy, *International Trade and Labor Standards: A Proposal for a Linkage*, New York, 2008, p. 126.

6. S. F. Diamond, Labor Rights in the Global Economy, A Case Study of NAFTA, in L. A. Compa and S. F. Diamond (eds), *Human Rights, Labor Rights, and International Trade,* Philadelphia, 1996, p. 201.

7. A. Bieler, I. Landberg, and D. Pillay, *Labour and the Challenges of Globalization, What Prospects for Transnational Solidarity?* London and Ann Arbor, 2008; C. Swidorski, From the Wagner Act to the Human Rights Watch Report: Labor and Freedom of Expression and Association 1935–2000, *New Political Science*, Vol. 25, no. 1, 2003, p. 55.

8. H. Lim, *The Social Clause: Issues and Challenges*, International Labor Organization, Bureau for Workers Activities, Geneva, 2001, p. 15; J. D. London, The Economic Context: Grounding Discussions of Economic Change and Labor in Developing Countries, in L. P. Hartman, D. G. Arnold, and R. E. Wokutch (eds), *Rising above Sweatshops, Innovative Approaches to Global Labor Challenges*, Westport and London, 2003, p. 49.

9. The OECD commissioned D. K. Brown, a scholar with strong personal views on these issues.

10. This assessment is shared by K. A. Elliott and R. B. Freeman, Can Labor Stands Improve under Globalization? Institute for International Economics, Washington, DC, 2003, footnote on p. 80.

Chapter Eleven

My Own Proposals

The conclusions reached in the previous chapter are not very encouraging. They are even alarming if we take into account the limits of the alternative solutions examined in chapter 5. Yet, even if the links proposed in this study were to be adopted and applied by all nations, this would not solve the non-trade-related problems deriving from poor labor conditions examined in chapter 3. Although these problems do not justify the establishment of a link between trade and labor standards, more has to be done in order to tackle them.

This chapter explains my own proposals to that end. It should be noted, however, that these problems can hardly be solved without implementing CLS in all countries of the world. The following proposals are not meant to substitute but only to prepare the ground for the adoption of adequate policies and the enforcement of minimum labor standards.

WITHDRAWAL OF GSP PREFERENCES

In 2003, the European Commission prepared a report (not published) analyzing the effects of the EU GSP scheme. This report compares the value of imports benefiting from GSP preferences to those from all countries and from developed countries. While imports to the European Union of dutiable products grew, over the period from 1997 to 2001 by 50 percent, imports from countries enjoying preferential treatment increased considerably faster (63 percent) than imports of the same products from countries not enjoying preferences (26 percent). These figures suggest that by and large, the GSP achieves its objective of enhancing the participation of developing countries in international trade. However, the efficiency of the EU special incentive arrangements concerning labor rights has been somewhat limited, as shown in chapter 6. Under these circumstances, the positive effect of increasing trade is likely to have a negative side effect in countries not fully implementing labor standards: a proliferation of violations of the latter.

In such cases, it would be appropriate to make wider use of the rules which allow the withdrawal of preferential treatment. For that purpose, the United States and the EU could coordinate their policies by agreeing to use the same benchmarks for assessing whether GSP preferences should be withdrawn. These benchmarks could be similar to the criteria proposed for link B.

So far, both the United States and the EU provide GSP preferences even to countries with notoriously poor records in terms of labor protection. They hesitate to withdraw GSP preferences for two reasons: because they are lobbied by those who take advantage of poor labor conditions in developing countries and because they do not want to put strain on the relations with the exporting countries concerned. Experience has shown that ethical arguments, if presented effectively and convincingly, may eventually prevail over economic interests and lobbying. The risk that withdrawal of GSP preferences may have a negative impact on relations with other governments is similar to the problem of how to deal with human rights issues. The human rights aspects of the matter which ultimately concern each and every consumer in developed countries may raise it to a politically more prominent level. A public explanation that GSP preferences could be responsible for poor working conditions in developing countries may encourage the governments of the United States and the EU to take action. This requires a well-organized campaign supported by those who are committed to improving the fate of labor in the world. In my view, such campaign could have a decisive impact.

Withdrawal of GSP preferences would have the consequence that importers have to pay normal duty rates. This would benefit the budget of the importing country. The idea of a more general withdrawal of GSP preferences would become more attractive if the additional income generated by those duties were to be used for development assistance earmarked for promoting compliance with CLS in exporting countries.

VOLUNTARY MINIMUM WAGES

Although this study does not find justification for establishing a link between trade and labor standards for a non-trade-related reason, the analysis in chapter 3 clearly shows that poor labor standards create problems, which are real and serious. It is therefore necessary to look for additional ways and means to solve these problems.

The factor that determines the livelihood of workers more than any other is the level of wages. CLS stipulate procedural requirements for the collective bargaining of wages, without fixing minimum levels. ILO conventions on minimum wages regulate the implementation of minimum wage policies, but do not provide any concrete guidance to what the minimum should be. Fair trade initiatives promise to provide fair income, but they do not propose criteria to determine the minimum level where income starts to be fair. Codes of conduct commit companies to pay local minimum wages, but they are, as shown in chapter 5, often extremely low.

There are also proposals to make direct income transfers to the working poor.[1] In general, it is better to attack a problem at its root than to solve it *a posteriori* through compensation. The easiest way to avoid the problems stemming from insufficient wages is to pay adequate ones.

The Minimum Level of Wages

There are many proposals for international minimum wages, and there are probably as many claims that they are not a good idea. I agree that minimum wages may have serious shortcomings if they are set too high. But I believe that minimum wages are nonetheless a good idea when real wages are otherwise far too low.

Admittedly, the determination of a minimum level of wages is ultimately based on subjective criteria. Notwithstanding, I believe that there is a bottom line: wages which do not suffice to lift a family out of poverty are too low. As stated in chapter 5, it takes an income of $240 per month to lift a family of four above the international poverty line of $2 per day. I fail to see any reason—economic or other—why people who make their labor available to employers should be denied a chance to escape poverty, to live a decent life, and to ensure a better future for their children. With a family income of less than $240 per month, child labor is likely to remain a necessity in many countries. Therefore, workers should be paid that amount, everywhere.

However, in very poor countries, it may not be possible to pay wages at that level. The level of wages that can be paid depends on the GDP per capita. It would be economically possible to pay wages reaching the level of at least 50 percent of the mean disposable income of a given country.[2] What is then the level of per capita GDP that would allow paying wages of $240 per month?

$240 for four people implies $60 per person. $60 per person per month corresponds to $720 per annum. If this amount is 50 percent of the mean disposable income, the latter would be $1,440. Assuming that the mean disposable income is 70 percent of GDP per capita,[3] $1,440 would correspond to a per capita GDP of $2,057. Hence, it is fair to say that countries with an annual per capita GDP in excess of $2,000 have no economic excuse for paying wages below $240 per month.

Certain employers such as MNEs could pay such wages everywhere, even in the poorest countries. As mentioned above, the share of labor in production costs and final sale prices of goods produced by or for MNEs in developing countries clearly show that there is considerable headroom for paying higher wages. In essence, it can safely be assumed that employers from developed countries operating in developing countries could pay wages of at least $240 per month.

Non-Binding Standards

Yet, minimum wages in many developing countries are below $240 per month. Afraid of losing a competitive advantage, the governments of most of these countries are extremely reluctant to raise legal minimum wages. It therefore makes sense to tackle the issue by using a non-binding approach instead. Defined along the lines explained above, non-binding minimum standards could serve as guidelines for remunerating workers. My proposal includes two such standards, the "wage above poverty standard" and the "dollar an hour standard."

The Wages Above Poverty Standard

Considering that the international poverty line is $2 a day and that one breadwinner's income must feed on average a family of four, wages should be at least be $8 per day ($240 per month). In countries with a per capita GDP below $2,000, this standard should instead be four times the amount of the national poverty line (per head) of the country concerned. This is the "wage above poverty standard."

The Dollar an Hour Standard

Wages are only fair if they correspond to a reasonable number of working hours. The relevant ILO convention, adopted many years ago, limits work to eight hours a day or forty-eight hours a week. This would limit the number of hours to roughly 208 a month. Wages of $240 would thus amount to approximately $1.15 per hour. This should be paid in all countries with a per capita GDP above $2,000, as well as by all foreign employers in all developing countries. In short, this is referred to as the "dollar an hour standard."

Using These Standards

It would be difficult to make these standards binding. But this does not imply that these standards could not be effective. They could provide a reference and a target, and also criteria for shame and blame. Governments who fix legal minimum wages below the wages above poverty standard would have to justify that policy. International organizations such as the World Bank and the IMF could check countries' policies against this standard and include this in their country reports. The ILO could use it to determine whether wages are fair.

Companies from developed countries could use the dollar an hour standard in a similar way as codes of conduct. Meeting the standard would help them improve their image. Fair trade initiatives could use the standard as a reference for fair income. Clear standards send clear messages and provide a stronger incentive for the consumer to give preference to goods that meet them. Since compliance with the dollar an hour standard is easy to verify, products could also be certified in a more reliable manner.

NOTES

1. C. Barry and S. G. Reddy, *International Trade and Labor Standards: A Proposal for a Linkage*, New York, 2008, p. 37.
2. This amount would correspond to a national poverty line calculated in accordance with the relative method. Countries using the relative method for calculating their national poverty line typically fix that line at 50 percent or 60 percent of their mean disposable income.
3. It is in developing countries, it is typically lower than in developed countries.

Final Remarks

This study advocates the adoption of two rules linking the multilateral trading system to CLS. One would be warranted by the effects of non-compliance with these standards on trade. It seems that at present, there is little interest in the adoption of a new rule providing protection against these effects. I can imagine a situation where trade negotiators and legislators will regret that they did not insist on making this a multilateral rule at an earlier stage.

The other rule is justified by the responsibility of importing countries for violations of CLS in exporting countries. Ultimately, this is the personal responsibility of each one of us. But we are not always fully aware of this responsibility. The fact that exporting countries are independent states makes us believe that only they are responsible for violations of labor standards in their territory. Another reason why we tend to be indifferent is that many countries where such violations happen are far away. In addition, the consumption of cheap goods seems to act like a drug on which we are becoming increasingly dependent. As a result, we prefer to turn a blind eye on the reasons why they are cheap. Moreover, given the number of people working under extremely poor conditions, we are inclined to regard these conditions as normal. However, what is fundamentally immoral can hardly be considered as normal. We have to realize that we are responsible for promoting immoral and inhumane working conditions in other countries if we import and consume more and more goods produced under such conditions. And that we have to take action, by adopting link B.

We have succeeded in giving capitalism a human face in Western countries. Now the issue is to make globalization more humane. Both the fight for better working conditions in Europe and the battle against slavery opposed economic interests and moral considerations. They were won because we gave preference to values such as human dignity. The choice concerns the shape of the world in which we want to live.

Summing Up

THE GAP BETWEEN TRADE AND LABOR STANDARDS

Trade has an impact on the level of labor protection in countries that trade with each other. Similarly, the level of labor protection has an impact on trade between countries. Aware of these implications, some nations decided almost a century ago to adopt international minimum standards. Labor standards are among the earliest internationally harmonized norms.

Trade benefits all countries if it is open and fair. Having learned this lesson, a group of countries adopted some seventy years ago a set of rules and disciplines for international trade. But they did not agree on a rule that would allow restricting trade with countries that do not comply with international labor standards.

Without such a rule, substandard labor conditions may have disastrous consequences. Poor labor conditions in one country may be an incentive for others to tolerate violations of their labor laws or even to lower their level of labor protection. And shipments from countries where labor conditions do not meet minimum standards can distort trade. This may result in increased exports from these countries, in higher investment, and ultimately in more violations of labor standards of the same kind.

Some of these risks have materialized and produced serious problems. In order to address them, proposals were made to link the rules of the multilateral trading system to international labor standards. However, none of these proposals was adopted, because

- exporting countries fear that compliance with labor standards raises production costs and takes away their competitive advantage;

- exporting countries and importers lobby the governments of importing countries to keep their markets open for cheap imports, including those which are cheap because labor standards are not met;
- other issues were given priority, such as the protection of intellectual property rights.

HOLLOW PROMISES AND ALTERNATIVE APPROACHES

Certain economists claim that there is an automatic solution to the problems stemming from substandard labor conditions. They argue that poor labor standards favor growth and that growth leads to better labor conditions. For a quarter of a century, free market fans and globalization enthusiasts have enjoyed the privilege to use the world as a laboratory to test these claims. What we know now is that on the whole globalization does not keep the promise that economic benefits trickle down and that the tide will raise all boats. The contention that there is an automatic solution is, at best, wishful thinking and, at worst, political blindness and cynicism.

Some of those who see a need to address these problems turn to another argument, that of human rights. While this argument may change political consciousness, it has little practical impact. The same is true of other policies that have been proposed and tested as alternatives to the normative approach of the ILO. Fair trade initiatives and codes of conduct are based on the erroneous belief that law enforcement can be privatized. They are no panacea nor substitute for a rules-based policy.

Meanwhile, some major trading partners have introduced links between trade and labor in their national trade laws. However, the effect of these unilateral measures is very limited, because WTO rules leave little room for treating imports from countries with different labor standards differently.

ASKING THE RIGHT QUESTION

The discussion of the merits of linking trade to labor standards has suffered from several weaknesses:

- until 1998, there was no consensus on a priority list of labor standards;
- it was taken for granted that linking trade to labor standards would mean *enforcing* labor standards;
- the merits of a link were exclusively evaluated in terms of *economic costs and benefits.*

The question is not whether it is good or bad to link trade to labor nor who would be the winners and who the losers. By the same token, it is irrelevant whether poor labor conditions are the work of corrupt governments or greedy CEOs, capitalism or globalization, trade or consumer preferences. The real question is this: Are there any problems stemming from poor labor conditions that need to be addressed and that only trade restrictions can solve?

THE ANSWER IS: YES, WE NEED TO BRIDGE THE GAP BETWEEN TRADE AND LABOR STANDARDS

There are two good reasons for linking trade to labor standards. One is social dumping. Social dumping is incompatible with one of the major principles underlying GATT and WTO: fairness. It is therefore surprising that the multilateral trading system has not made it actionable. Apparently, many countries exposed to social dumping are at present prepared to accept this. They would be well advised to reconsider their position.

The other reason for establishing a link between trade and labor standards concerns the responsibility of importing countries. Increasing imports of goods produced under substandard labor conditions are an incentive for the exporting country to produce more goods under the same labor conditions, and ship them to the same country. This results in a proliferation of violations of labor standards, for which the importing country shares the responsibility. There is a need to adopt a link between trade and labor standards enabling the importing country to cap imports in order to escape the blame.

Abbreviations

ACP	African, Caribbean, and Pacific Group of States
AIP	Apparel Industry Partnership
CAFTA	Central American Free Trade Agreement
CBERA	Caribbean Basin Economy Recovery Act
CCC	Clean Clothes Campaign
CEARC	Committee of Experts on the Application of Conventions and Recommendations
CEDAW	Convention on the Elimination of All Forms of Discrimination against Women
CEO	Chief executive officer
CITES	Washington Convention on International Trade in Endangered Species
CLS	Core labor standards
CRC	Convention on the Rights of the Child
DSB	Dispute Settlement Body
DSM	Dispute Settlement Mechanism
EBA	Everything But Arms
EFTA	European Fair Trade Association
EPZ	Export Processing Zone
ETI	Ethical Trading Initiative
ETUC	European Trade Union Confederation

ETUF/TCL	European Trade Union Federation of Textiles, Clothing, and Leather
EU	European Union
EURATEX	European Apparel and Textile Organization
FIFA	Fédération Internationale de Football Associations
FLA	Fair Labor Association
FLO	Fairtrade Labeling Organization
FTA	Free Trade Agreement
GDP	Gross National Product
GSP	General System of Preferences
HS	Harmonized Commodity Description and Coding System
ICCPR	International Covenant on Civil and Political Rights
ICERD	International Convention on the Elimination of All Forms of Racial Discrimination
ICESCR	International Covenant on Economic, Social, and Cultural Rights
ICFTU	International Confederation of Free Trade Unions
ILC	International Labor Conference
ILO	International Labor Office; International Labor Organization
ILRF	International Labor Rights Fund
IMF	International Monetary Fund
IPEC	International Program for the Elimination of Child Labor
LDC	Least developed country
MAI	Multilateral Agreement on Investment
MFN	Most favored nation
MNE	Multinational Enterprise
NAALC	North American Agreement on Labor Cooperation
NAFTA	North American Free Trade Agreement
NAO	National Administrative Officer
NEWS!	Network of European Worldshops
NGO	Non-Governmental Organization
PPM	Production and processing methods

OECD	Organization for Economic Co-Operation and Development
SAAS	Social Accountability Accreditation Services
SAI	Social Accountability International
SAP-FL	Special Action Program to Combat Forced Labor
SDT	Special and Differential Treatment
SPS	Sanitary and phyto-sanitary
TBT	Technical Barriers to Trade
TPRM	Trade Policy Review Mechanism
TRIPS	Trade-Related Intellectual Property Rights
UDHR	Universal Declaration of Human Rights
UNCTAD	United Nations Conference on Trade and Development
UNCTC	United Nations Commission on Transnational Corporations
UNDP	United Nations Development Program
UNICEF	United Nations Children's Fund
UNIFEM	United Nations Development Fund for Women
UNITE	Union of Needle Trades, Industrial, and Textile Employees
USTR	United States Trade Representative
WCL	World Confederation of Labor
WIPO	World Intellectual Property Organization
WRC	Workers' Rights Consortium
WTO	World Trade Organization

Bibliography

Agusti-Panareda, J., F. C. Ebert and D. LeClercq, Labour Provisions in Free Trade Agreements: Fostering their Consistency with the ILO Standards System, International Labour Office, Geneva, 2014.

Alatas, V., and L. A. Cameron: Should Nike And Reebok Pay Higher Wages? The Impact of Minimum Wages On Employment In A Low Income Country, Research Paper of the Department of Economics of the University of Melbourne.

Alben, E., GATT and the Fair Wage: A Historical Perspective on the Labor-Trade Link, *Columbia Law Review*, Vol. 101, p. 1410.

Alston, P., Labor Rights Provisions in US Trade Laws, "Aggressive Unilateralism"?, in L. A. Compa and S. F. Diamond (eds), *Human Rights, Labor Rights, and International Trade*, Philadelphia, 1996, p. 73.

Amato, T. A., Labor Rights Conditionality: United States Trade Legislation and the International Trade Order, *New York University Law Review*, Vol. 65, 1990, p. 79.

Amnesty International, Global trade, labour and human rights, Amnesty International United Kingdom, London, 2000.

Arnold, D. G., and L. P. Hartman, Worker Rights and Low Wage Industrialization: How to Avoid Sweatshops, *Human Rights Quarterly*, Vol. 28, No. 3, August 2006, p. 676.

Azariadis, C., and J. Stachurski, Poverty Traps, in P. Aghion and S. Durlauf (eds), *Handbook of Economic Growth*, Los Angeles, 2002.

Bagwell, K., and R. W. Staiger, The Simple Economics of Labor Standards and the GATT, National Bureau of Economic Research Working Paper, no. w6604, 1998.

Barrientos, S., and S. Smith, Do Workers Benefit from Ethical Trade? Assessing Codes of Labour Practice in Global Production Systems, *Third World Quarterly*, Vol. 28, No. 4, 2007, p. 713.

Barry, C., and S. G. Reddy, *International Trade and Labor Standards: A Proposal for a Linkage*, New York, 2008.

Bhagwati, J., Policy Perspectives and Future Directions: A View from Academia, in Proceedings of a Symposium, International Labor Standards and Global Economic Integration, United States Department of Labor, Bureau of International Labor Affairs, Washington, DC, 1994, p. 57–62.

Bieler, A., I. Landberg, and D. Pillay, *Labour and the Challenges of Globalization: What Prospects for Transnational Solidarity?* London and Ann Arbor, 2008.

Brown, D. K., A. V. Deardorff, and R. M. Stern, Pros and Cons of Linking Trade and Labor Standards, Paper prepared for the Murphy Institute Conference on "The Political Economy of Policy Reform," Nov. 2001, p. 13.

Brown, D. K., International Trade and Core Labour Standards, A Survey of the Recent Literature, OECD Labour Market and Social Policy Occasional Papers No. 43, Paris, 2000.

Brown, D. K., International Labor Standards in the World Trade Organization and the International Labor Organization, *Review*, Federal Reserve Bank of St. Louis, issue July 2000, p. 105.

Brown, D. K., A. V. Deardorff, and R. M. Stern, Child Labor: Theory, Evidence, and Policy Options, in K. Basu, H. Horn, K. Román, and J. Shapiro, *International Labor Standards: History, Theory, and Policy Options*, Malden, 2003.

Busse, M., Do Labor Standards Affect Comparative Advantage in Developing Countries? *World Development*, vol. 30, 2002, no. 11, p. 1921.

Cavanagh, J., L. Compa, A. Ebert, B. Goold, Z. Selvaggio, and T. Shorrock, Trade's Hidden Costs: Worker Rights in a Changing World Economy, International Labor Rights Education and Research Fund, Ithaca, 1988.

Charnovitz, S., The Influence of International Labor Standards on the World Trading Regime, *International Labour Review*, Vol. 126, No. 5, Sept.–Oct. 1987, p. 565.

Collingsworth, T., International Workers Rights Enforcement, Proposals Following a Test Case, in L. A. Compa and S. F. Diamond (eds), *Human Rights, Labor Rights, and International Trade*, Philadelphia, 1996, p. 233.

Compa, L. A., and S. F. Diamond (eds), *Human Rights, Labor Rights, and International Trade*, Philadelphia, 1996.

Diamond, S. R., Labor Rights in the Global Economy, A Case Study of NAFTA, in L. A. Compa and S. F. Diamond (eds), *Human Rights, Labor Rights, and International Trade,* Philadelphia, 1996.

Cullen, H., The Limits of International Trade Mechanisms in Enforcing Human Rights: The Case of Child Labour, *The International Journal of Children's Rights*, 7: 1999, p. 1–29.

Duhigg, C., and D. Barboza, In China, Human Costs are Built into an iPad, *The New York Times*, January 25, 2012.

Duhigg, C., and N. Wingfield, BITS; Apple In Shift, Pushes An Audit Of Sites In China, *The New York Times*, February 14, 2012.

Ehrenberg, D. S., From Intention to Action, An ILO-GATT/WTO Enforcement Regime for International Labor Rights, in L. A. Compa and S. F. Diamond (eds), *Human Rights, Labor Rights, and International Trade*, Philadelphia, 1996, p. 163.

Elliott, K. A., Fin(d)ing Our Way on Trade and Labor Standards? Institute for International Economics, Washington, DC, Policy Brief 01–5, 2001.

Elliott, K. A., Labor Standards and the Free Trade Area of the Americas, Institute for International Economics, Washington, DC, Aug. 2003.

Elliott, K. A., and R. B. Freeman, Can Labor Stands Improve under Globalization? Institute for International Economics, Washington, DC, 2003.

Emmerij, L., Contemporary Challenges for Labour Standards Resulting from Globalization, in W. Sengenberger and D. Campbell (eds), *International Labour Standards and Economic Interdependence*, International Institute for Labour Studies, Geneva, 1994, p. 326.

European Commission, Commission Communication to the Council: Development cooperation and the observance of certain international standards governing working conditions, COM (78) 492 final of 10 November 197.

European Commission, Communication from the Commission to the Council, the European Parliament and the European Economic and Social Council: Development countries, international trade and sustainable development: the function of the Community's generalized system of preferences (GSP) for the ten-year period from 2006 to 2015, COM (2004) 461 final of 7 July 2004.

European Commission, Proposal for a Regulation of the European Parliament and of the Council applying a scheme of generalized tariff preferences, Explanatory memorandum, COM (2011) 241 final of 10 May 2011.

Ewing, K. D, The Sense of Measure: Old Wine in New Bottles, or New Wine in Old Bottles, or New Wine in New Bottles?, in *Dialogue & Debate: Labour, Constitution and a Sense of Measure: A Debate with Alain Supiot, Social & Legal Studies*, 2010, 19(2), p. 231.

Fields, G., The Role of Labor Standards in US Trade Policies, in A. V. Deardorff and R. M. Stern (eds), *Studies in International Economics: Social Dimensions of US Trade Policies*, Ann Arbor, 1999, p. 167.

Flanagan, R. J., *Globalization and Labor Conditions, Working Conditions and Worker Rights in a Global Economy*, Oxford, 2006.

Foner, P. S., *History of the Labor Movement in the United States*, Vol. 7, *Labor and World War I, 1914–1918*, New York, 1987.

Friedman, M., The Social Responsibility of Business to Increase Its Profits, *New York Times Magazine*, September 13, 1970, p. 30.

General Agreement on Tariffs and Trade, Preparatory Committee (GATT), Prep. comm. (86) SR 14 (23 May 1986).

Greenhouse, S., and J. Kahn, U.S. Effort to Add Labor Standards to Agenda Fail, *The New York Times*, December 3, 1999.

Gross, J. A., (ed), *Workers' Rights as Human Rights*, Ithaca, 2003.

Gross, J. A., and L. Compa (eds), Human Rights in Labor and Employment Relations: International and Domestic Perspectives, Labor and Employment Relations Association, Champaign, 2009.

Gross, J. A., Takin' It to the Man: Human Rights at the American Workplace, in J. A. Gross and L. Compa (eds), *Human Rights in Labor and Employment Relations: International and Domestic Perspectives*, Labor and Employment Relations Association, Champaign, 2009, p. 32.

Hartmann, L. P., D. G. Arnold and R. E. Wokutch (eds), *Rising above Sweatshops, Innovative Approaches to Global Labor Challenges*, Westport and London, 2003.

Hayek, F., *Law, Legislation and Liberty: A New Statement of the Liberal Principles of Justice and Political Economy*, London, 1980.

Hensman, R., Fine-Tuning the Linkage Proposal, in C. Barry and S. G. Reddy, *International Trade and Labor Standards: A Proposal for a Linkage*, New York, 2008, p. 122.

Herzenberg, S., In From the Margins, Morality, Economics, and International Labor Rights, in Compa, L. A., and S. F. Diamond (eds), *Human Rights, Labor Rights, and International Trade*, Philadelphia, 1996, p. 113.

Hilgert, J., A New Frontier for Industrial Relations: Workplace Health and Safety as a Human Right, in J. A. Gross and L. Compa (eds), *Human Rights in Labor and Employment Relations: International and Domestic Perspectives*, Labor and Employment Relations Association, Champaign, 2009, pp.43–68.

Howse, R., The World Trade Organization and the Protection of Workers' Rights, *The Journal of Small and Emerging Business Law*, Summer 1999.

Hudec, R. E., Like Product: The Differences in Meaning in GATT Articles I and III, in T. Cottier and P. Mavroidis (eds), *Regulatory Barriers and the Principle of Non-Discrimination in World Trade*, Ann Arbor, 2000.

Independent Commission on International Development Issues, North-South: A program for survival, The Report of the Independent Commission on International Development Issues, Cambridge, 1980.

International Labour Organisation, The Dilemma of the Informal Sector, Report of the Director-General to the International Labor Conference, Geneva, 1991.

International Labour Organisation, Defending Values, Promoting Change, Report of the Director-General to the International Labor Conference, Geneva, 1994.

International Labour Office, Global Wage Report 2008/09, Minimum wages and collective bargaining: Towards policy coherence, Geneva, 2008.

International Labour Office, International Institute for Labor Studies, Studies on Growth with Equity, Making recovery sustainable: Lessons from country innovations, Geneva, 2011.

International Labour Office, Working Party on the Social Dimensions of the Liberalization of Trade, Country studies on the Social Impact of Globalization, Final Report, document GB.276/WP/SDL/1, 276th Session, Geneva, 1999.

International Labour Office, Report of annual reports under the follow-up to the ILO Declaration on Fundamental Principles and Rights at Work, Governing Body, 310th Session, document GB.310/3, Geneva, 2011.

International Labour Office, Report of the Working Party on the Social Dimension of Globalization, Governing Body, 310th Session, document GB.310/16, Geneva, 2011.
International Labour Organisation, Press release ILO/97/10 of April 23, 1998.
International Labour Organisation, Your voice at work, Global Report under the follow-up to the ILO Declaration on Fundamental Principles and Rights at Work, Geneva, 2000.
International Labour Organisation, Stopping Forced Labor, Global Report under the follow-up to the ILO Declaration on Fundamental Principles and Rights at Work, Geneva, 2001.
International Labour Organisation, A Future Without Child Labour, Global Report under the follow-up to the ILO Declaration on Fundamental Principles and Rights at Work, Geneva, 2002.
International Labour Organisation, Organization for Social Justice, Global Report under the follow-up to the ILO Declaration on Fundamental Principles and Rights at Work, Geneva, 2004.
International Labour Organisation, A global alliance against forced labor, Global Report under the follow-up to the ILO Declaration on Fundamental Principles and Rights at Work, Geneva, 2005.
International Labour Organisation Equality at work: Tackling the Challenge, Global Report under the follow-up to the ILO Declaration on Fundamental Principles and Rights at Work, Geneva, 2007.
International Labour Organisation, Freedom of association in practice: Lessons learned, Global Report under the follow-up to the ILO Declaration on Fundamental Principles and Rights at Work, Geneva, 2008.
International Labour Organisation The Cost of Coercion, Global Report under the follow-up to the ILO Declaration on Fundamental Principles and Rights at Work, Geneva, 2009.
International Labour Organisation Equality at work: The Continuing Challenge, Global Report under the follow-up to the ILO Declaration on Fundamental Principles and Rights at Work, Geneva, 2011.
International Labour Organisation, 349th Report of the Committee on Freedom of Association, Governing Body, 301st session, document GB.301/8, Geneva, 2008.
International Labour Organisation, 371st Report of the Committee on Freedom of Association, Governing Body, 320th session, document GB.320/INS/12, Geneva, 2014.
Kolben, K., Labor Rights as Human Rights? *Virginia Journal of International Law*, Vol. 50, issue 2, p. 449.
Krugman, P., In Praise of Cheap Labor, *Slate*, March 20, 1997.
Kucera, D., Core Labour Standards and Foreign Direct Investment, *International Labour Review*, Vol. 141 (2002), No. 1–2, p. 31.
Ladbury, S., and S. Gibbons, Core Labour Standards, Key Issues and a Proposal for a Strategy, report submitted to the UK Department for International Development, 2000.
Langille, B. A., Labour Standards in the Globalized Economy and the Free Trade/Fair Trade Debate, in W. Sengenberger and D. Campbell (eds), *International Labour Standards and Economic Interdependence*, International Institute for Labour Studies, Geneva, 1994, p. 332.
Leary, V. A., The Paradox of Workers' Rights as Human Rights, L. A. Compa and S. F. Diamond (eds), *Human Rights, Labor Rights, and International Trade*, Philadelphia, 1996, p. 37.
Lim, H., *The Social Clause: Issues and Challenges*, International Labor Organization, Bureau for Workers Activities, Geneva, 2001.
Liubicic, R. J., Corporate Codes of Conduct and Labeling Schemes: The Limits and Possibilities of Promoting International Labor Rights through Private Initiatives, *Law and Policy in International Business*, Vol. 30, No. 1, 1998, p. 111.
MacPherson, C. B., Elegant Tombstones, A Note on Friedman's Freedom, *Canadian Journal of Political Science*, Vol. 1, No. 1 March 1968, p. 95–106.
Marshall, R., Trade-Linked Labor Standards, *Proceedings of the Academy of Political Science*, Vol. 37, 1990, No. 4.
Martin, W., and K. E. Maskus, Core Labor Standards and Competitiveness: Implications for Global Trade Policy, *Review of International Economics*, 9 (2), 2001, p. 317.

Maskus, K. E., Should Core Labor Standards Be Imposed Through International Trade Policy? The World Bank Development Research Group, Policy Research Working Paper 1817, Washington, DC, 1997.

Maupain, F., New Foundation or New Facade?, The ILO and the 2008 Declaration on Social Justice for a Fair Globalization, *The European Journal of International Law*, Vol. 20, 2009, No. 3 p. 823.

McFadyen, J., NAFTA Supplemental Agreements: Four Year Review, Institute for International Economics, Working Paper 98–4, Washington, DC.

McIntyre, R. P., *Are Workers Rights Human Rights?* Ann Arbor, 2008.

Miller, J., Why Economists Are Wrong about Sweatshops and the Antisweatshop Movement, *Challenge*, Vol. 46, No. 1, January–February 2003, p. 93.

Moore, M., The WTO: what is at stake? 6th John Payne Memorial Lecture, European Business School London, March 12, 2001.

Moran, T. H., Beyond Sweatshops, Foreign Direct Investment and Globalization in Developing Countries, Washington, DC, 2002.

Moran, T. H., Trade Agreements and Labor Standards, Policy Brief 133 from the National Academy of Science, Washington DC, 2004.

Mosley, L., and S. Uno, Racing to the Bottom or Climbing to the Top? Economic Globalization and Collective Labor Rights, *Comparative Political Studies*, Vol. 40, No. 8, August 2007, p. 923.

Myerson, A. R., In Principle, a Case for More Sweatshops, *The New York Times*, June 22, 1997.

Novitz, T., Workers' Freedom of Association, in J. A. Gross and L. Compa (eds), *Human Rights in Labor and Employment Relations: International and Domestic Perspectives*, Labor and Employment Relations Association, Champaign, 2009, pp. 123–154.

Organization for Economic Cooperation and Development, International Trade and Core Labour Standards, Paris, 2000.

Organization for Economic Cooperation and Development, Trade, Employment and Labour Standards: A Study of Core Workers' Rights and International Trade, Paris, 1996.

Organization for Economic Cooperation and Development, Working Party of the Trade Committee, Codes of Corporate Conduct: An Inventory, D/TC/WP(98)74/FINAL of April 29, 1999.

Organization for Economic Cooperation and Development, Codes of Corporate Conduct: Expanded Review of their Contents, Directorate for Financial, Fiscal and Enterprise Affairs, Working Paper on International Investment, No. 2001/6, May 2001.

O'Rourke, D., Outsourcing Regulation: Analyzing Nongovernmental Systems of Labor Standards and Monitoring, *The Policy Studies Journal*, Vol. 31, No. 1, 2003, p. 1.

Palley, T. I., The Economic Case for International Labor Standards, *Cambridge Journal of Economics*, Vol. 28, No. 1, 2004, p. 21.

Palley, T. I., The Child Labor Problem and the Need for International Labor Stands, *Journal of Economic Issues*, Vol. 28, No. 3, September 2002, p. 601.

Palma, J. G., Globalizing Inequality: "Centrifugal" and "Centripetal" Forces at Work, UN Secretariat, Department of economic and social affairs, Working Paper No. 35, ST/ESA/2006/DWP/35, September 2006.

Polaski, S., Trade and Labor Standards, A Strategy for Developing Countries, Trade, Equity, and Development Paper, Carnegie Endowment for International Peace, Washington, 2003.

Radin, T. J., Levi Strauss & Co.: Implementation of Global Sourcing and Operating Guidelines in Latin America, in L. P. Hartman, D. G. Arnold, and R. E. Wokutch (eds), *Rising above Sweatshops, Innovative Approaches to Global Labor Challenges*, Westport and London, 2003, p. 254.

Ratner, S. R., Corporations and Human Rights: A Theory of Legal Responsibility, *The Yale Law Journal*, Vol. 111, No. 3 (2001), p. 443.

Robertson, R., D. Brown, G. Pierre, and M. L. Sanchez-Puerta (eds), Globalization, Wages, and the Quality of Jobs, Five Country Studies, The World Bank, Washington, DC, 2009

Rodrik, D., Labor Standards in International Trade: Do They Matter and What Do We Do About Them? in R. Z. Lawrence, D. Rodrik and J. Whalley (eds): *Emerging Agenda for*

Global Trade: High Stakes for Developing Countries, Overseas Development Council Essay no. 20, Washington, DC, 1996.

Rodrik, D., Democracies Pay Higher Wages, *The Quarterly Journal of Economics*, Vol. CXIV, Issue 3, August 1999, p. 707.

Ross, R. J. S., *Slaves to Fashion, Poverty and Abuse in the New Sweatshops*, Ann Arbor, 2004.

Sachs, J. D, *The End of Poverty, Economic Possibilities for Our Time*, New York, 2005.

Sengenberger, W., and D. Campbell (eds), *International Labour Standards and Economic Interdependence*, International Institute for Labour Studies, Geneva, 1994.

Shotwell, J. T., (ed), *The Origins of the International Labor Organization in Two Volumes*, New York, 1934.

Srinivasan, T. N., Trade And Human Rights, Center Discussion Paper No. 765, Economic Growth Center, New Haven, Dec. 1996.

Steele, D., The Living Wage Clause in the ETI Base Code—How to Implement It? Project Archive of the European Initiatives on Monitoring and Verification of Codes of Conduct in the Garment and Sportswear Industry, 2000.

Stern, R. M., Labor Standards and Trade Agreements, Research Seminar in International Economics, Discussion Paper no. 496, Ann Arbor, 2003.

Stiglitz, J. E. and A. Charlton, *Fair Trade For All, How Trade Can Promote Development*, Oxford, 2005.

Swidorski, C., From the Wagner Act to the Human Rights Watch Report: Labor and Freedom of Expression and Association, 1935–2000, *New Political Science*, Vol. 25, no. 1, 2003, p. 55.

United Nations Children's Fund, Children at Work, UNICEF East Asia and Pacific Regional Office, Bangkok, 1994.

United Nations, Office of the High Commissioner for Human Rights, The Corporate Responsibility to Respect Human Rights, An Interpretative Guide, prepared by the UN Special Representative on Business and Human Rights, Geneva, November 2011.

United Nations Conference on Trade and Development, GSP Newsletter, Geneva, Number 6, November 2005, UNCTAD/DITC/TNCD/MISC/2005/5.

United Nations Development Fund for Women, Progress of the World's Women, Biennial Report 2000.

United Nations Development Programme, International cooperation at a crossroads: Aid, trade and security in an unequal world, Human Development Report 2005.

United Nations Development Programme, Sustainability and Equity, A better future for all, Human Development Report 2011.

United Nations Human Rights Council, Mandate of the Special Representative of Secretary-General on the issue of human rights and transnational corporations and other business enterprises, Resolution 8/7 of June 18, 2008.

United States General Accounting Office, International Trade, Comparison of the US and European Union Preference Programs, Report of the Chairman, Subcommittee on Trade, Committee on Ways and Means, House of Representatives, Washington, DC, June 2001, GAO-01-647.

Weston, B. H., Child Labor in Human Rights Law and Policy Perspective, in J. A. Gross and L. Compa (eds), *Human Rights in Labor and Employment Relations: International and Domestic Perspectives*, Labor and Employment Relations Association, Champaign, 2009, p. 74.

Wingfield, N., Apple's Profit Doubles on Holiday iPhone 4S Sales, *The New York Times*, January 24, 2012.

Woolfson, C., The Sense of Measure and Societies "Without Limit," in *Dialogue & Debate: Labour, Constitution and a Sense of Measure: A Debate with Alain Supiot, Social & Legal Studies*, 2010, 19(2), p. 226.

World Bank, The World Development Report, A Better Investment Climate for Everyone, Washington, DC, 2005.

Index

About the Author

Wolfgang Plasa is a former official of the European Commission. He gathered most of his professional experience in the area where trade policy joins development policy. As a member of the EU Delegation in Geneva, he participated in GATT, WTO, and ILO activities as well as in the negotiations of the Uruguay Round. In the late 1990s, he managed the Generalized System of Trade Preferences (GSP) of the EU. He drafted Council Regulation No 2501/2001 which is one of the first legal texts of the EU to establish a link between trade and labor standards.

Wolfgang Plasa was head of the EU Delegations in Chile and Algeria, where he was responsible, *inter alia*, for trade policy and for the implementation of EU development assistance. He also visited many countries in Asia and Latin America, where he saw the reality of sweatshops. In 2009, Wolfgang Plasa was offered a fellowship at Yale University where he did research into the issue of trade and labor standards. Being increasingly fascinated by the subject matter, he undertook to write this book.

www.ingramcontent.com/pod-product-compliance
Ingram Content Group UK Ltd.
Pitfield, Milton Keynes, MK11 3LW, UK
UKHW041125071026
15587UKWH00009B/221